Speaking Parables

Speaking Parables

A HOMILETIC GUIDE

David Buttrick

Westminster John Knox Press
Louisville, Kentucky

Scripture quotations, unless otherwise indicated, are from the New Revised Standard Version of the Bible, copyright © 1989 by the Division of Christian Education of the National Council of the Churches of Christ in the U.S.A., and used by permission. The parables have been translated by the author.

HarperCollins Publishers, Inc.: Selected parables from the Gospel of Thomas from *The Nag Hammadi Library in English,* 3rd completely revised ed., by James M. Robinson, General Editor. Copyright © 1978, 1988 by E. J. Brill, Leiden, The Netherlands. Reprinted by permission of HarperCollins Publishers, Inc.

Acknowledgments can be found on pages 239–240.

Book design by Drew Stevens
Cover design by Kevin Darst & Jennifer K. Cox

First edition
Published by Westminster John Knox Press
Louisville, Kentucky

This book is printed on acid-free paper that meets the American National Standards Institute Z39.48 standard.

PRINTED IN THE UNITED STATES OF AMERICA
00 01 02 03 04 05 06 07 08 09 — 10 9 8 7 6 5 4 3 2 1

Library of Congress Cataloging-in-Publication Data

Buttrick, David, 1927–
   Speaking parables: a homiletic guide / David Buttrick.
     p. cm.
   Includes bibliographical references and index.
   1. Bible. N.T.—Parables—Homiletical use. I. Title.
BT375.2 .B89 2000
226.8'06—dc21
                                         99-048398

For Betsy

Contents

Preface

Years ago my father, George Arthur Buttrick, wrote a book entitled *The Parables of Jesus*. Although the book is still being published, Father tried to stop sales because he believed the scholarship was dated and he feared misleading ministers. The book contains inspiring pages, but Father's realism should be honored—scholarship *has* changed.

I would not attempt to replace Father's book. Trying to compete with an illustrious parent is foolish. We need neither defend nor correct parents. We are all poor sinners and, thus, we all flunk parenting. Nonetheless, we can be grateful for parents, and delight in remembering their humor, their keenness of mind, their winsome ways, and above all, their faithfulness. I am sure I write on parables because once upon a time Father stirred my interest. But now I am writing a different book with different aims. I am interested in homiletic strategy: How can we preach parables? I am also interested in theology: What is the mysterious "kingdom" parables declare?

I have lectured on the parables in several settings: The Pastors' School of Furman University where I was welcomed by Chaplain James M. Pitts, and the Alumni Lectures at Emmanuel School of Religion where Bruce E. Shields is the excellent homiletician. Most recently, I delivered the C. M. Nicholson Lectures at Atlantic School of Theology in Canada, where President William Close and his wife Doris were gracious in their welcome. I enjoyed the company of faculty members Martin and Barbara Rumscheidt as well as Mary Schaefer. Thomas McIllwraith and his associate Beth Bruce were most hospitable.

In 1992, I was honored to deliver the George Arthur Buttrick Lectures on the parables at the Bay View Assembly in Michigan. Bishop Emerson S. Colaw was my host. The Buttrick Lectures were generously established by David Dykhouse in honor of his father and of mine. The trip to Bay View has resulted in pleasant summer visits with Polly and Bill Jones of Louisville and Walloon Lake.

On occasion I have been able to teach the parables in some detail: Twice at the splendid College of Preachers in Washington, D.C., where Shelagh Casey Brown directed the programs, and twice in seminars at the Vanderbilt Divinity School. I enjoy students, and learn from them more than they may guess. As always, I am intensely grateful to those I have been privileged to teach.

I need to say thank you to some helpful people.

Anne Womack, Associate Director of the Divinity Library, located, documented, and copied my published sermons from long ago.

Nancy Weatherwax, a graduate student in theology and an ace researcher, diligently tracked down some of my more elusive citations.

Indexes were compiled by homiletician-to-be Laura Hocker Barbins. Laura is remarkable; she likes to index and does so wonderfully well. She also has an editorial eye and checked the entire manuscript for overlooked errors.

I have had two readers, both Crumplers. Paul C. Crumpler, an insightful churchman, read chapter one. His son, the Reverend David Paul Crumpler, an able preacher, read chapter three. Both readers offered helpful corrections for which I am grateful.

I must offer special "huzzahs" for Stephanie Egnotovich, Executive Editor at Westminster John Knox Press, who is always smart and always gracious. What would absent-minded writers do without whiz-bang, clear-eyed, sane editors?

A few years ago I wrote a little book, *Preaching Jesus Christ,* dedicated to my wife. To my dismay, the book went out of print. So once again I dedicate a volume to Betty More Allaben Buttrick. We are getting old—although she claims that "over the hill" is always five years older than she. With age we weather into statements of who we are. Betty displays her courage, patience, love, and more faith then she would ever admit. Her face calls me out of myself. Her laughter edges me toward God's remarkable joy.

I publish these pages in the final year of my teaching at Vanderbilt University. Good colleagues. Good students. What will I do without them?

D.G.B.

The Divinity School
Vanderbilt University

Introduction

Usually a writer comes clean in an epilogue, making summary statements, admitting theological bias, and the like. Why wait for an epilogue? Let us be "up-front" about such matters.

You are about to read, perhaps use, a book about parables. So we shall begin with some remarks on the parables of Jesus. I will be looking at thirty-three parables, only twenty of which can be traced back to Jesus with assurance. What about the other parables, those that seem unlikely—for example, the parable of the Closed Door that used to be labeled "Wise and Foolish Virgins," or the parable of the Planted Weeds? I discuss both and warn preachers away from reading doctrine in them. I will not argue that because they are in the Bible they are thereby "baptized" by canonical status. Canonical status, though a guard against nonsense, should never be turned into a tablet of stone.

You will also discover that I am critical of some parable interpretations. Matthew draws a reprehensible conclusion from the parable of the Unmerciful Servant after the fellow ends up being tortured: "So will my heavenly Father do to you unless everyone of you forgives your fellow human from your heart." Look out, Matthew has handed us dreadful theology. Later, by chaining together parables of the Treasure, the Pearl, and the Fishnet, I suspect Matthew has misunderstood all three. I will be as candid with regard to a few of Luke's somewhat moralistic readings. Do I suspect that the Gospel writers sometimes have misunderstood the parables of Jesus? Yes I do. Will you and I also misread the parables? Absolutely.

Some of you may be troubled by my insistence that Jesus himself never told any of the second-coming parables that herald an apocalyptic "Son of Man." A smart book by Douglas R. A. Hare, *The Son of Man Tradition,*[1] has convinced me that in all likelihood Jesus never used the term "Son of Man." Furthermore, recent research into the early "Q" source suggests that second-coming parables may be secondary material. I have no wish to remove the category of "judgment"; it is a biblical idea that must never be discarded. But notions of judgment ought to be appropriate to a God whose nature is love. The judgments of love may be awesome, but they do not end in the dark with "weeping and grinding of teeth" as Matthew seems to have supposed.

The Bible as a Gift

Should these observations unsettle you, I had better be open. I receive the Bible as a gift, indeed a gift given by God via devout writers, preachers, prophets, and apostles back through the years. "Gift" is a much better term than "authority." Gifts can be full of joy and usefulness; good heavens, you can hardly wait to unwrap a gift. Gifts are treasured in their use, we remember givers with gratitude. While I delight in scripture and enjoy studying and restudying the Bible, and while I read scripture with excitement, finding more and more insight into the mystery of God, I do not bother with the notion of "authority." We revere the Bible because it brings us good news of God and not because it is superperfect. The Bible is *not* an inerrant "Word of God." The idea is silly.

Deeper still, I rather suppose that high-powered ideas of biblical authority are a theological error. To want an inerrant Bible is an old temptation endorsed by the serpent in the Eden myth when suggesting a nosh from the forbidden tree: "You will not die; . . . you will be like God, knowing good and evil." We are human and we cannot know like God. "To err is human," and biblical authors are emphatically human.

But more, God's sovereignty is exercised with divine modesty and love, not in despotism. If the cross is in any way a disclosure of God, then God's sovereignty is expressed, as the apostle Paul suggested, in the helpless "foolishness" of Jesus Christ crucified. Vertical notions of biblical authority frequently feature images of enthroned domination. So "gift" is better, for gifts can be filled with both love and a kind of shy, deferential generosity. What's more, gifts can be shared with partying and laughter—as can the Bible.

Can we ever be sure of our interpretations? We cannot. If I criticize Matthew I do so knowing I am as prone to error as anyone. We are all inadequate sinners who reach for grace. But with Matthew I share faith and, I do hope, some slight degree of faithfulness. Still more, I am at table with Matthew, breaking the "bread of life" and sharing "the cup of salvation." At table is probably where we are meant to interpret scripture. Together let us receive the parables as gift.

Methodologies

I will be drawing on the research of others. As we go along, I will try to tell you names in footnotes or in brief references. I have read the books listed in the bibliography at the end of the book, so you will notice that I have been instructed by more than seventy parable scholars. Although five of my books have been largely exegetical in character, I would not pass myself off as a professional exegete. I have relied on many scholars to teach me.

I owe a special debt to a friend, Bernard Brandon Scott. Ministers ask bibliographic advice: "What books would you suggest on . . . ?" On parables I am particularly eager to recommend Scott's *Hear Then the Parable: A Commentary on the Parables of Jesus*.[2] Responsible preachers/interpreters will want to own several good books on parables, but Scott's work is a *must*. Because the book treats parables as scenarios for retelling and analyzes the structural movement of each narrative, it is especially helpful to those who, in turn, must interpret and, in a way, redesign the parables of Jesus.

Though I draw on a collection of scholars, I read the parables as someone who teaches preachers and has an interest in theology. You will discover some of my interpretations risk a reading different from the scholarly consensus, but then I will warn you so that if you wish you can discard my position as uninformed, wrongheaded, scurrilous, badly mistaken, or whatever. I have no desire to mislead you, but I do want you to engage parables and, as well, the people who write about parables. Parables are exciting, they are fun to work with, and they should prompt lively give and take.

My approach will be eclectic. I have been taught by some fine historical critics and have enjoyed learning all I can about biblical background. But in the 1960s, I did graduate study in literary criticism and poetics. Thus I have been enthusiastic about newer critical methods, in particular with those that engage language—literary approaches, structural analysis, rhetorical criticism, reader-response analysis, and the like. But in the "commentary" sections of the book I do not forget I am writing for working priests, ministers, and active lay teachers who interpret parables on a week to week basis. I try to avoid esoterics.

Parables and Preaching:

Why are the parables important? Why have they generated shelves of books in every century? Quite simply, the parables comprise a huge percentage of Jesus' teaching. If we wish to know him, to get at his ways of thinking, we will have to study the parables. Of course, most of you who will be working your way through the book will want more; through preaching, teaching, and talking, you will be trying to form a community into "the likeness of Christ."

Be warned. I do not view parables as helpful wisdom for daily living, like mottoes hung on a kitchen wall to encourage nice behavior. Parables are not "conventional wisdom." I do not view parables as Jesus' sermon illustrations, homely stories of everyday life to help us grasp the things of God. Parables are not very religious. I do not view parables as swell stories for "narrative preaching." Parables are frequently too talky to be good stories. I do not view parables as therapeutically useful. Parables do not resolve personal ambiguities, or provide for self-acceptance.

I believe parables are powerful. They may be designed for a kind of group conversion. Parables usually begin rather tritely, depicting our everyday world in an everyday way, but then in most cases there is something surreal that disrupts our world and hints at a wider, more mysterious world—as well as a more astonishing God. Parables may well move us toward what Jesus called the "kingdom of God." If I am at all correct, then speaking parables is a tricky, exciting craft. Ministers who do not want to devote themselves to preaching will probably prefer some other approach. But preaching parables is an excitement you shouldn't want to miss.

A Vocation of Meaning

These days ministry is a peculiar vocation. Ministers and priests are more parochial than they once were. They serve their parishes but often without a wider concern for the world God loves. Too easily they can be devoted to institutional management or, worse, institutional preservation. They become program people. If they do not thrive on institutional management, ministers can focus on the needs of people; they will comfort, counsel, and busy themselves with the growth and well-being of the individuals under their care. What we do not see much of these days are ministers who are first and foremost devoted to preaching and teaching and reaching out with the Word of God. Nowadays therapy and management consume the clergy.

We live at a time when the huge, worldwide, human problem is meaninglessness. Properly, the defining task of ministry is meaning. Years ago Paul Tillich argued that in early centuries of the church, the urgent problem was death. Given an average ancient lifespan of less than thirty years, Tillich was surely correct. In medieval years the problem became guilt: How can we stand acquitted before the judgment of God? Churches set up penitential rites and often preached forms of judicial atonement. People still die and people still struggle with guilt, but now, according to Tillich, the overriding concern is meaninglessness. We are assaulted with news "every hour on the hour," but cannot assemble the disparate news items into any sense of overall meaning. Without meaning, people give themselves to proximate goals, year by year as they grow older: I will finish school, I will buy a car, I will get a job, I will get married, I will make money, I will breed children, I will start an IRA, on and on until, oops, there's an obituary. The great liturgical cry of our age: "I don't have a clue!"

I view ministry as a vocation of meaning. Preaching and teaching and talking are all ways of speaking meaning. Ministers are meaning-givers not merely for a parish, but in everything ministers do everywhere. All of which means ministers must study every day of their lives. They can. They can because laypeople can manage churches very well, design programs, write church newspapers, and all the rest. Laypeople also are excellent at giving comfort, visiting the sick, and helping others in wonderful ways. Ministers can assist, giving meaning to programs and deep meaning to desperate people in crisis moments. These days ministers are beset; too many demands assail them. But they may be dodging their primary concern—meaning.

Enough tirade.

"A Homiletic Guide"

The book you now are reading is subtitled, "A Homiletic Guide." The word "homiletic" may require explanation. Here are a few random thoughts:

1. Although preaching need not begin with scripture, many preachers preach from biblical passages. "Raw" scripture, however, is insufficient; scripture must be interpreted.

2. The interpretation of the Bible is ultimately a theological task. Protestant Reformers Luther and Calvin wrote volumes to provide theology for the understanding of scripture. Today, in the absence of theology, people seem to be reading the Bible through their political or cultural loyalties, particularly when engaged in public debate.

3. Protestants have argued that the Bible is self-interpreting, with one part illuminating or correcting another. The argument fails because there is no consistent "biblical theology"; instead there are many, often incompatible, theolog*ies* in scripture.

4. In actual practice (as Bultmann noted long ago) we come to scripture with some sort of "pre-understanding," not only of what the Bible is, but of something we usually call the "gospel." Our grasp of "gospel," however inchoate, has been formed within some sort of theological tradition.

5. To be responsible, we must set our understandings of "gospel" within a developed systematic theology that seeks to articulate faith for our contemporary world in a comprehensive way. The shibboleth that theology is a Greek speculative invention contrary to biblical faith is nonsense.

6 Preaching seeks to speak faith to particular social contexts, and, to do so, must discern "signs of the times." Thus homiletics will have to interpret human situations, social behavior, and cultural products (film, art, music, literature, etc.) as well as scripture. Paul Tillich spoke of "A Theology of Culture."

So homileticians are busy people. Let us count the ways: Homiletics is engaged in biblical exegesis, in interpreting texts for gospel preaching, in defining "gospel" with theological depth, in analyzing contending cultural ideas, and, in the light of rhetorical wisdom, determining how to speak the gospel to our society, both in church and beyond—whew! It's a great life, even if you weaken! In this book, we will be engaged in homiletic theology, seeking to understand the parables of Jesus.

The Book's Shape

The book you now are reading has two parts. Part 1 begins with three introductory chapters:

Chapter 1 provides a general approach to parables. The chapter will address questions such as: How many parables are there? How many come from Jesus? Where did Jesus learn parables? What are parables?

Chapter 2 is all about "kingdom." I struggle with the topic, as does everyone who ventures to write about *basileia tou Theou,* "kingdom of God." Jesus' preaching spreads across pages in our Bibles, and the Jewish basis for his preaching fills book after book of the Hebrew Bible. I struggle not only because I am frequently dumb, but because the subject is awesome and essentially mysterious. I invite you to struggle with me.

Chapter 3 turns to the task of preaching or teaching parables. The chapter looks at problems in interpreting parables, in designing sermons, in choosing illustrations, and so forth—technical homiletic stuff. The chapter has been difficult to write. Some years ago I published a big book on preaching with the catchy title, *Homiletic*.[3] In the book I devoted some five hundred pages to technical stuff on assembling sermons. I have no desire now to reiterate the earlier book. As an author, however, I am happy to advise you to buy the book and learn what you can learn. If you read *Homiletic,* you will understand better the critical discussion of parable sermons.

Part 2 of the book is a kind of commentary on thirty-three different parables. In each case, I will provide a new translation from the Greek, a brief survey of scholarship, and then suggestions with regard to preaching the parable. The parables are arranged according to source—Mark, Matthew, Q, and Luke—with brief introductions to each of the sources. In discussing the parables, I do not provide detailed exegeses. But I do try to get at the major problems scholars have run into, and to explain disagreements in interpretation. But basically I am interested in theological issues and homiletic strategy. After all, I am writing for you who preach or teach or talk to others about parables.

Titles, Translations, References, Sermons

Titles

How can we refer to the parables? The Bible does not supply titles, and the many books on parables hand out different labels. Shall we label a well-known Matthean parable "The Last Judgment" or "The Sheep and the Goats"? Do we refer to "The Wise and Foolish Virgins," "The Ten Girls," or the "Closed Door"? In general, I have adopted titles given parables by the Jesus Seminar and published in *The Parables of Jesus: Red Letter Edition*.[4] To their list I have added "Children in the Market," "Empty House," "House Builders," "Weather Report," "Friend at Midnight," and "Undeserving Servants."

Translations

I have deliberately tried to capture some feel for the Greek colloquial because, after all, the parables are written in "street-corner" *koine* Greek. I have changed time references to match our mode of timekeeping (e.g., third hour = nine o'clock), and also I have attempted to suggest monetary values, though economies then and now are quite different. I have translated "master" as "boss" when feasible. The Greek word *doulos,* slave, is a peculiar problem. Slaves in the first century were often managers, financial officers, educators, sales representatives, and the like. So, for example, I have changed the dishonest "steward" to a "manager" and the unforgiving "servant" to an "agent." At the same time, I have tried my best to show respect for Greek syntax and vocabulary range. There are translations of the parables you may prefer. The Jesus Seminar has issued *The Complete Gospels,*[5] which is quite colloquial and a bit freer than mine. At the other extreme, there is a careful, if somewhat wooden, translation in Richmond Lattimore's *Four Gospels and the Revelation.*[6] The New International Version is quite fine but, unfortunately, works from a different Greek text.

The phrase *basileia tou theou,* "kingdom of God," is a special problem. The word "kingdom" is both sexist and anachronistic—fairy tales speak of kingdoms. In 1998, I published *Preaching the New and the Now,*[7] a book on the kingdom of God, and I used several different terms—realm, social order, rule, as well as kingdom. I follow the same practice here in the second chapter, "The Mysterious 'Kingdom of God.'" But in the parable texts, reluctantly, I translate *basileia* as "kingdom." I considered "empire," a word that may imply an emperor, just as kingdom implies a king. The word could be helpful, for "empire" might convey a touch of threat as the *basileia* probably did in first-century Israel. In a recent book, Stephen J. Patterson uses "empire" quite successfully.[8] But I finally decided to go with "kingdom," the term used in most biblical translations. Not only does "kingdom" match parables that feature a "king," but the harsh "k" seems to work better in contemporary translation than the softer "em" sound.

References

Though I have taught Christian scripture courses in theological schools, I am not a professional biblical scholar. Therefore I have drawn on the work of many scholars, from older standard works by Dodd and Jeremias to more recent studies. You will come across their names—Scott, Crossan, Herzog, Bailey, Derrett, Drury, Donahue, and many others. At the end of the book you will find a bibliography. In the exposition, citations of parable scholarship are by date and page; for example, the reference "Crossan 1975, 78" would indicate page 78 in John Dominic Crossan's *The Dark Interval,* published in 1975, and listed in the bibliography. Other references not listed in the bibliography are documented by endnotes.

Sermons

I include some fourteen sermons that I have delivered over the course of forty years (1958–1998). With only slight modification to introduce inclusive language, the sermons are taken from actual preaching manuscripts, "warts and all." I selected the sermons because they are on parables and not because I regard them as especially fine. Indeed I am embarrassed by a few. Sermon manuscripts are oral scripts that preachers usually modify in delivery; they are not written for publication. Even so, some of the sermons were published and, if published, then I have reproduced the published version (again with a concern for inclusive language). When submitting sermons for publication in years past, I have been lazy, for I have usually transcribed the original preaching script with virtually no modification. A few of the sermons were edited down in length, abbreviated to fit one single page of the magazine *Presbyterian Life.*

In presenting the sermons, I designate the introduction and conclusion and then number the paragraphs in the body of the discourse. Paragraphing matches sections of each sermon that focus on particular ideas. These sections—I call them "moves"—are not separate "topics," nor are they didactic "points," but are designed like the back-and-forth shifts in a conversation; thus they are *moves* in a mutual *movement* of thought.

As I look back at the sermons, old and new, I find myself being critical. There are mistakes a preacher in his twenties could make, but there are also mistakes made by an old man who should know better. So after each sermon, I review the sermon critically, section by section. Perhaps preachers will be reassured to know that *all* preachers make mistakes. Together, maybe we can learn to do better.

The sermons are datable. All sermons are particular; they address people who live at a particular time in a particular place. Sermons are not intended to be religious essays for all time. Like bird flight, they are spoken, heard, and are gone. Thus, for years I have resisted publishing many sermons. But now here are some. All the sermons were actually preached. They are untitled. Unless some church demanded a bulletin title, I avoided the practice.

You may be interested to trace changes in preaching from early sermons to the more recent, from 1958 when I preached on Children in the Marketplace to 1998 when I delivered a sermon on the Dishonest Steward. I have listed information on where and when each of the sermons was preached in the bibliography.

Join me. Let's go to work together. As old-time preachers used to say, together "Let us learn from the Lord." Perhaps, poking around with parables— odd, old stories handed down from Jesus—perhaps we'll be changed.

PART 1

1

The Parables of Jesus

Everyone who hangs around churches has heard of the parables of Jesus. They are familiar. Have they not contributed to our language? We speak of helpful neighbors as "Good Samaritans" or label wayward youngsters "Prodigal." We use the word "talent" because of Matthew's famous parable. Parables are preached in sermons and studied in church school classes on a regular basis, year after year. They have been allegorized, psychologized, and sometimes reduced to pointed "lessons" on moral behavior. But, mysteriously, after twenty centuries they still generate retelling and still are puzzling.

As we stumble into a new millennium, parables are as exciting as ever—indeed they are more so. About twenty-five years ago scholars began taking a second look at the parables, but with somewhat different critical methods. Though historical research into first-century customs continues, providing helpful background information, newer methods of research—structural, literary-critical, rhetorical, sociological—have changed our understanding of parables, often radically. More recently, contextual approaches have raised troubling questions of meaning; perhaps parables generate a range of interpretation, for, obviously, people read parables differently depending on situations. Will impoverished migrant fieldhands understand the parable of the Vineyard Laborers in the same way as affluent American entrepreneurs?

Parables, however, are not Rorschach ink blots in which we read our own reflected psyches. Yes, a Marxist can interpret parables with revolutionary insight and Freudians can find all sorts of psychological meanings; both readings have been done insightfully. But parables are still attached to the figure of Jesus and in some manner articulate his purposes. So if we study the parables, we may find ourselves captured by his imagination. No wonder that year after year, century after century, the parables have held our interest. If the figure of Jesus is in any way a "disclosure model" for God, then parables—sometimes roguish, sometimes hilarious, sometimes deeply moving—may be a way into the Presence.

Although there are helpful books on preaching parables, most of them seem to draw on historical-critical research done during the first three quarters of the twentieth century. But exciting literary studies of the parables have been published in the past twenty-five years. Thus, there may be reason for yet another homiletic/theological look at the parables of Jesus.

The Parables: What and Where

What are we talking about when we speak of the parables of Jesus? Here is what the author of *Hodge Podge: A Commonplace Book* has written on parables: "If I'd been challenged to guess how many parables there are in the Bible, I'd have said a dozen or perhaps fifteen. There are actually sixty-four."[1] He sounds quite positive, but most scholars are not. Are all figures of speech parables? John Drury, who includes many of the brief similes, counts more than sixty in Matthew alone, at least another sixty in Luke, and around twenty more in Mark.[2] Jeremias lists only forty parables, but he does not count duplicates.[3] So how many parables of Jesus are there? Answer: It depends on what you count and how you count them. In the Hebrew Bible, the word *mashal* seems to label everything—images, riddles, metaphors, allegories, wordplays, brief similes, puns, as well as terse stories most of us call parables. In the Christian scriptures, the Greek word *parabole* serves a similar function.

We will study thirty-three parables. If you count duplicate versions (parables that show up in more than one Gospel), we will be covering fifty. But I will not look at brief metaphors such as "You are the light of the world," "It is easier for a camel to go through the eye of a needle than for a rich man to enter the kingdom of God," "No one sews a new patch on an old garment." Are these short sayings parables? Probably. But I am limiting our study to parables with some sort of minimum movement of plot. Thus we will step beyond simple comparisons or brief rhetorical images.

We will be studying parables that display some degree of "story." But we are not thereby limited to longer parables. Sometimes there can be plot in a single sentence:

> The kingdom of heaven is like treasure hidden in a field, which, finding,
> a man rehides, and in his joy goes and sells everything he has and buys
> the field.

Although the parable is no more than a sentence, it has a moving plot. The narrative begins with finding treasure, moves then to hiding the treasure, then elation, then to selling everything, and finally to buying the field. Of course, most of the well-known parables have developed plots with different characters and actions and, sometimes, obvious motivations. We will be particularly interested in the structural movement of plot within the parables.

The Jewish Context

Where did Jesus pick up the practice of telling parables? Obviously he learned from his own Jewish heritage. The Talmud contains parables; so does Midrash. Jewish parables are clever, often paradoxical; they are "traps for contemplation." So Jesus did not invent the parable; he learned to speak in parables by being Jewish.

Some years ago, a somewhat romantic British scholar wrote, "[T]he Gospel parables are virtually a new and highly original form, both as regards purpose and content. Indeed, one of the striking things about the teaching of Jesus, its method and its content, is its newness when compared with the newest approach to it elsewhere in the Bible."[4] The quote is one of many in which Christian scholars have praised Jesus for innovative parables. Either they are touted as being new or they are celebrated as a bright high point of parable design beside which other parables, particularly Jewish parables, pale. But arrogance, particularly Christian arrogance, is seldom charming, especially when it is wrong!

Jesus' parables are thoroughly Jewish. Their form is Jewish, their style is Jewish, and their patterns of thought are Jewish. In some ways they may seem different, but the differences do not lead us away from a Jewish context. Look at the component parts of a rabbinic parable:[5]

1. *Setting*. What prompts the telling of a parable? The Jewish *mashal* was addressed to a life situation or, often, to an exegetical situation, namely, the interpretation of a text. For the most part, Jesus' parables appear to have been situational.
2. *Hermeneutic imagination*. The teller juxtaposes an image analogous to the setting. Thus a situation is interpreted and, by an act of imagination, a parable is posed. Almost always the phrase "is like," *mashal le,* is used. No wonder Jesus' parables also feature "is like," as in "The kingdom of God is like . . . ," or "What is like this generation. . . . "
3. *Mashal*. The parable itself will be a brief pattern of images or a structured story. Usually the stories are detached from specific places or named people much as in fairy tales. No wonder many of Jesus' parables begin, "A certain man. . . , " with no name or place provided.
4. *Nimshal*. A follow-up instruction or explanation of the parable, often beginning with "likewise," *kakh,* and concluding with a scriptural citation. Presumably many of these are secondary, for in actual life situations an audience simply might be left to puzzle over the story on its own.
5. *Audience*. Presumably an audience must think out the parable and what it may have to do with the situation or scriptural citation. The result should be insight as the audience catches on to the same understanding

as the speaker. Sometimes some brief statement with regard to the listeners' response is included.

Here is a parable told by a rabbi as part of his eulogy at the untimely death of another rabbi.[6] Thus the parable addresses a situation:

Mashal   It is like a king who had a son whom he loved more than anything else. What did the king do? He planted an orchard for his son. When the son obeyed his father, the king would go around the entire world, and whenever he saw a beautiful plant he would plant it in the orchard. And whenever the son angered his father, the king would uproot all the plants.

Nimshal   Likewise: When Israel performs the will of the Holy One, blessed be He, He goes through the entire world, and whenever he finds a righteous gentile, He takes him and joins him to Israel, like Jethro or Rahab. And whenever Israel angers Him, he removes the righteous from them.[7]

In the situation (the untimely death of a righteous rabbi), the parable will be powerful. The two basic parts of the Jewish *mashal* are present: the *mashal* itself and the *nimshal*. With the *nimshal* an audience would catch on to the speaker's imaginative analogy and understand the meaning of the *mashal*.

Here is another parable, offered as a commentary on a biblical text, namely, the food laws in Leviticus 11.[8]

Mashal   Rabbi Tanhum ben Hanilai said . . . To what may this be compared? To a physician who went to see two sick people, one whose life was not in danger and the other who was near death. The physician said to the one whose life was not threatened: "You should not eat such and such things!" And in the case of the other man near death, he said to the people: "Give him whatever he wants to eat!"

Nimshal   So it is with the people of the world who are not chosen for life in the world to come: "Every creature that lives and moves shall be food for you . . . " (Gen. 9:3). But to the Israelites, who are there to live in Gan Eden: "These are the living things which you may eat among all the beasts that are on earth" (Lev. 11:2).[9]

David Stern has written a comprehensive study of the rhetoric and poetics of the rabbinic parables, applying contemporary literary analyses to the ancient form. He compares the rabbinic parables to the parables of Jesus and concludes, "Jesus used the parable in essentially the same way as the Rabbis employed the mashal."[10] So where did Jesus get the form of the parable? He learned parables by being a Jew.

Is There a Difference?

I have argued that Jesus' parables are in continuity with the Jewish *mashal* tradition. He used parables in much the same manner as did the rabbis. Yet, in a way, Jesus' parables do seem different. Why?

Though parables are a form of wisdom literature, Jesus was not a wisdom sage. Most rabbinic parables were used to interpret the paradoxes of scripture or to offer insight in puzzling human situations, often morally ambiguous ones. But though parables are "wisdom" materials, Jesus seemed to be using them in a prophetic vocation. So at the outset let us recognize that a wisdom form is being used with prophetic purpose. Thus the *mashal* is altered by the purpose of its use. But we do not step out of a Jewish milieu, for wisdom and prophetic traditions are both within a Jewish heritage. Jesus was clearly Jewish; he did not have a magic "Christian" brain.

The transmission of parables is complicated. Prior to our Gospels there were collections of sayings, notably Q and an early stratum of the *Gospel of Thomas*. These collections compiled parables of Jesus but seldom offered descriptions of the original situations in which they were spoken. As a result, by comparing triple versions of a parable—in Mark, Matthew, and Luke—we can spot a variety of settings that have been designed most often by the different Gospel writers. If original settings have been lost, then a recovery of original meaning may be elusive indeed. Luke may tell us the story of the Good Samaritan, but almost certainly he has supplied a new setting and, therefore, a new interpretation of the parable. Luke is addressing Gentile readers; with a Jewish audience, the parable might have had a different meaning.

Moreover, many *nimshals,* interpretations that may have been attached to original parables, are also lost. Obviously the allegories that sometimes follow parables are usually the work of Gospel authors—for example, Mark's labored allegory of the soils (Mark 4:14–20) and Matthew's equally pedantic explanation of the Planted Weeds (Matt. 13:37–43). Having lost the original settings, the new context for parables is a Christian Gospel writer's story of Jesus.

There may be still another difference beyond the prophetic use of a wisdom form. All the Gospels seem to express some sort of split consciousness, a feature we will examine when we study the notion of a "kingdom of God." Mark, the earliest Gospel, appears to be based on the apocalyptic idea of two aeons. Thus Mark sees Jesus as the herald of a new aeon that will replace the sociopolitical orders of our temporal world. And Matthew, a Jewish/Christian Gospel,[11] views his little community as a "new Israel" created by God to replace an old unfaithful Israel. Luke's split is a bit more complex but still is discernable: God by Word and Spirit is transforming the whole world, namely, the Roman Empire, by conversion. So the Gospel writers use parables as a witness to change; they open to us something new, something Jesus preached—the "kingdom of God." Sometimes the kingdom seems to be forming in the midst of our commonplace world; at other times it may be coming from God's future to displace our social order.

Because of split consciousness, the parables are apt to seem culturally disruptive within the Gospel narratives.

Though Jesus is using a conventional Jewish parable form, in prophetic activity he employs the form somewhat differently than did the sages. Because original situations may be lost, the parables are placed within Gospel narratives that appear to be the products of Christian (split) consciousness. Thus parables may appear to be countercultural. Nevertheless, the parable form itself—paradoxical, clever, often witty—is decidedly Jewish.

Are All the Parables from Jesus?

A few years ago, the Jesus Seminar focused on the words of Jesus, including his parables. As you may have heard, Seminar scholars voted on each parable with different colored "stones." Red meant, "That's Jesus!"; pink, "Sure sounds like Him"; gray, "Well, maybe"; and black, "There's been some mistake." According to the Seminar, five parables seem to be sure things, fifteen are probable, six somewhat unlikely, and six are simply not from Jesus even though they may be attributed to him in biblical texts.[12]

To push the question: Can we ever have the actual red-letter words of Jesus? Not likely. So the Seminar went further and rated parables by the percentage of the text that might be attributed to Jesus and the percentage that could be considered redactional, an editorial elaboration. In some cases the Seminar picked out particular verses that could scarcely have been original. Nevertheless, the Seminar thought that twenty of the parables probably traced back to something Jesus may have said.

Most of the parables have been woven into Gospel stories of Jesus and thus have context. Both Matthew and Luke tell the story of the Lost Sheep, but Matthew tells the parable in connection with lapsed church members. Luke tells the same story, but as a reply to Pharisees who question Jesus' eating and drinking with known sinners. While these settings may tell us what the parable may have meant to Luke and to Matthew, most scholars are unsure of the historical validity of such contexts. In fact, school children in the first century were taught how to make up stories in which significant sayings could be passed along. Thus we do not know where or when or to whom parables were actually spoken. Before Mark, Matthew, or Luke wove parables into their different stories of Jesus, parables probably circulated without any narrative location in collections like Q. As a result, most parable scholars take parables out of context and, by analyzing clues within the text itself, suggest some sort of original meaning. Of course, they also look at the parable in context so as to see how each Gospel writer understands the parable.

No doubt parables have been subject to change both in oral transmission and as they were written down. If someone tells you a joke, you will remember the plot and the punch line. When you retell the joke in a new setting, probably you will change the wording and details of the story in different ways, though preserving the basic structure and the punch line. Semitic oral cultures regard language with respect and, therefore, show great care in transmitting phrases, stories, and the like. Nevertheless, inevitably, different people will tell the same story differently, particularly in different settings. Because language on a printed page is more formal than speech, oral tradition is usually edited when written down, as, for example when copyeditors nowadays change many *don'ts* into *do nots*. Would parables undergo similar changes both in oral transmission and in transcription? Probably.

If you turn to the parable of the Feast (page 156) you will see Matthew's version of the parable, with his additions italicized. Presumably the parable is from Q; thus we can compare Matthew with Luke and spot additions readily. Finding additions and deletions in the parables is the work of redaction criticism. Can we construct original parables, restoring the actual words of Jesus? No, not with one hundred percent certainty. But in many cases we can use informed scholarship to restore the basic structural design of an original parable.

A Sharp Eye for Change

Begin by seeing what we have to work with. Parables show up in the Synoptic Gospels as well as in some extrabiblical sources such as the Gnostic *Gospel of Thomas*. Thus we can do some comparing of texts. Most scholars accept a fairly simple source theory:

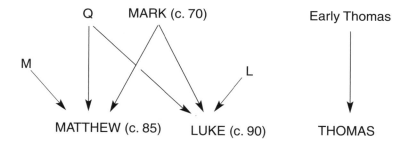

Mark, the earliest Gospel, was used by both Matthew and Luke. Synopses of the Gospels will let you see texts side by side so you can spot the changes Matthew and Luke made in drawing from Mark's Gospel.[13] But Matthew and Luke shared another source that scholars have named Q. While we do not have an actual copy of Q, we are able to reconstruct its contents.[14] In addition, Matthew seems to have used another source (or sources) as did Luke, and scholars label these materials "M" and "L," respectively.

What about *Thomas?* Around 1900, papyrus fragments of an unknown Greek Gospel were discovered in Egypt. More recently, in 1945 a complete Coptic text of the same Gospel was discovered in the Gnostic collection at Nag Hammadi, Egypt. Putting discoveries together we can presume that an early Greek text of the *Gospel of Thomas* circulated prior to Mark, about the same time as Q. There are fifteen parables collected in *Thomas;* some appear to have been expanded by Gnostic editors, but others appear in a form that may predate our Synoptic Gospels. These parables can be lined up and compared to parables in Mark, Matthew, and Luke.

Some years ago Joachim Jeremias, a great parable scholar, drew up a list of reasons editorial changes were made in the parables.[15] Some of them are listed here in order to help you become parable "detectives":

1. *Translation.* Scholars used to suppose the parables were spoken originally in street-corner Aramaic and then translated into a Greek text. But now scholars suspect that Jesus may have been bilingual. Nevertheless, translation may have been involved and, no matter how carefully done, translation *always* alters meaning to some degree.

2. *Representational changes.* Jeremias lists a few changes, instances when Palestinian customs are replaced by customs of the Greek world. For example, Luke (12:58) changes "synagogue official" (Matt. 5:25) into "bailiff." And Matthew's Palestinian cloudburst flooding a wadi (7:25) becomes a river overflowing in Luke 6:48.

3. *Embellishment.* Good storytellers fool around with a story, frequently exaggerating or adding episodes. Compare the Entrusted Money in Matthew and Luke (pp. 171–72). In my translation, Matthew's three servants are given different amounts of money—ten, four, and two thousand each—but in Luke there are ten servants with only a thousand dollars each. With the Feast (pp. 156–57), Matthew has a king and a wedding banquet; Luke has a host and a dinner party. Almost every parable that shows up in more than one version displays signs of elaboration.

4. *Influence of Hebrew scripture and folktale.* When Mark recounts the story of the Tenants, his description of the vineyard is drawn from Isaiah 5 and, of course, includes a quote from Psalm 118:22–23. Likewise Mark's parable of the Seed and Harvest cites Joel 3:13. The parable of the Leaven mentions three measures of flour, an allusion to stories of Abraham and Gideon and Hannah. The Mustard Seed parable quotes from Ezekiel 17 and Daniel 4. As for folktale: Is the Fishnet influenced by a tale from Aesop's collection? Probably.

5. *Change of Audience.* Here we are referring to the audience in the biblical text. For example, take the parable of the Lost Sheep (pp. 152–56). In Matthew the parable is addressed to disciples and told in connection with rules governing church discipline. In Luke the parable is told to critics who have accused Jesus of eating with sinners. Thus the parable changes its rhetorical shape along with the imagined audience.

6. *Hortatory use of parables by the church.* Obviously the Good Samaritan is used to encourage compassion for neighbors: "Go and do likewise." In Luke the story of the Feast is used to advocate feeding the poor and hungry. Luke uses several parables to urge prayer, for example, the nagging widow and the Unjust Judge. According to Luke, the parable teaches us "to pray all the time and not lose heart."

7. *Influence of the church's situation.* Some parables change along with changes in the life of the church from Mark (c. 70) to Matthew (c. 85) to Luke (c. 90). For example, compare the parable of the Returning Master in Mark 13:33–37 and Luke 12:35–38. In Mark there is urgency—"watch and pray" because the second coming of the Lord is imminent. But in Luke the second coming has been transformed; we are waiting for a wedding party and a master who will enter and party with us. The Feast in Matthew has been historicized to refer to the failure of Judaism and the inviting of a "new Israel," namely, Matthew's congregation. In Luke the same parable has an extra recruitment of guests, perhaps to represent Luke's Gentile congregation.

8. *Allegorization.* Several parables are allegories, such as the Wheat and Weeds, and the Tenants. Sometimes allegories are spelled out, as when Mark interprets the Sower by listing the different kinds of soil. At other times the allegory is built in, as with the Tenants when an only son (Jesus?) is killed and thrown out of the vineyard.

9. *Collection and conflation of parables.* Parables are chained, as, for example, when Matthew 13 puts together the Treasure, the Pearl, and the Fishnet; or when Luke 15 chains the Lost Sheep and the Lost Coin with the Lost (Prodigal) Son. In the chains, Gospel writers have recast parables in a parallel style in order to indicate similar meaning.

10. *Setting.* We have said that Q and an early version of *Thomas* collected the parables but without settings. In turn, Gospel writers have inserted the parables into a story of Jesus, but often in quite different ways. For example, Mark tells the seed parables early in chapter 4, whereas Matthew collects them in his crucial chapter 13 where they become turning-point parables.

In general, most scholars accept Jeremias's list of redactional reasons. The list can help us all understand changes we may encounter when we study parables, particularly parables that show up in more than one Gospel.

Of course, there is a more profound way of studying parables. If we can isolate a collection of authentic Jesus material, then we can begin to get hold of his ways of thinking and speaking and even his theological convictions. Thus armed, we may judge materials accordingly (these fit, these do not). If, overall, Jesus does not seem to worry much over who is in and who is out at the judgment, we can be suspicious of the Planted Weeds; it does not seem to fit the "mind" of Jesus. Sometimes we can line up parables with the other teachings of Jesus. Does "Love your enemies" relate to the story of the Good Samaritan? Could the parable of the Leaven be a storied version of "Tax collectors and prostitutes are going into the kingdom of God ahead of you"?

Looking for editorial revisions may trouble some Christians, particularly those who wish to affirm some sort of scriptural inerrancy. But for others, learning to work with parables will be liberating and exciting, as we search the meanings Jesus Christ gives us, meanings which are for us the substance of revelation.

The Scenarios of Jesus

Let us look at parables as scenarios for speech rather than as literary works on a Bible page. Parables were originally speech. As Luther was fond of remarking, Jesus did not write any books. Though parables now appear in print, they wound their way into our Bible via oral transmission; they were told and retold, and retold again many times. Obviously we cannot claim to possess the actual words of Jesus. We can suppose, though, that in many cases we have a scenario—the moving structure, the humor, the punch line—of an original parable. When a parable such as the Sower appears in Mark, Matthew, Luke, and *Thomas,* we can spot the basic structure or plot of the story, and then track the various elaborations as each Gospel tells the parable in a slightly different way. Read the late, great scholar Norman Perrin:

> [Parables] survived the subsequent process of transmission very well,
> while, at the same time, the process of interpretation was so obvious and
> so much at variance with the original thrust of the parables themselves,
> that the original form and thrust of the parables have not proven diffi-
> cult to reconstruct.[16]

The parables themselves have survived. And as we have seen, it is fairly easy to spot interpretive additions. But though we can spot elaboration and obvious changes, we still cannot go back to recover the actual words of Jesus. What we can reconstruct is a Jesus scenario, a kind of script for retelling—what Perrin called "the original form and thrust." Scenarios have structure and with a structure we can retell parables in our own way to our own more modern audiences. And maybe, just maybe, we can beg the Spirit, the same Spirit that was in Christ Jesus, to further our words as well.

Are Parables Allegories?

Before we can proceed, we must have some understanding of what parables are and how they work.

The question "What is a parable?" goes back in Christian history as far as chapter 4 of the Gospel of Mark. According to Mark, Jesus tells a parable about a farmer sowing seed. Then the disciples, who are somewhat thickheaded in Mark's Gospel, ask Jesus about why he speaks in parables. Jesus tosses off an enigmatic reply:

> You have been given the secret of the Kingdom of God, but for out-siders, everything comes in parables, so that 'they may look, but not per-ceive, and may listen and not understand, lest they turn again and be forgiven.'   (Mark 4:11–12 DGB)

Notice that Jesus' response includes a quote from the call of Isaiah (Isa. 6:10). The split between an in-group ("you") and "outsiders" sounds like mystery cult stuff, while the dismay over those who see but do not see, hear but do not under-stand might match Mark's own discouragements—how few people respond to the gospel message!

Of course, almost immediately Mark hands out an allegorical interpretation of the Sower, which does not stress the farmer or the seed but instead identifies different types of soil. In effect, Mark explains the secret meaning of Jesus' para-ble to initiates, namely, the disciples. In so doing, Mark tipped centuries of Chris-tian interpretation in the direction of allegory.

Allegory is actually a system of similes. Usually the allegory itself represents a whole: for example, the whole church, the whole world, the whole of human history. Within the whole are component parts (A, B, C, D), each an obvious sim-ile. Thus readers are meant to identify each part and its significance. The system is bound to be a bit pedantic. Some parables have been allegorized in transmis-sion (just as many are allegorized in preaching), but scholars are convinced orig-inal Jesus parables were *not* allegories.

Both Mark and Matthew offer allegorical interpretations of parables. Here is the most obvious:

> His disciples approached him, saying, "Explain to us the parable of the weeds of the field." He answered, "The one who sows the good seed is the Son of Man; the field is the world, and the good seed are the chil-dren of the kingdom; the weeds are the children of the evil one, and the enemy who sowed them is the devil; the harvest is the end of the age, and the reapers are angels. Just as the weeds are collected and burned up with fire, so will it be at the end of the age. The Son of Man will send his angels, and they will collect out of his kingdom all causes of sin and all evildoers, and they will throw them into the furnace of fire, where there will be weeping and gnashing of teeth. Then the righteous will shine like the sun in the kingdom of their Father. Let anyone with ears listen!   (Matt. 13:36–43, NRSV)

The explanation is really a series of equal signs: the field = the world, the good seed = the children of the kingdom, the weeds = children of the evil one, and so forth. The parable of the Planted Weeds addresses a problem in the Matthean church: what to do about members of the community whose moral behavior is decidedly below par—throw them out or wait for the judgment? The explanation, though put on the lips of Jesus, displays Matthew's own unmistakable style and concludes with a favorite catchphrase, "weeping and gnashing of teeth."

Mark has a similar allegorical explanation attached to the parable of the Sower (Mark 4:13–20), although, in contrast to the Planted Weeds, most scholars believe that, in some early form, the Sower was an authentic parable of Jesus.

The allegorization of parables seems to take two forms: (1) lining up parables with features of churchly experience and (2) lining up parables with a reading of history. Mark reads the Sower allegorically as referring to the ways in which people hear and respond to the church's preaching. Matthew reads the Wheat and the Weeds as referring to the moral lives of church members. Both allegories are lined up with situational experience.

But there are many parables that have been historicized, particularly by Matthew. Matthew obviously reads the Vineyard Laborers as a historical allegory in which all-day workers are Israel and end-of-the-day workers are the new Israel of the Matthean church. A similar historical allegory is read into the parable of the Feast. And all the Gospel writers seem to have historicized the Tenants. The Tenants are Israel—Israel that has persecuted the prophets, killed John the Baptist, and crucified Christ. Who are the new tenants who will take over? Why, obviously, Christians.

What about Mark's peculiar notion that parables are for an in-group with in-group meanings, but deliberately obscure to the worldly ("they may look, but not perceive, and may listen and not understand, lest they turn again and be forgiven")? Although the idea appeals to Mark's own frustration with regard to the few who respond to Christian preaching, it is theologically suspect. Would a God of love who wants to be known speak in allegorical code only for a selected churchly in-group? A double-predestinarian mind might embrace such a position, but biblically the position is untenable. God is love; God wants to be known; therefore, God speaks to *all* humanity. We must be suspicious of allegorical definitions of parables.

Because of the allegory of the soils in Mark 4, many preachers in the past supposed that Jesus himself endorsed allegorical interpretation. Thus great preachers—Irenaeus, Tertullian, Clement of Alexandria, Origen, Augustine, Aquinas, and, though he protested, Luther—often engaged in allegorical interpretation of the parables. Was the oil and wine that the Good Samaritan applied to the victim's wounds an anticipation of the Christian sacraments? Was the innkeeper in the same parable the apostle Paul (Augustine) or a symbol of the Christian church?

John Calvin rejected allegorical method. He rehearsed some allegorical readings of the Good Samaritan and then concluded:

> [T]hey make out the Samaritan to be Christ, because He is our protector: they say that wine mixed with water was poured into the wound because Christ heals us with repentance and the promise of grace. And a third cunning story has been made up, that Christ does not immediately restore health but sends us to the Church, that is the inn-keeper, to be cured gradually. None of these strikes me as plausible: we should

have more reverence for Scripture than to allow ourselves to transfigure its sense so freely. Anyone may see that these speculations have been cooked up by meddlers, quite divorced from the mind of Christ.[17]

Calvin may have complained but, in spite of his protest, allegory continued for centuries. Archbishop Trench's thick *Notes on the Parables of Our Lord,* filled with allegorical readings, was first published in 1841, but has been sold throughout the twentieth century and only recently has gone out of print.[18] Trench was dismayed by Calvin's strictures that he claimed "would leave the parables bare trunks, stripped of all their foliage and branches, of everything that made for beauty and ornament." The pleasures of allegory, he argued, should not be denied.[19] But, in general, twentieth-century parable interpreters have sided with Calvin.

Are Parables Jesus' "Sermon Illustrations"?

At the end of the nineteenth century, a splendid scholar, Adolf Jülicher, wrote a two-volume work on the parables.[20] He flatly rejected allegory, although from reading Aristotle he did suppose the parables were similes of a sort.

Jülicher launched an attack on allegorical method. First, he proved on philological grounds that the allegory of the soils in Mark 4:14–20 was not written by the speaker of the parable itself (presumably Jesus), but was evidently a first-century "sermon" added to the parable of the Sower. As a result, Mark's allegory of the soils was no longer the model for parable interpretation. Thus Jülicher sharply separated parable from allegory.

But Jülicher went further. First, he argued that instead of the many meanings of allegory, parables were similitudes, or simple comparisons—A is like B—and therefore they had only *one* central message or meaning. He went on to insist that parables are "authentic" because the terms of comparison (A is like B) are clear and uncomplicated; there is nothing hidden. Allegory, in contrast, is "inauthentic" because, in the terms of comparison, we are dealing with a hidden "code." Thus, for Jülicher, parables are not riddles or paradoxes or puzzles to solve. In parables the comparisons produce immediate meaning—"products of the moment." Parables need no explanation; their lessons could be grasped at once by anyone.

Second, Jülicher insisted that in parables Jesus used stuff from everyday life in Palestine—women baking bread, shepherds tending sheep, farmers sowing seed, neighbors borrowing bread, a host planning a dinner party. The stories Jesus told are stories of day-to-day experiences that people would recognize and to which they could relate easily. Jülicher seems to picture Jesus as a nice German folk preacher in a peasant parish, telling simple stories to make plain the things of God to plain people.

Jülicher was a remarkable scholar. He liberated parables from a thicket of allegory and, as a result, both preachers and scholars nowadays read parables as stories of everyday life with single meaning. For nearly eighty years, Jülicher's understanding of parables has held the field. Subsequent books have urged preachers to "Seek the one main point of the parable. Do not seek allegorical significance in the details."[21]

Although Jülicher set parables free from the esoterics of allegory, inadvertently he may have moved them toward banality. If you look at the "main points" that Jülicher distills from the parables, you will find yourself dazzled by the trivial! Jülicher reads the parable of the Dishonest Steward (Luke 16:1–8) and announces, "Determined use of the present is a prerequisite for a happy future." He unpacks the parable of the Entrusted Money (Matt. 25:14–30) and sums it up with "Reward is only earned by performance." And after studying the Good Samaritan, he observes, "The most important duty for man is to love."[22] You read Jülicher's interpretations and wonder why anyone would bother to crucify Jesus, except to end boredom. The parable "lessons" have all the wild excitement of rhetoric at a Rotary convention. Could God's word be tedious? Can you imagine Moses coming down from Sinai, from the cloud and the glory, reading banal mottoes from the tablets of stone? Jülicher, though a wise scholar, was an early-day theological liberal; inadvertently he trivialized the gospel message.

Jülicher picked up critics, of course, the most important being a scholar named Paul Fiebig, who chased Jülicher's almost prejudicial dismissal of Jewish parables.[23] In reply Fiebig translated around four dozen rabbinic parables pointing to similarities of form and arguing against Jülicher's single-point-of-comparison theory. By setting rabbinic parables side by side with the Jesus tradition, Fiebig demonstrated the paradoxical, edgy, often witty character of the Jewish parables. Parables in rabbinic literature were not simple, clear "sermon illustrations." Despite such criticism, in general, Jülicher's position has been accepted through most of the twentieth century—(1) simple, single meanings (2) in stories of everyday life.

During the 1960s, the two most important works on parables were by C. H. Dodd and Joachim Jeremias. Both elaborated Jülicher's position, though correcting his theological naiveté. Dodd argued that parables should be interpreted in the historic context of Jesus' ministry and, above all, must be aligned with his overall teaching. According to Dodd, Jesus taught a "realized eschatology." The kingdom was realized in Jesus' presence, so those parables that seem to anticipate a future judgment are best understood as addressing the crisis of Jesus' own ministry.[24] Jeremias, who also accepted Jülicher's work, displays great erudition in digging up background in first-century Palestinian life, but he believed Jesus aimed parables at the future coming of an eschatological kingdom of God.[25]

A Second Look at Parables

What is behind the big shift in recent parable study? Answer: New ways of studying the biblical texts. For many years the Bible has been interpreted by historical-critical methods. Scholars have attempted to reconstruct the historical character of the first-century world in order to understand the Christian scriptures. The preoccupation with history derives in no small part from the notion of "revelation in history," a theological idea that, of late, has all but faded away. There are newer critical methodologies now to help us read the Bible—rhetorical criticism, literary criticism, structural criticism, reader-response criticism, sociological criticism, and so forth. Lately many of the leading parable scholars have approached the texts as literary critics looking at how the language works. As a result, they have questioned Jülicher's basic assumptions.

Are Parables Stories of Everyday Life?

If the parables are merely stories of everyday life in Palestine, then life in those days must have been mighty peculiar. Here are some of the stories:

1. A woman misplaces a small coin, spends all day searching and when she finds the coin throws an expensive late-night party with neighbors to celebrate.
2. A woman bakes bread in a tiny clay oven, following a "sacred" recipe that calls for around sixty pounds of flour! She produces enough bread to fill a modern-day bakery truck.
3. A boss pays one-hour workers the same salary as twelve-hour workers and then is furious when a grievance committee complains.
4. A shepherd leaves ninety-nine sheep unprotected to chase after one stray.
5. A man sells everything to buy a field to get a treasure that, according to law, reverts to the field's original owner anyway.
6. A "fool" builds his house in the middle of a sandy arroyo.
7. A farmer carefully seeds a field but then abruptly quits, neglecting the field completely.
8. A gardener begs time to fertilize an absolutely dead tree.
9. A boss congratulates a manager for marking down the boss's own collectible invoices.
10. A formal dinner party ends up packed with "street people."

If these and other equally peculiar parables represent daily life in biblical times, then first-century Palestine was an odd place indeed.[26] The consistently surreal character of the parables cannot be written off as humor or as mere "Semitic exaggeration."

Even stranger, these same parables all start out quite normally in ways that do reflect everyday life in first-century Palestine: Farm laborers are hired during harvest time, an owner demands an audit from his manager, formal dinner invitations are sent out to an impressive guest list, farmers seed fields, a woman misplaces something valuable, another woman bakes bread. We read the parables and recognize our world. But then in almost every case, there is something bizarre, something out of place, something unexpected and quite incredible that disrupts the normal world, indeed, something *surreal*.[27]

All of us live in an everyday world, a world constructed in consciousness, a commonplace world with conventional social meanings. Even more, as religious people we share conventional notions of God shaped by our common liturgical heritage. So how do the parables work? At the outset we find ourselves in an image of our world, a world under the gaze of our conventional God. But then without warning, something odd occurs that does not seem normal in our world—workers are paid the same for one hour as for twelve hours, a gardener heaps fertilizer on an absolutely dead tree, a formal dinner party is packed with bums, and so forth. Suddenly, shaken, the image of our world is no longer quite sure. Perhaps we may begin to sense a hidden, mysterious dimension to things with a very different logic. Could there be a "kingdom of God"? And could the God of the "kingdom" be strangely different from the "god" of our conventional religious faith? Paul Ricoeur noticed the extraordinary in parables long ago; he labeled it "extravagance":

> This trait [extravagance] has not been emphasized, even where the "real-ism" of the parables has been insisted upon. The parables tell stories that could have happened or without a doubt have happened, but it is this realism of situations, characters, and plots that precisely heightens the eccentricity of the modes of behavior to which the kingdom of heaven is compared. The *extraordinary in the ordinary:* this is what strikes me in the dénouement of the parables.[28]

Notice we are dealing with stories that are strange and often paradoxical, stories that are as clever as many rabbinic parables, stories that are not quite like simple sermon illustrations. The parables are not teaching devices, each with a lesson to be learned. No, the parables are designed to *do*. They may even be designed for conversion!

Are Parables Stories with a Single Meaning?

One of Jülicher's odd ideas, a notion he picked up from Aristotle, is that para-bles are simple similes—A is like B. Most modern parable scholars reject such a definition.[29] Instead they argue that parables are more like metaphor. Look at the difference in a simple example:

1. She has nails like tiger's claws.
2. She is a caged tiger.

Now look at another example:

3. Cotton candy looks like a puffy pink umbrella.
4. They walked the street in little white dresses, holding high their cot-ton candy; umbrella to ward away a world of tears.

Notice examples 1 and 3 call for recognition: Fingernails are like animal claws and cotton candy on a rolled cardboard stem is shaped like an umbrella. Similes deal with the obvious. But examples 2 and 4 force you to think. Why would the woman be a caged tiger? Repression, pacing, fury—what? The metaphor is a mystery. In example 4 we have a more visual system, with some action and a more complicated understanding of "umbrella"; you are forced to consider the juxtaposed images. If parables are simple similes (A is like B), they can be didactic, containing nothing more than obvious lessons to be learned. This was Jülicher's mistake. But suppose, in spite of the word "like," parables function with metaphorical power, forcing us to consider why the kingdom of God might be like a boss who pays one-hour workers the same wage as all-day workers. As my colleague Sallie McFague observes, "Metaphor . . . is *the* way of human knowing. It is not simply a way of embellishing something we can know in some other way. There is no other way."[30]

So what about single meaning? Jülicher seems to have had a didactic definition of parables. To him, parables were teachers, each with a single lesson. But as modern biblical critics have analyzed parables, they are neither didactic nor do they have single meaning. Instead, as we have already noticed, they seem to have *action* as they travel in a listening consciousness. Not only can we diagram the plots of parables episode by episode, but we can chart listeners' reactions to the same twists and turns of plot. Look at the odd parable in Luke 13:6–9, the brief story of the Barren Tree:

PLOT	REACTION
1. A tree is certified dead, with no fruit for seven years.	Acknowledging the tree is absolutely dead.
2. "Cut it down; the tree is taking up good space."	Recognizing logic of the owner's command.
3. Gardener's request: a year more to fertilize.	Absurd! The tree is dead.
4. Application, namely, a time for repentance.	Seeing God's absurd merciful patience.

Each episode in the plot is significant as part of a unified narrative, and each episode registers in consciousness as we listen. Yet we are not allegorizing a sequence of separate meanings: the dead tree =, the owner's command =, the gardener's proposal =. All the parables we will be studying can be said to display plot movement.

To say that parables do not have lessons, fixed truths that can be cracked out of a story shell and learned, does not mean that parables can be reduced to inner effect or turned into Rorschach inkblots in which we do nothing more than read our own reactions. Parables force us to think deeply. The result of our thinking can be a profound new understanding of world and God and self. Thus, in a way, parables have meaning, but not a meaning that can be reduced to moral or theological principles.

Parables Against the World

I have suggested Jesus used a familiar Jewish wisdom form, the parable, but used the form prophetically. To be a prophet in Israel was to speak for God over against moral neglect and the easy idolatry of popular religion. Such protest is based on Israel's calling to be holy as a Holy God's covenant partner. Prophecy also looks toward "Zion," the fulfillment of all God's promises. But to say that Jesus is prophetic does not mean Christians can set Jesus against his own Jewishness as if Christianity were something redemptively new. Prophets spoke for God within their Jewish heritage, recovering primal Jewish meanings and critically recalling Israel to its true religion.

If Jesus is speaking parables in a prophetic ministry, then there is bound to be a degree of over-againstness to the parables; they will trouble us now even as they must have troubled Jesus' audience long ago. After all, they are parables of the kingdom, and the whole idea of kingdom is a society ordered by God and ruled by God's own gracious and demanding love. Thus they are bound to be socially disruptive. If parables are innocent, loving, little sermon illustrations, Jesus' death on the cross is absolutely inexplicable. So as we study the parables, we will see them as set against the conventional social meanings of our age as much as once they were prophetically critical of first-century Israel.

Parables and Teachings

We should not be surprised that Jesus' other teachings are frequently as prophetically sharp as the parables. We are no longer under the sway of a theological liberalism that viewed teachings of Jesus as grand, religious ideas for us all to live by. When Luke has Jesus announce, "Blessed are the poor," and then follow up with "Woe to you who are rich," the teaching is no more acceptable now than it was when first spoken. Certainly, "Blessed are you who weep" runs counter to the "pursuit of happiness" the Declaration of Independence endorses. What about "Love your enemies"? Will we be willing to apply the words to Saddam Hussein? Most clergy are quite happy with the idea that Jesus' teachings, including the parables, are "interim ethic," teachings designed for a community awaiting an imminent end of the world. Thus we can regard the words of Jesus as extreme, as superhigh ideals, to be scaled down to fit into our everyday world— Don't be too rich, too happy, too lustful, too angry, too judgmental; indeed, don't be too much of anything!

The teachings of Jesus are as "extravagant" and as troubling as the parables. They are also prophetic, though couched in wisdom forms. Here is an example from Matthew 5:38–41 suggested by John Dominic Crossan.[31]

> You have heard it was said, "An eye for an eye and a tooth for a tooth."
> But I'm telling you, Do not resist evil. But if anyone smacks you on the
> right cheek, turn to him the other as well; If anyone takes your shirt in a

lawsuit, let him have your topcoat as well; And if anyone commandeers you for one mile, go two for him.   (DGB)

Crossan notes that Jesus is using a traditional "case law" form. After a general rule ("Don't resist evil") there are exceptions to the rule. Exceptions are expressed in a formula, "*If . . . then . . . ,*" manner. Examples of the formula can be found one after another in Exodus 21—22.

Jesus' use of the traditional formula is surprising. First-century Palestine was a land occupied by Roman troops where a Jew might get the back of a hand across the face or be commanded to lug Roman baggage like a slave. But Jesus' words are sweeping, "Don't resist evil." Even now the command is troubling. Are there to be no exceptions? Are there not times when religious people should—indeed, must—resist evil? But look at Jesus' "*If . . . then . . .* " forms!

> *If* anyone smacks you on the right cheek, *then* turn to
>   him the other . . . .
> *If* anyone takes your shirt in a lawsuit, *then* let him have
>   your topcoat . . . .
> *If* anyone commandeers you for one mile, *then* go two . . . .

The exceptions turn out to be extravagant examples of no exceptions at all. But notice that like many parables, we have a prophetic message wrapped up in a traditional form.[32] For most parables we can find parallel teachings, and the teachings help us to read the parables and, of course, vice versa.

In parables Jesus still speaks prophetically to us. His images call us to thoughtfulness. We must put his words together with the notion of God's social order, what Jesus called *basileia tou Theou,* "kingdom of God," and see what he is trying to say to us. Yes, to *us.*

2

The Mysterious
"Kingdom of God"

Jesus preached the kingdom of God. Many of his parables begin, "The kingdom of God is like . . ." And the prayer he handed to his disciples, our "Lord's Prayer," asks God to make the "kingdom come." But what exactly is the kingdom of God? Parables are enigmatic stories. Metaphorically they are set beside the idea of a kingdom of God, but the idea of kingdom is itself mysterious. Could "kingdom of God" also be a metaphor, a metaphor in which we can live?

The Provenance of "Kingdom"

Where does the idea of a kingdom of God come from? Jesus did not make up the idea; as a Jew, he inherited it. You will find the notion forming in the Hebrew Bible where, again and again, God is hailed as "King." Take a look at Psalms 96, 97, 98, 99; they all celebrate God as a king:

> The LORD is king; let the peoples tremble!
>   He sits enthroned upon the cherubim; let the earth quake!
> The LORD is great in Zion;
>   he is exalted over all the peoples.
> Let them praise your great and awesome name.
>   Holy is he!
> Mighty King, lover of justice,
>   you have established equity;
>   you have established justice
>   and righteousness in Jacob.
> Extol the LORD our God;
>   worship at his footstool.
>   Holy is he!   (Ps. 99:1–5)

Underlying the idea of kingship is covenant; originally there was YHWH and a chosen people, Israel. The idea of territory, a promised land, was added. Thus, there was God, a covenant people, and the land—an image was taking shape. But soon, when the several tribes of Israel came together, though they had been given God's law at Sinai, they needed centralized government. God was reluctant, but Israel begged for a king. Israel's first king was the tormented Saul; its second king was a shrewd power politician, David; its third king was Solomon, whose legendary wisdom managed to get him in trouble with God. But with the idea of kingship, Israel had a religious metaphor to overrule any political pretensions: God was the true king and Israel was God's kingdom.

Early in the sixth century B.C.E., Israel was overrun and its people taken into exile. How could Israel sing the Lord's song in a strange land? The exile forced a revision of Israel's faith. God the king was no longer a territorial ruler housed in Jerusalem's temple; no, for God was with them even in far-off Babylon. God, their God, was king of the universe.

In exile, Israel began to write down dreams of Zion. Someday Israel would return in triumph. Once more God would be enthroned, and God's kingdom would draw in all the people of earth. At the end of the exile, Israel's dream seemed to be coming true. In a battered land, done in by impoverishments of exile, Israel came home to rebuild a temple for God.

How hard it is to hold onto a dream when, over and over, your little land is swept by invading armies. Israel was overrun by Persians and Greeks and finally by the Romans. So, for many, the idea of a divine kingship floated into a far-off eschatological future. God's kingdom became the stuff of "someday," spelled with a capital S. Yes, there was a kingdom; after all, they were back in the land God had promised long ago. And yes, they were still people of the covenant. But Israel was occupied by pagan armies. And, to be truthful, the land itself was scarcely a land of milk and honey and money. The kingdom of God waited consummation; it was a not-quite-yet kingdom. For pietist Pharisees, it would be a kingdom of the righteous; for proto-Zealots, it was a kingdom to be claimed by political force; for the apocalyptic fringe, it was an imminent kingdom—soon God would evict conquering empires and establish a holy realm.

Jesus came preaching. Was he apocalyptic? Albert Schweitzer said so.[1] Certainly Paul and Mark, our earliest writers, seem to have been apocalyptic Christians. But recent Jesus research has made us less certain; the earliest layer of Q, the collection of teachings shared by Matthew and Luke, while ethically intense, is not exactly apocalyptic. The teachings appear to be couched in a wisdom style. All we can say with certainty is that Jesus, a prophet, showed up preaching a kingdom of God. In our Bibles, the phrase "kingdom of God" is found almost exclusively in the Synoptic Gospels. The concentration of the phrase establishes that Jesus preached, calling people to live in the kingdom, either as a kind of new age community forming in the midst of our world or as the advanced guard of a kingdom scheduled for imminent arrival. But was he apocalyptic? We cannot say for sure. But, without doubt, he was a radical, prophetic figure who was crucified as a threat to both the empire and organized religion. Probably he is still both.

A Split Consciousness

There appears to be some sort of split consciousness in each of the Christian Gospels.

Mark, the earliest Gospel, is an apocalyptic work. Written around 70 C.E., the time of the fall of Jerusalem, Mark's Gospel senses that the world of Israel, God's world, is falling apart. Were they living in the midst of the "great tribulation," a kind of cosmic seizure before the coming of God's promised kingdom?[2] Certainly the little apocalypse in Mark 13 predicts an end-time era of contention, trial, and persecution. Mark expects the church will face tribulation, perhaps martyrdom. But Mark wants readers to be emboldened by their royal Lord—his sufferings, his trial, his faithfulness before the cross. But in view of the resurrection, Mark believes we are living on the verge of *parousia;* soon Christ will return to establish a righteous rule of God. The Gospel of Mark sees us in the midst of crisis; an old aeon is in its death throes, a new aeon will soon come upon us. In Mark, we are involved in cosmic drama: "The kingdom of God is at hand."

Matthew shares some of the same urgency, but with a peculiar focus on Israel. For him, the split is a split between an old and a new Israel. According to Matthew, the old Israel has failed to acknowledge its Messiah. So Matthew regards his little community of faith as true Israel, and he calls upon his people to live God's law in a much more rigorous way. In the Sermon on the Mount, Jesus, a new Moses, instructs true Israel in patterns of piety and morality. In the crucial chapter 13, a chapter full of parables, Matthew argues that as Israel has refused Jesus as Messiah, now his community of Christian Jews must fulfill God's purposes. Over the last half of Matthew's Gospel there is a sense of moral urgency—the judgment is coming. Notice, once again, we confront a split between old and new.

Luke's split consciousness is more difficult to recognize. Mark's apocalyptic crisis has been eased in Matthew and Luke, but the sense of a major shift in God's history underlies both Gospels. Luke is a child of the empire. As scholars have noticed, he plays down the role of Rome in the trial and crucifixion of Jesus. Is Luke compromised by his citizenship? Not really. He depicts Jesus as an Imperial Lord Jesus, whose arrival will clearly "transvalue values" of the empire. The poor, the estranged, the rejected are to be elevated, while the powerful will be brought down and the rich sent away empty (Luke 1:52–53). With the ascension narratives, Luke exalts the Imperial Christ to a position of rule; Jesus Christ, who was crucified, is the world's true emperor. Under the direction of the word and led by the ever astonishing Spirit, Luke seems to look for a colonizing transformation of the social order. How will the conquest occur? Oddly enough, through preaching the word and being led by the Spirit. In Luke's thought the church is a prototype of God's new order.

Thus, in the Pauline letters, in the Synoptic Gospels, and in the Gospel of John, we bump into a huge sense of social change. The new is replacing the old—

the new garment, the new wine, the new covenant, the new life. Liberation theologies have stressed freedom, but freedom is from something old, perhaps old as Eden, and true freedom is for a new social order. The sharp sense of a new consciousness undoubtedly goes back to the words of Jesus. Again the question: Was Jesus apocalyptic? He was certainly prophetic, if not apocalyptic — prophetic and apocalyptic are, after all, gradations on a radical continuum. Jesus called disciples, significantly twelve, to form a new social order. He taught a radical ethic of love. Thus the sense of new that underlies all the Gospels does seem to have come from him.

Obviously there was great excitement connected with the early Christian enterprise. Men and women left their families to spread news of God. In many cases they did so with apocalyptic urgency, for they were sure the present age would end soon in chaos and dismay. They believed God was bringing something new into being, a new social order: The kingdom is at hand — come join the new order! Early Christians prayed, "Lord, come!" They baptized new converts into the kingdom of God, or, more exactly, into Eucharist, a symbolic presence of the kingdom, and a prototype of the promised great feast on Mount Zion. As persecutions commenced — under an old order resisting change — Christians died often eyeing the risen Christ, certain of God's ultimate triumph. We can analyze the sociological factors, but sociology alone cannot explain the early Christian movement. What cannot be denied is the enormous excitement generated by the notion of a new social order, the promised kingdom of God.

Parables and Kingdom

Are all the parables "kingdom" parables? Technically no. Some parables are aimed descriptively: "To what shall I liken this generation?" Others appear to relate to the character of the Christian life; for example, the Rich Farmer, the Two Children, the Rich Man and Lazarus. Only a few begin with the famous phrase, "The kingdom of God is like . . ." C. H. Dodd provides the arithmetic:

> In Mark two parables are so introduced, those of the Seed Growing Secretly and of the Mustard Seed. In Luke again there are two, the Mustard Seed and the Leaven. As these two also occur in Matthew with the like introduction, we may take it that they stood in the common source ("Q") of the first and third Gospels. In Matthew there are eight other parables introduced in this way.[3]

Only one-third of the parables we will review actually begin with reference to the "kingdom of God." Yet, as Dodd suggests, the parables of Jesus are all kingdom parables. Certainly we can insist that all the parables should be set beside the mystery of God's eternal purposes. Some may draw a contrast between God's intended social order and "this generation." Others may suggest patterns of life in God's new social order. Still others may probe the mystery of God-with-us per se.

In studying the parables, we will assume they are metaphorical stories designed to open deep thoughtfulness about God-with-us and the purposes of God that even now are unfolding among us, purposes that ultimately will be fulfilled. Thus all the parables of Jesus are kingdom parables.

An Embarrassing Kingdom

There is no doubt that Jesus preached a *basileia tou Theou,* "kingdom of God." As we have seen, the kingdom was not a new idea, but was shaped during YHWH's long love affair with recalcitrant Israel. Think of the wonderful visions that light up the prophets—Isaiah 9, 11 and 35; Jeremiah 31:31–34; Ezekiel 36, 37; Zechariah 8:

> Thus says the LORD: I will return to Zion, and will dwell in the midst of Jerusalem; Jerusalem shall be called the faithful city, and the mountain of the LORD of hosts shall be called the holy mountain. Thus says the LORD of hosts: Old men and old women shall again sit in the streets of Jerusalem, each with staff in hand because of their great age. And the streets of the city shall be full of boys and girls playing in its streets. . . . Thus says the LORD of hosts: I will save my people from the east country and from the west country; and I will bring them to live in Jerusalem. They shall be my people and I will be their God, in faithfulness and in righteousness　(Zech. 8:3–8)

For Israel, the kingdom, a sociopolitical image, was both here and now and yet to come. Jesus announced the same kingdom of God; many of his words seem to speak of a social order forming among us, while almost as many sayings wave toward a future on the way.

Now for the embarrassing question: Where on earth is the kingdom Jesus promised? You look around at our broken world, ripped by warfare, stifled by greed, and it doesn't much look like a kingdom of God. Is Christian faith based on the rantings of an early day idealist who, to be truthful, may have been loony? How can we handle the fact that no new social order has dropped out of the skies, and, as Thomas Hardy once observed:

> After two thousand years of mass,
> We've got as far as poison gas.[4]

The problem is not merely a homiletic difficulty to be overcome by citing examples of a few nice people doing a few nice things. No, Jesus preached the kingdom of God, a bright, right social order and it has not appeared, ever, anywhere. Such embarrassment seems to undercut Christianity *per se.*

Proposed solutions have been many. We can say (1) the kingdom has come, but is invisible, (2) the kingdom has come, but it is different from Jesus' vision, (3) the kingdom is up in heaven, (4) the kingdom is a helpful dream (only if understood by "Christian realism"). The various solutions—and there are probably more[5]—testify to the church's embarrassment with Jesus' kingdom preaching.

There is no doubt that Jesus spoke of a *basileia tou Theou*. Further, there is no doubt that his image of kingdom was in continuity with Jewish understandings—kingdom was God's kingdom, a sociopolitical image, both now and someday. If Jesus was looking to the future, he rewrote the timetable, for he preached "the realm of God is *at hand*." If he was referring to a kingdom now, he preached the "now" with prophetic urgency. In either case the blunt question remains: Where? Where on earth is the kingdom of God?

The Question of Where

In the nineteenth century, a controversy between Adolf von Harnack and Alfred Loisy defined two of the options. Either we must deny the sociopolitical character of Jesus' vision, thus separating him from his heritage in Israel, or we must argue that a rather different sociopolitical reality appeared. Harnack, a great historian of Christian thought, opted for an invisible kingdom:

> The kingdom of God comes by coming to the individual, by entering his soul and laying hold of it. True, the kingdom of God is the rule of God; but it is the rule of the holy God in the hearts of individuals.[6]

Harnack denied that there was any social or historical dimension to the kingdom. Perhaps he could have added the words "by faith" to his definition; obviously, they were intended. For many Americans, religion is a "habit of the heart"; thus Harnack's position is still attractive though it is assuredly unbiblical. Yes, we may be aware of living in God's social order, and such awareness can be in our minds so as to affect our emotions, but there is a difference between an individual inner awareness and an external social order. Dissolve the external reality and the inner awareness becomes nothing more than fantasy. No wonder Catholics have accused Protestants of a "fideist heresy," embracing inward faith without a social reality.

According to Alfred Loisy, a great Catholic biblical scholar, Harnack's version of Christianity "was as a soul without a body."[7] Loisy, in contrast, supposed that "Jesus foretold the kingdom, and it was the church that came."[8] The logic is simple: Jesus announced a new social order and the church, an actual worldwide social institution, arrived to fulfill the prophecy. At least the Catholic position respects the sociopolitical character of the kingdom image; God's kingdom is neither individual nor insubstantial.

But the problem is obvious; in spite of the church's pomp and ceremony, when vestments are stripped away, the church can be dismayingly human. These days the church includes celebrity televangelists, aggressive fundamentalists, popemobiles, thoughtless church promoters, big-steeple prides, homiletic laziness, predatory clergy, denominational competition, sectarian nuttiness, and organized right-wing ranting that upsets almost every American religious body.

The gap between Jesus' vision and the institutional church is simply too great. Besides, the kingdom Jesus announced was a world-sized kingdom and not merely a religious option within the world. We can imagine that the church will enlarge and a world-sized ecclesial "kingdom" finally arrive, but such a position would trap the church into a triumphal-conquest mentality quite antithetical to the gospel message. Perhaps we can say that the church is called to be the living sign of a coming kingdom, but at all costs we will have to avoid talk of identity: the church is emphatically *not* the kingdom of God.

Perhaps both positions are in error. If we look objectively at the world, there seems to be no sign of a kingdom of God, particularly these days when America has been partially settled by secularism: Our nation spends more than forty percent of its income on military matters while poor people are struggling on a very inadequate minimum wage; our nation still relishes the death penalty but is incapable of providing universal health care; our nation builds walled enclaves for the rich while the poor scratch for affordable housing. The negative evidence is overwhelming—where is a kingdom of God? Ministers can give examples of little one-to-one acts of Christian kindness, but they do not add up to a worldwide kingdom. As for looking inward, people examining themselves in a mirror of self, even under the rubric "spirituality," are too solipsistic to qualify as a kingdom of God! But notice what we are doing: We are looking at self and world as human products. Can anything that bears a human trademark be other than ambiguous? We are sinners all.

Suppose we begin differently. First, let us admit that the kingdom of God is God's project. The metaphor "kingdom of God" represents God's ultimate purpose for the human world, a purpose God seeks to realize interactively with us somewhat-free human creatures. The prophets portrayed God's purpose in stunning images of reconciliation: nations dropping their emblems to enter a Holy City, the lion and the lamb snoozing side by side, all humanity partying on top of Mount Zion. The world God intends is a world that lives in the glad exchanges of neighbor love, a world in which God and humanity live in mutual delight, free from destructive powers, free in the wideness of mercy. We do believe that God is bringing such a world into being; the promises of God are sure. Though God's activity is not obvious in the social world, nonetheless, it is sure. If we are to locate signs of the kingdom of God we will spot those movements that seem to reflect in advance aspects of the future God is bringing about. As human movements, they will always be ambiguous, but nevertheless they can be moving toward God's purpose. To pick an example, we will turn away from the "victim's rights" people demanding more executions, and look for those groups who are trying to liberate the land from a death-penalty mentality. To cite another, God's kingdom is shalom, peace; therefore peace movements surely are involved in God's kingdom project.

Secondly, let us agree with those like theologian Edward Farley who recognize that underlying both self-awareness and the social world is a pattern of interacting human beings.[9] When we look at ourselves in self-awareness, we are viewing a self-image shaped by human interaction. When we assess the social world, the so-called "lived world," we sense that patterns of activity and attitude are products of primal human interactions. We are all centered selves, for we see the world *around* us. Therefore we tend to regard others around us as ordered by our needs, dreams, and purposes. But, of course, the others around us are also centered selves in a world, with their personal desires and dreams. We often collide. But, instead, we can recognize ourselves in the faces of others—our mortality, our aloneness, our fears, our wonders, our vulnerabilities. A kingdom of God must form within the underlying interacting structures of human beings together, and with human beings who somehow sense in their interactions the transcendent presence of the Other, the mysterious Other we sometimes call God. If the underlying interhuman realm is redeemed, both self-awareness and the social world will be transformed.

What can we say of the kingdom of God? The kingdom of God is *in process;* it is a happening. The kingdom is happening wherever God is redemptively involved with human beings, which is to say everywhere!

The Question of When

Because we human beings have memory and anticipation, we tend to describe kingdom in a linear way. We locate the idea on a time line. When will the kingdom arrive? What is the ETA, the estimated time of arrival? We read the Jesus material, teachings and parables, and we are puzzled. There seems to be a huge sense of urgency in Jesus' words, but about what? Does he refer to a kingdom now forming among us, or to a kingdom on the way coming from God's future? About all we can say is the kingdom is TBA, to be announced, for the schedule seems quite uncertain.

Perhaps we need to think of time differently, scrapping the linear model. Could we view time as, let us say, the design on a vast tapestry, with woven strands of color emanating from one cluster of events to another where, transformed into different colors, the strands project toward still other clusters? We seem to be imagining interacting clusters of events happening on an open field. We might even go further and imagine the tapestry to be made of fabric layers. Such an image of time and event might help to get us out of a linear trap. How easy it could be to say, yes, the kingdom is here insofar as the strands of color are being woven interactively by God and humanity into the fabric of time, and someday we will see these strands forming some great social design. Meanwhile we live in the midst of God's quite mysterious interweaving.

Neither a vertical model (the kingdom is up in heaven) nor a horizontal model (the kingdom will come at the end of time) is entirely helpful. The Bible seems to say that God's kingdom is now because God is now, and yet God's kingdom is still forthcoming because God may be said to have purpose. Certainly we can say that we live in an interweaving of human intentions and God's purposeful, if improvisational, grace. Are the parables of Jesus metaphors flung up before the mystery of God, a God interactively weaving divine purpose into the free field of human affairs? Perhaps. But however we may depict time, we believe kingdom is *happening*.

Let us try another image: A novelist may set up a fictional world and expand that world with Dickensian improvisation, creating many different characters in many different places. What's more, in chapter one the novelist may start a story in which the characters and the places can happen. At a certain point, many novelists sense that in their plotting they have turned toward denouement, their characters are being drawn toward some conclusion. Perhaps the author may have some sense of how the story should work out, but of course there are contingencies, promptings of character and bindings of events that shape the conclusion. Perhaps Jesus was saying that human affairs are now being drawn purposefully toward some great conclusion. Said he, "The kingdom of God is at hand."

But our model is still too linear. Perhaps God's kingdom has been intended from the beginning, and is somehow built into creation. Therefore the human world will always be reaching to actualize the divine purposes while, at the same time, denouement is drawing humanity toward the future. The idea that the future can be a presence with us may seem strange. Jean-Paul Sartre imagines he is to meet his friend Pierre in a café at 4:00. He arrives a little late, looks around, does not see Pierre, and says to himself, "He is not here." He looks at faces of people coming into the café. "Could this be Pierre coming in?" He realizes that if Pierre were present, the ambience of the café would be organized around him. But now everything seems to be organized around his absence and his coming. Pierre is thus future-present![10] The image is suggestive, if a bit too personal. Instead we should imagine a huge Jewish/Christian community at table anticipating a coming banquet with God on Mount Zion. Everything we do, our words and our actions, are because the kingdom, God's great denouement, is coming toward us. Strands of life projecting from creation are entwining with lines of purpose drawing us toward God's future. So the kingdom is happening. We live *now* in the happening of the kingdom.

Scanning the Tombstones,
Searching the Skies

The big problem with social vision is obvious. We die. No matter how exciting a social prospect may be, many older human beings have already begun counting years left on their fingers; if lucky, on toes as well. But fingers and toes only add up to a double decade. Death does put a damper on social dreaming, doesn't it? We can be benevolent and want a better world for our children and our children's children. Nevertheless, given the sputtering few breaths we are allotted in life, end-term visions may be less than captivating.

Of course, we cannot help dreaming if only because we are frequently beset. We suffer from diseases and, thus, can dream a disease-free world. War is a chronic human problem; wouldn't it be wonderful if peace, shalom, were full-time? Racism in America is a subtle, terrifying tragedy; can we not dream a free, familial society? Poverty hampers more than half the human world; wouldn't it be splendid if cash and property could be shared? As for ourselves, most of us would be delighted to be delivered from our hang-ups, our inabilities, our crippling inhibitions, and the like; yet self-help sales multiply because, when it comes to personal engineering, we are frequently helpless. So we are bound to dream a better, brighter, sweeter world. For centuries, human beings have fashioned full-scale visions out of their longings.

But social visions may push further than deprivations and dreams. There is a primal sense of "ought," as philosophers from the Greeks to Kant to those of the present day have noticed. Probably the sense of justice, of rights, of fairness is something that has been developing through the centuries. Biblical visions of the kingdom always feature justice, and not merely justice, but justice for the poor, the defenseless, and the overlooked. Life ought to be an equal-opportunity employer. Life ought to be reasonably free for all. Life ought to be designed to encourage sweet amity. Our world is spectacularly unjust as well as cruel, so we long for a justice that ought to be.

But, though we dream, and maybe even dream some of God's dreams, we die. No wonder people schedule a kingdom of God in the hereafter, and Christian hymnbooks are packed with songs of heavenly fulfillment. Marx, of course, saw the danger. A handout heaven can be designed to keep the poor in place. Anticipate ivory palaces, and you can put up with a slum. Look forward to a heavenly fish fry, and you can live in hunger. Marx accused a bourgeois Christian church of dealing in such socially damaging dreams. Of course, there is another side to the issue: If you are desperately oppressed, a little "opiate of the people" can be a comfort! Maybe one reason the Bible uses here-and-now metaphors for the kingdom is to keep hope connected to some sense of social reality.

What about dying? The mortality rate still runs around one hundred percent. The answer to the problem of dying is a series of statements. If God is love, would God trash what is beloved? If God seeks a harmonious human race in love with one another within wide mercy, would God junk huge batches of humanity every instant? If death is ultimate, it would be an absolute contradiction of "God is love." Yet there are few if any biblical texts that suggest a vertical, heavenly location for kingdom. No, most texts seem to suggest that kingdom will be realized horizontally at the end of time. So what should we imagine? Will we wake as if from a long sleep, rub our eyes, and step into a new "world"? Will there be a "new heaven and a new earth"? Although W. H. Auden announced gleefully, "I wouldn't be caught dead without a body!" perhaps consciousness will provide embodiment in some unusual manner. Who knows? The book of Revelation pictures a throne room full of singing. But these are acts of imagination; they are woven metaphors. Jesus himself was reticent with regard to the hereafter, suggesting only that it will be new and different (Mark 12:18–27). All we can say is that God's word will be kept and that God's promised kingdom will be, but no one knows where or when. The Bible does not cater much to literalists!

Obviously, the Bible does use here-and-now stuff as metaphor for a kingdom of God; the visions include lions and lambs, burning military uniforms, weapons converted into farm implements, boys and girls playing in a city's streets, deserts blossoming, and lots of full-scale partying. The images multiply but are not very precise—perhaps to leave room for the improvisations of grace. But the images are quite concrete, no doubt to convey a sure sense of reality.

Why would we need anything more?

The Problem with High Ideals

More than a hundred years ago, biblical scholars Johannes Weiss and Albert Schweitzer argued that moral advice found in Christian writings was "*interims-ethik.*"[11] They pictured early Christians as all agog, expecting an imminent end of the world with the cataclysmic arrival of a kingdom of God. As a result, they embraced a radical ethic designed for a brief interim. The position put forth by Schweitzer and Weiss impressed many mid-century ethicists and theologians. If the primitive Christian ethic was extreme, then a more mature church must now seek to compromise radical kingdom teachings with things as they are. After all, Jesus' breakthrough kingdom has not arrived. One biblical scholar put it bluntly, "Jesus does not provide a valid ethics for today."[12]

What do we do with the notion of a kingdom of God? Many Christians in the twentieth century accepted the kingdom of God as a high ideal, the image of society as it ought to be, but an image to be modified by calculated compromises with things as they are. The Sermon on the Mount with its perfectionist ethics—love enemies, do not worry over practical needs, don't judge, don't hate, don't lust—is an ethic for the kingdom of God which, unfortunately, has not come. So, according to Reinhold Niebuhr, Christians must develop a casuistry to modify perfectionism with what he called "Christian realism."[13] Otherwise, the kingdom of God could become nothing more than a naive, often misleading utopianism.

Preachers bought the argument. If they preached on lust (Matt. 5:27–30), they admitted right away that, according to Freud, all of us lust; therefore what the teaching means is "don't lust too much." Or if they preached on Matthew 6:25–34, "I tell you don't worry about your life, what you will eat, or about your body, what you will wear," they giggled a bit over the advice because, after all, how can anyone avoid anxiety when "there's always more month left after the money runs out?" Their sermons ended up urging people not to worry excessively. Quite systematically, we who preach compromised Jesus' teaching in the name of Christian realism. If Jesus' words were impossible, they could be modified, morally eased, so as to be practically useful. Besides, preached rigorously, such teaching could only increase guilt, which in turn might undercut the good news we preach these days—"Smile, God loves you."

By treating kingdom passages as ideals—every society needs a batch of high ideals—we completely sabotage the notion of the kingdom. Are we to suppose Jesus deliberately preached a perfectionist ethic because he thought it would be good for societies to have high ideals to compromise? If not, then are we forced to admit that Christianity was founded by an unrealistic apocalyptic nut? To argue that Christian realism must deliberately compromise kingdom teaching implies that *realism* rather than kingdom is our actual norm. But what if the church is called to be a radical witness, a living sign of the kingdom? Or suppose that *real* realism is the acknowledgment that God is, we are, and our world is God's world. Niebuhr was right to underscore structures of human sinfulness within the social world as well as within the stymied self, a sinfulness that defies all our kingdom dreams. Human beings are ever ambiguous, and, therefore, we are very dangerous to one another. Nevertheless, as God works among us by Word and Spirit, kingdom can be happening, a living process, and thus, more than a package of pleasantly lofty ideals.

Part of Reinhold Niebuhr's struggle was caused by his attempt to apply kingdom teachings to ordinary individual human beings. Individuals on their own, Niebuhr observed, are incapable of not hating, not judging, not lusting, not worrying, and so forth. But Jesus' teachings are not addressed to individuals on their own; they are "you all" language, spoken to communities with a shared faith-consciousness. Thus they are calling for conversion to a new social order. There is a difference between "don't lust" addressed to an individual (when, realistically, all of us lust), and addressed to a community. The command calls for a community to reconceive itself as "brothers" and "sisters" so lust will not deform common life. As for anxiety over the basics of life, we are to be a sharing community living beyond ideas of private property, so that no one will go hungry, need clothing, or suffer untended in illness. Can such communities actually function in our world? Only with difficulty. But as witnesses to the coming of the kingdom, we should try to form ourselves into a sign, indeed a sacrament, of the kingdom. A calling of God addressed to a people is something more than a dreamy idealism. We are called to participate in the kingdom's happening.

The Disappearing Kingdom of God

A startling fact: We have not preached the realm of God. We have preached kingdom parables but in peculiar ways. We have turned them into pointed lessons in individual morality, or therapeutic advice for the living of life. But have we preached the kingdom of God as a sociopolitical image? Well no, not really. Inasmuch as Jesus was centrally concerned with the *basileia tou Theou,* we have failed to preach his preaching. What was crucial to him has been silenced by us. Why?

One reason for the neglect of kingdom preaching is its association with the "L" word—liberal. These days in America it is fashionable to be "postliberal."

Nineteenth-century social liberalism was full of misguided optimism; it was theologically thin. Overlooking the hard truth about human nature, turn-of-the-century Christians viewed the kingdom as either morally attainable or achievable through missionary efforts ("the kingdom of God in our generation!"). Such naiveté soon crumbled in the twentieth century with two world wars, a great Depression, and, above all, the Holocaust. Now we live with shadows in our eyes, for who can be innocent after the Holocaust? But instead of correcting naive liberal theology while keeping the realm of God central to our preaching, we scuttled the whole idea.

No doubt, the notion of a kingdom of God was also diverted by the rise of therapeutic personalism. As we have noted, nineteenth-century revivalism urged a personal appropriation of Jesus. The concern was translated into a therapeutic personalism when news of Freud floated to America in the 1920s. Then in the 1950s another European import drifted into our pulpits—existentialism. So for most of the century, preachers have preached a gospel for individuals in their individual self-awareness. Obviously, such a gospel must either scuttle the idea of a realm of God or, following Harnack, turn it into inwardness.

Meanwhile, beginning primarily in the 1940s, in the backwash of the Depression, we saw the rise of the biblical theology movement, often with a Barthian trademark. We were determined to turn our congregants into biblical people, indeed, to preach a biblical world for them to enter. Although the kingdom of God is clearly a biblical idea, somehow it was shuffled away. Our churches prospered. As mainline Christianity became fairly well-heeled, the social radicalism of the kingdom of God was set aside, replaced by either a gospel of therapeutic concern or the gospel of a full-service church. The coming of a kingdom of God has never been attractive to those who have invested heavily in here-and-now social adjustment.

Instead of looking to God's future, we have turned back and tried to burrow ourselves in a biblical world. We have declared a therapeutic Jesus, but forgotten what he was talking about, namely, a realm of God. Without social vision, America seems frozen in political gridlock, trying to fend off God's future while holding on to the cash and the power. But truthfully, if God is working purposefully in human affairs and the kingdom is happening, then a reactionary America is in serious trouble with God. Our land desperately needs social prophecy on the one hand and social vision on the other; both derive from preaching the realm of God.

The church has become strangely isolated. Our public voice has gone silent. There is little evangelism in mainline churches, except for institutionally oriented church growth programs. Our message is strictly Bible stuff for church-pew people. We don't speak out in the world or take on social issues that, in the light of the gospel, may be urgent. We seem to want to take people out of the world into church, and then further back into the biblical world, a strategy that probably is the exact reverse of God's purpose for us!

God help us.

The God of the Parables

When most people think of God they think big! They also think *all:* God can do all, know all, be all, begin all, end all. God is ultimate, eternal, perfect in goodness, truth, and beauty. Sometimes we add the word "sovereign" to remind ourselves that God rules everything. What we are doing is rehearsing what are usually labeled "attributes of God." Notice that God's attributes always seem to be reversals of our finite selves. We cannot do anything we want; for example, we cannot drop-kick the U.S. Capitol building into space, though the idea may have a certain appeal. We cannot know everything; how could we be in on everyone else's secrets? We are mortal: we live a span of days and then we die. We are dependent on food and drink, air to breathe and shelter from the elements. No one yet has accused any of us of being perfect in "truth, beauty, goodness" or anything else. So how do we think of God? God is not finite and God is not fragile. No wonder we rattle off a list of latinate terms: God is omniscient, omnipotent, omnipresent, immutable, immortal, and so forth. We think very big.

When God is lined up with parables, we are bound to suppose God is represented by the authority figures in the stories—the father of the prodigal son, the vineyard owner who hired laborers, the host who has planned a great feast, the landowner with rebellious tenant farmers. But we must be cautious. There is a parable involving a judge, and though God is surely our judge, the judge in the story is corrupt. So we reverse logic and say, "Our God is not a *corrupt* judge; indeed, our God is incorruptible!" Or what about the parable of the Entrusted Money? There is an authority figure distributing talents to servants. But remember how he describes himself? "I harvest where I haven't sown, and gather where I haven't scattered"—apparently the man is ruthless. Again we reverse logic and say, "But our God isn't ruthless." Of course, there are parables that do not directly feature authority figures—for example, those that begin, "To what shall I liken this generation . . . ?" Nevertheless, there are parables that do seem to suggest the character of God. There are clues to the mystery of God in the parables of Jesus:

1. The God figures in parables do not seem to be fiercely concerned with what we call morality. The father in the Prodigal Son does not seem to worry that his young son has been off whoring in a far country. The boss whose manager marks down the accounts payable to save his own neck praises the man for his dishonest shrewdness. The owner who hires workers for his vineyard ignores fairness and pays them all the same, those who worked only one hour and those who worked twelve. In the great Feast, the host invites in riffraff for his banquet, thus ignoring social propriety. The publican, a big-time racketeer, is justified by God outside the temple courts.

2. The God of the parables seems willing to give up sovereignty, yes, and honor as well. Look at the father of the prodigal. Though it will

slice landholdings and reduce his social status, he hands over a chunk of inheritance to his demanding young son. Then, when the disgraceful boy returns broke, he forgets his dignity, hauls up his robes, and rushes out to kiss him. Though villagers would regard the boy as despicable, the father throws a huge party for everyone to celebrate the prodigal's return. When an older brother sullenly accuses the father of favoritism, the father replies, "Dearest child, everything I have is yours." Thus the father has ignored honor, lost sovereignty, and, having given up everything, may well be destitute. Such patterns do not seem to line up with the usual attributes of God.

3. At the time of Christ, society was patriarchal. Images of God were masculine and moral examples were also masculine. Fathers were clan chiefs, jealous of any threat to their prerogatives. But as Bernard Brandon Scott has observed, power characters in parables are much more feminine, at least as "feminine" was defined in the ancient world.[14] Jesus told parables that featured women—a woman baker who produces enough leavened bread in her tiny clay oven to fill a bakery truck twice over; a woman who searches all day for a lost coin and then, when she finds it, throws a lavish party for the neighborhood. Are these women images of God? And what of the father in the Prodigal Son who gushes and kisses and fusses and, finally, serves up a banquet?

4. The God figures in the parables seem to be appallingly patient with wickedness. They defer judgment: the gardener who wants to keep on fertilizing a dead tree; the manager who condones a crook; the landowner who lets tenant farmers beat up his agents, even killing one of them, but continues to send more agents and finally, as a last resort, dispatches his own son. These parables certainly do not display decisive sovereign power. Yes, there are judgment parables, for example, the Closed Door and the Last Judgment. Most of these parables show up toward the end of Matthew and are suspect; that is to say, many scholars do not believe they come from Jesus. But in parables generally assigned to Jesus, authority figures seem to avoid any rush to judgment.

5. The God of the parables seems to like partying, particularly in the Lukan collection. In a rather feminine way, the God of the parables provides food. The one startling example is what Luke does with the story of "Be on watch, for you don't know when the master of the house will come." Luke's master shows up, puts on an apron, and serves dinner! There are associations with food and celebrative partying in many, many parables. In a paternalistic world, the parables portray a self-giving, feminine figure who does not stand on honor, and who abdicates power again and again. The parables portray a God we have not yet come to terms with.

We say our God is omnipotent, omniscient, omnipresent, and we define these words by the word "any." God can do *any*thing, know *any*thing, be *any*where. We define God in terms of absolutes and then, oops, forget love. God is love. There are things love will not do. There are secrets love will not try to know. There are places love will not invade. If God is love, then God will do *only what is loving*. To say, "God can do *any*thing," is inappropriate, for there are many, many things love cannot do! In parables, we meet a God of radical love.

A World with Worlds within

Actually Jews and Christians, children of a common religious heritage, are two-world people. With everyone else, we live in a shared social world, a world full of meanings. Meanings are formed in consciousness by words, political slogans, conversations, novels, advertising, TV images, and so forth. But at the same time, we live in a world formed in religious communities by preaching and teaching, by rituals, by the hymns we sing and the religious texts we hear or read, by the interaction of our lives together. The two worlds are *always* intermixed. The attempt on the part of somewhat sectarian Christians to crowd people into a separate "Bible world," or even a Christian "faith world," is absurd. We live in one social world with everyone else, including sweet, secular neighbors. The idea that religious people should inhabit a separate "religious world" is an attempt to ghettoize us, denying our common humanity. No, the world of religious meaning (could it be the "now" of the kingdom) overlaps, or better, is interwoven with the shared social world. Maybe religious meanings restructure the social world in consciousness as God's world, created by God, sustained by God, and given purpose by God. But because they are *within* the social world, religious meanings will always seem somewhat visionary, indeed unrealized. Thus, in a way, the kingdom is always both now and yet to be—a happening.

Is life in the kingdom a matter of conversion? Perhaps. Although we must understand conversion is not a divine "zap," but socialization that occurs as we hear words of faith, see profound, probing works of art, experience ritual, interact with other members in a faith community. Conversion is not an internal combustion that occurs without the assistance of others. To live in a realm of God, a religious world intermixed with a social world, is to hope for eventual redemption of our common life. The mysterious interhuman realm, the realm that underlies both self and society, somehow must be redeemed.

We noted earlier that we are centered selves. In consciousness the world seems to surround us. Therefore we tend to regard others in the world as subservient to our centered selves. Why? Because our needs, dreams, desires are central to us. Thus we may regard others as threats to the sovereignty of our centered selves. To centered selves, even the idea of God may be peripheral. We are seldom aware of God and, inevitably, tend toward idolatry. Why are acts of worship so crucial? Because in worship we are addressed by God, reminded of who God is and what God has done, and, in return, acknowledge God as our true center.

Moreover, we recognize neighbors as part of God's world with us. News of God through parables and preaching is crucial. Parables disrupt our world, the world of centered selves, and relocate us in what Jesus called "the kingdom of God."

On Believing While You Preach

Maybe we who preach must be converted. We cannot preach about a kingdom of God as if it were something somewhere out in the world beyond us. Remember, the kingdom is a happening, and we live within its happening. If you speak of kingdom "out there," you will mislead yourself and your congregation. Instead you must speak of a kingdom happening all around us.

Moreover, in earlier chapters we discovered that parables are designed *to do*. Our sermons must be designed to deconstruct the social world in which we live and open sudden glimpses of another world, the real world, God's world. In God's world conventional moralities are irrelevant, and certainly "getting somewhere" or "being somebody" or "having something" is absurd. All our human competitions, claims, and rights fade away. All the labels—race and nation and sexuality and economic class—all are quite passé. All these are the stuff of centered selves.

The vision, God's social order, is like a great, grave formal dance, in which we human beings, children of God, interrelate. We serve and are served, we give and are given, we acknowledge others and are acknowledged by them, all in a high, holy, courteous pattern of love.

To such a vision we can say, "Amen."

3

Preaching Parables

Parables have been preached for centuries. At first they were probably retold as stories in a rabbinic fashion. But soon they were interpreted as allegorical mysteries, with each detail explained: What was the real meaning of the prodigal's return—the robe, the ring, the sandals, the fatted calf? In the nineteenth century, parables began to be preached as didactic lessons drawn from everyday life. In every era, the parables have been preached. Now it is our turn. How will we preach parables in the twenty-first century?

Ways of Preaching Parables

All preachers preach parables. We preach parables if we follow a lectionary because most lectionaries include them all. But even without a lectionary we preach parables because they have always been a substantial part of the church's "homiletic canon." In the last century or so, parables have been preached in three primary ways: verse by verse, in a textual-topical system, and in a life-situation scheme.

Verse by verse. Some preachers still work their way through every parable, verse by verse, explaining biblical background and opening up meanings for each verse. The procedure, particularly espoused by conservative pulpits as properly biblical, will provide biblical background but, at the same time, may produce a disconnected set of meanings that do not necessarily coalesce into a message. Inevitably, the method will tumble into allegory with each verse having a separate theological meaning. The result can be interesting in the same way that a necklace made of pearls, bottle caps, jelly beans, and buttons might be interesting. But along the way the narrative meaning of the parable may disappear.

Textual-topical system. Other preachers will distill some single topical meaning from each parable. Then they will apply the distillation to our lives by making points. Back in the seventeenth century, some preachers began with a single verse, text, first offering biblical study, then distilling theological truth, and finally, making practical applications (usually moralities for the living of life). The practice has continued down through the years, although often with the first two sections reduced. A preacher will look at the story of a gardener dealing patiently with a dead tree (Luke 13:6–9), distill a truth from the parable (e.g. "the patience of God"), and then make points: (1) God is patient with our moral progress, (2) God is patient allowing repentance, (3) God is patient waiting for our love.

The real problem with the method is that preachers objectify the parable as if it were the shell-like container for some eternal truth. The parable itself never becomes contemporary in our lives; it is rhetorically pointed at and, thus, kept at a distance. Can you see what is lost in the procedure? The unfolding movement of story—in a word, plot. Plus different preachers may distill different central ideas from the same parable. Does the barren tree disclose God's patience? Or is the parable referring to impending judgment? Or could the parable be saying that our lives will be examined for moral "fruit?" Any one of these distilled topics could produce a series of applied points. Are parables merely shells to be cracked open for some kernel of wisdom? A point-making homiletic reads a parable, grabs some sort of topic and then, of all things, throws the parable away!

Life-situation approach. Life-situation preaching, popularized by Harry Emerson Fosdick, has spread widely. The method was born of concern for the pulpit's practical helpfulness. Fosdick took what was then labeled "The New Psychology" and looked at the day-to-day problems of human beings. He then provided insights from the Bible, which themselves were often couched in categorical points.[1] It is only a short step from Fosdick's method to the "positive thinking" therapeutic preaching of the past half century. The scheme begins by describing a human problem or situation, often with psychological insight, and then turns to a biblical passage that offers meaningful help for "the living of these days." Sometimes such preaching can be diagnostically sharp and genuinely helpful. But notice how the method domesticates parables; they are turned into helpful hints for daily living. Luther argued that the gospel message is always *extra nos*. We do not originate the message because it is a message given by God, an alien, divine Word from beyond our lives. Life-situation preaching, however helpful, traps parables within the daily round of human experience. But parables should not be psychologized, should not be domesticated, and, above all, must not be trivialized. After all, the kingdom of God is not religious Prozac!

In this brief survey, current homiletic strategies appear to fail. The verse-by-verse system atomizes parables, separating parts and moving toward allegory. The textual-topical system objectifies parables, distilling a topic and applying "truths" in categorical points. The life-situation approach domesticates parables into helpfulness, thus preventing any encounter with the living God. How are we going to preach parables?

"I Love to Tell the Story"

Can we set down some ground rules? Perhaps. Parables are stories and, presumably, they ought to move along episodically like a story. But what kind of narrative technique can we use? Can we modernize the parable and retell it by making up a parallel modern story? Almost always such attempts prove ludicrous. If we retell the Prodigal Son, having the young boy go off to Paris for a fling while the older boy stays faithfully on the farm, the story loses too much and meanings change. For example, the "far country" in the parable is despised Gentile territory. Is a young son who wants an advance on his inheritance greeted with absolute horror nowadays? Not really. What equivalent will we find for a Jewish boy tending pigs? As for the father's wild hullabaloo of a welcome, can we find parallels that will be as undignified, unwise, and bizarre? Trying to retell parables will usually end up in undesired laughter as well as inaccurate interpretations.

Yet, to be truthful, we cannot take people back and get them to live in the biblical world as some homileticians would have us do.[2] To do so would mean countless explanations of biblical background, turning our sermons into pedantic Bible study classes. Weighted down with explanation, the parables would cease to have immediacy; they would lose narrative potency. Maybe congregations admire a minister's research—"Our minister knows so much!"—but God help the minister who is eager for such admiration. So we are in a quandary. We know we must retain narrative movement to our parable sermons. The question is, How?

The usual solution is to preach as if we and our congregation are hearing and reacting to the parable together. The sermon can then move along, episode by episode like a good story, yet permit us to respond, thinking through each episode as it is heard. The device is very much like telling stories to children. Again and again you interrupt your story line, stopping to explain, to react, or to ask your young audience for their responses. So we can overhear a parable *with* our congregations. What a relief not to have to be teachy, or worse, preachy. What's more, by responding to the story together, ministers are able to use illustrations and associations prompted by the episodes in the parable. Here is an example from a sermon on the Vineyard Laborers (pp. 115–18). A move is concluding in which we have reacted to paying all the workers the same money, those who work one hour and those who work twelve. Then in the parable the vineyard owner flares in anger and throws the grievance committee out of his vineyard. Here are the sections:

[Move end]   When you hear the parable, you do feel outraged: Are some of us rewarded for what we do, and others for what they don't do? Forty dollars for one hour; forty dollars for twelve! Our rage is justified: God, you don't play fair!

[Move start]   How does God answer? What does God say? God says, "Take your pay and get out of my church!" That's what the boss said in the

parable: "Take yours and get out of here!" We're shocked. Here is
God rejecting us, God's own faithful people. Didn't God call us
into the church and promise us the kingdom for doing right? And
we've tried, God knows we've tried, Sunday after Sunday, singing
praise, saying prayers, paying our cash in the collection plates. We
have a right to expect a nod of approval, or at least a kind word.
Back in the nineteen fifties, Harvard Business School did a study
on worker motivation. Do workers work for money or is there some
other reward they are after? According to the study, the lure wasn't
pay, it was recognition. That's it! We are not asking for a starry
crown or a gown of angel gauze. And we are not expecting a double share of happiness. All we want is a little heavenly recognition.
Instead, God spits out a sharp rebuke: "Take your pay and get out!"
Get out of my church! We hear the words and we don't understand.

The sermon is following the plot lines of the parable, and yet we are responding
with a congregation. At the same time, notice we are able to draw into our
response the example from Harvard Business School without undue disruption.
Most parables can be preached as if we, congregation and minister, are hearing
a story together.

Another option is to stay in the story to a greater degree, but to interpret the story
by using contemporary metaphor. The technique is often heard in brilliant black
preaching, telling the biblical story but, again and again, drawing in contemporary language and contemporary images. The trick is to be responsible. Here are
two moves from a sermon on the Prodigal Son (pp. 204–7):

[Move 1]   Let's be honest. The younger son, the prodigal son, is a stock char-
             acter. The younger son is scarcely original. There are thousands of
             stories about scapegrace younger sons. We see him on the television
             soaps. Perhaps we see him in ourselves. He is a rogue, a thorough-
             going rascal. Doesn't he con his father out of a bundle of cash? Too
             bad you've lived so long, Dad; how about an advance on the old
             inheritance? Then, with a bulging wallet, he's off and running. See
             him run, with a Benny Hill smirk on his face, off to where the action
             is. Talk about wine, women, and song. He quaffs wine like water,
             sings every ribald song, and, as for women, well, they may be
             expensive, but every growing boy should have a hobby. How was
             it Saint Augustine described his own wild oats? "The sizzling . . .
             of unholy loves," he wrote. Well, the young son in the story sizzles;
             he sizzles, that is, until the cash runs out. Then there he is, broke,
             hungry, and homeless. "Prodigal" is too nice a word for him; to be
             truthful, the boy is a bum.

[Move 2]   But, mark this, the prodigal son is not stupid. Like most rogues, he
            has a shrewd, canny, calculating mind. Here he is hungry while, in
            his thoughts, he could picture his father's farm hands feeding on
            three square meals a day. Aha! he says to himself, I know what I'll
            do. I'll go to Daddy and sound religious: "I've sinned against
            heaven and in your sight. . . . Please pass the mashed potatoes!"
            Look, we want the story to be about conversion; we want a religious
            motive and a religious reward; after all, the story is in the Bible.
            But to be honest, is the prodigal son all that religious? There was a
            wonderful show some years ago about a Salvation Army soup
            kitchen where bums could line up for a handout lunch. One old bum
            in line advises a young tramp standing behind him, "Always eat
            good," he says. "Take a dive for Jesus every day!" Leave your reli-
            gion behind when you hear the story of the Prodigal Son, and you'll
            have to agree; if he's converted, it's not much more than a soup
            kitchen conversion. I'm hungry. Father's farm hands are eating
            well. . . . I know what I'll do! Listen, the prodigal son may be a
            rogue, but he isn't dumb.

The story unfolds: The young son gets the cash, goes to a "far country," and
messes up! Then he decides to return home to his father. We are not so much
overhearing a story with our congregation as we are telling the story. But look at
all the contemporary language and imagery. "Too bad you've lived so long, Dad;
how about an advance on the old inheritance"—such inner dialogue is more fun
than a labored explanation about how asking for an inheritance is wishing a
father dead. Notice contemporary references—bulging wallet (first-century people didn't have wallets), Benny Hill (they didn't have raunchy television comics
either). The language is fairly flip, as is the prodigal son himself. But notice also
a reference to Saint Augustine to hint at possible redemption. The same technique is employed in the language on the subsequent move—"three square meals
a day," "go to Daddy and sound religious," "please pass the mashed potatoes,"
"take a dive for Jesus."
    Later, when the prodigal returns, his father roars out orders,

> "Get him a three-piece suit," he shouts, "tasseled loafers, and a dozen
> new shirts. Put a ring on his finger, my own signet ring. Sell the stock
> portfolio," he roars, "let's party tonight!"

We are telling the story, but deliberately using contemporary language and contemporary images. In every case, we are trying to do so responsibly—a fatted
calf in first-century Palestine would be equivalent to emptying the stock portfolio. Notice that we are not going to tell the parable all the way as a contemporary
twenty-first century parable, because making up a modern version of a biblical
story seldom works. But we can tell a biblical story, fully aware that it is a

biblical story, yet intrude with contemporary images and contemporary language. Some biblical purists may view the technique as almost sacrilegious, but great preachers have seldom worried too much over textual purity.

If we listen to a story unfolding or retell a story with contemporary imagery, we must do so *with* our audience. We must *be* them as much as possible. Such a stance will not be difficult. After all, preachers are children of the age as much as their listeners. We have been brought up in America circa 2000 C.E., thus we have grown up in a secular sphere using a language we have learned. Our congregations have the same sort of background. We must never tell parables as if we were learned religious teachers and our people were secular unbelievers. Self-righteousness in a pulpit is always out of place. Instead we must hear and react to the unfolding plots of parable stories in a representative way.

Making Do

In the previous chapter I argued that parables are designed not only to mean but to *do*. Parables are not allegories with secret coded God-meanings hidden in every verse. Nor are parables didactic teaching devices, each with an eternal lesson to be learned. I suggested that parables are developed metaphors forcing hearers to think deeply. I also noticed that virtually all Jesus' parables seem to feature some sort of extravagance, a surreal element designed to disrupt our sense of world. Parables seem to be designed for conversion. Like *Alice in Wonderland,* if you tumble into a new world, you know that somehow you must change.

If we design homiletic plots for preaching, we must ask how we can enable the parables to *do* what they intend to do. Thus as we begin to work with a parable we must ask not only, What does the parable mean? but also, What is the parable trying to do in our consciousness?

If we read the parable of the Sower (pp. 66–68), where an incompetent farmer throws most of his seed into rock piles, thorn bushes, and right down the center of an interstate, we must design a section in our sermon that expresses incredulity at the farmer's blundering ways. No wonder nothing seems to grow! But then, inexplicably, there is seed producing a crop—thirty, sixty, a hundred times more. We must find a way to surprise us all with the miraculous harvest. In addition, noting that the whole parable seems to be lined up with the church's evangelical preaching, particularly with dismay over scant success in recruiting citizens for the kingdom, we must weave the parable plot into a discussion of proclamation. Wow! What a creative puzzle to solve.

Let us take a look at another parable, the Vineyard Laborers. The parable tells of an owner who hires field hands to help bring in grapes at harvesttime. He goes out several times during the day to recruit workers, so that some field hands work all day and others only an hour. Then the surreal detail—everyone is paid the same wage. No wonder workers protest. But when they complain they are tossed out of the vineyard. You cannot preach the parable by trying to explain, rationalizing the owner's behavior. To do so would be to kill the surprises, indeed, the shocks that have been deliberately installed in the story. When a parable hands you an exciting disruption, for heaven's sake don't toss it aside. In God's world everyone is *called* and everyone is *beloved;* it is a free-grace world. In our world we talk of earning and deserving. Clearly the two systems of thought are meant to collide in preaching the parable. A preacher must design a collision in the minds of a congregation. There's an exciting task!

If we are going to preach parables, let's preach with excitement, the excitement of craft and challenge. If parables are merely packaged lessons, moral or religious truths to be handed over to congregations, preaching could be a terrible burden. But suppose that parables are dynamic systems designed to change the "world" we live in and, thus, change our ways of living as well. Then preaching is an excitement. More, preaching is an excitement we share with God.

How Far, How Near, How Wide

When we preach parables, a factor to be considered is what might be termed "distance." Are we hearing the parable unfolding as if for the first time? Do the twists and turns of plot surprise us? Is the parable immediately powerful, move after move, or are we standing back looking over the parable with a much more contemplative disposition? If we stand at a distance our lens may be wider, taking in more of our own experience, with less immediate attention to the text of the parable. Here is a first move from a sermon on the parable of the Rich Farmer (pp. 191–92):

> Question: What do you do with a bumper crop, the kind of crop that happens every twenty years or so? What do you do with prosperity? Answer: You become a capitalist—which is what the farmer in the parable did. We Americans tend to admire the man; he was an entrepreneur, tearing down in order to build bigger barns for bigger crops for bigger profits. And what's the motive? You don't have to have an MBA to figure out the motive: self-interest. He was providing for his own security. A few weeks ago while wandering the library of a management school, we came across a sign on the wall of a student carrel reading, "Self-interest Makes the World Go Round." Would you believe it was written in Gothic type? Listen, in an age of downsizing, a future free from money worries sounds pretty good—eat, drink, and enjoy! Could anyone describe the American dream any sweeter? Food enough, wine on the table, and time—time for ourselves. What do you do with a bumper crop? Easy, you become a capitalist.

Here we have backed off from the first-century story; now we are brooding on American prosperity and the "American Dream," with the problem of the parable very much in the distant background.

On the other hand, here is an example drawn from the parable of the Feast (pp. 161–64), in which the text itself seems to preach directly to us:

> But please note: "They came both good and bad alike," says the parable, and we are shocked. Did the king in the parable have no moral values? Didn't he care what kind of people he welcomed? And can this be an image of the God we worship? Yes, it can! God doesn't check references. God doesn't demand a placement test. Our neat, too neat notions of morality God sweeps aside. It doesn't matter what you've been or what you've done or how much of a mess you've made of your life. We are none of us good in the sight of God, but all of us are loved and invited to God's table. Did you read about the little girl who was found weeping because she couldn't attend a party for handicapped children? "I can't get in," she cried. "There's nothing the matter with me." On that basis we are all eligible, for there is something the matter with all of us. Call it evil, call it sin, call it what you will, but none of us, no none, is good enough to deserve God's invitation. Yet it comes to each of us personally, and it comes now.

Here we are experiencing the power of the text as a direct word speaking to us. Preachers must determine a stance—"distance" with a wide or narrow lens. The first example uses a wide lens and stands away from the parable being preached; the second example follows the text closely and lets it preach to us directly.

Shifting the Scenery

Though parables are stories and have plots, it is more helpful to think of them as dramas, scene by scene. Dramas are acted out for an audience and made of action and dialogue; so are parables. The parables are not like novels, which may spend much time on inner thoughts of characters, their feelings, and, of course, on detailed descriptions of scenery. Parables do none of these things. Their focus is on act and speech; background situations are usually sketched in no more than a sentence. Moreover, telling parables is not exactly like telling stories. Storytellers can ramble; they can smooth out plot episodes into a kind of continual story by providing transitions. In contrast, parables move abruptly with rare economy and sharp dramatic changes.

There is virtue in thinking of parables as drama. We will change scenes crisply, avoiding smooth transitions. We will design sermons dramatically—curtain up, curtain down, then curtain up again—letting the scenes bump against each other with little if any transitional language. Here are some examples of an abrupt conjunction of moves:

[Move end]   The kingdom of God is like a banquet. No black-suited saints with blacker Bibles, no prim souls, grim and repressed, but of all things, a party. Remember the old hymn we sometimes sing in church?

> They stand, those halls of Zion,
> All jubilant with song,
> The song of them that triumph,
> The shout of them that feast.

There it is: Joy! The kingdom of God is joy to enter. "Like a feast," said Jesus, and a wedding feast at that.

[Move start] Well, perhaps that's why it fooled the invited guests in the parable. And perhaps that's why it fools us too. When you come right down to it, there are more important things in life than parties.

Here is another example from a sermon on the parable of the Sower (pp. 66–68). It concludes a move expressing discouragement over the lack of response to the message of the gospel. The next move will speak of God's power to use our words:

[Move end] When the world seems tone deaf to the gospel, we turn off. Instead of scattering seed, we've kept our church lawns well-mowed. How easy, oh how easy it is to become discouraged, to lose heart.

[Move start] But hold on: Hey, take a look at the end of the parable. Look, thirty times, sixty times, a hundred times — a harvest! God takes our foolish leftover, throwaway seeds and turns them into triumph. There's a harvest coming.

You will find that almost all the parable sermons we have included have sharply defined moves. The scenes are separate. Each has a different focus. Moods change suddenly along with style. In the example above, see the dragged out despair in "How easy, oh how easy it is to become discouraged, to lose heart," but then the rather gleeful rhythms of "Hey, take a look at the end of the parable. Look, thirty times, sixty times, a hundred times — a harvest!"

Sometimes the moves have very different points of view. Look again at an earlier example from a sermon on the Vineyard Laborers:

[Move end] Are some of us rewarded for what we do, and others for what they don't do? Forty dollars for one hour; forty dollars for twelve! Our rage is justified: God, you don't play fair!

[Move start] How does God answer? What does God say? God says, "Take your pay and get out of my church!" That's what the boss said in the parable: "Take yours and get out of here!" We're shocked.

The move that ends looks at how everyone is paid the same in the parable. Along with the all-day workers, we are outraged. But then God directly addresses us, the congregation, and we are shocked. The angle of focus changes. As you study the sermons in this book, you often will see such point-of-view changes, usually happening as the scenes shift. Incidentally, point-of-view shifts, like the changing camera angles in contemporary films, are intrinsically exciting.

Keep the Order or Reorder

Another crucial decision: I have suggested that we must be guided by the plot of the parable. At the outset you will be wise to write down the sequence of episodes in each parable you intend to preach. In analyzing plot, sometimes you will reduce the sequence. For example, in Matthew's parable of the Entrusted Money there are three servants given money (storytellers love triads), but actually they can be reduced to two types—investor and saver. Or in the parable of the Vineyard Laborers there are several recruiting trips to hire workers—at dawn, nine, twelve, three, and finally at five. But the recruits are reducible to all-day workers and latecomers. In setting up the plot of a parable, you compress repetitions.

Plots begin when the action begins, in effect, when the curtain is raised. So you don't want to spend too much time introducing characters or describing the scenery; most such matters can be dealt with in an introduction or as the plot moves along. But because parables are often not much more than conversational dialogue, you will soon learn to treat dialogue as an aspect of plot. For example, the story of the Dishonest Steward (p. 209) could be charted:

1. Manager dismissed for crookedness
2. Predicament: "What am I going to do? I can't dig."
3. Solution: Marking down bills, "Quick, write 250 gallons!"
4. Boss's improbable praise

Though it is no longer than a single sentence with no dialogue, the Treasure parable (p. 100) is complicated:

1. Finding a treasure in a field
2. Being elated
3. Reburying the treasure
4. Selling everything
5. Buying field

The Vineyard Laborers breaks down in action and dialogue:

1. Hiring all-day workers
2. Hiring leftover last-hour workers
3. All paid the same, says a grievance committee
4. Boss's anger: "Take your pay and get out!"
5. Boss: "Didn't you bargain for a day's pay?"
6. Boss: "Are you jealous because I am generous?"

Preachers must think of parables as scenarios, play scripts for a drama. Because meaning is structural, plot is crucial.

Of course, in charting plots, please remember that somehow parables refer to the mystery of God-with-us. Thus parables may relate to a theological field of meaning. After you have studied a parable, think through what the parable means in relation to the mystery of God. For example, the parable of the Vineyard Laborers begins with employment; workers are hired by the vineyard owner. Does the recruiting relate to the idea of "call"? Are all of us called by God? Certainly God's love is for all humanity. Thus no one can earn more love from God than any other person. But we do persist in thinking of earned reward; no wonder we resent it if others with less religious merit seem to prosper in grace. All of a sudden, as we think our way around a theological field, we begin to see how the parable may relate to the mystery of a loving graceful God versus our demand for reward.

What about the parable of the Sower? Mark clearly relates the parable to spreading news of the gospel. Apparently Mark is dismayed by the lack of response. Thus the theological field would seem to be the church's evangelical calling; we are to preach good news of the kingdom of God. But now, as in any age, the response isn't smashing—most Americans are prospering according to the world's ways and are not crowding into church doorways. Nevertheless, all humanity ultimately will be drawn into God's love. We set the parable into a theological field and it begins not only to make theological sense but becomes homiletically exciting. (Notice that I refer to a "theological field" and not to verse-by-verse theological meanings.)

Please realize that plots can be reordered. When we preach parables we don't have to begin at the beginning, as if we were tracing our way, verse by verse. Compare, if you will, nineteenth-century and twentieth-century novels. Most nineteenth-century novels—for example, Thackeray's *Vanity Fair*—begin at the beginning and, episode after episode, continue to the end, as if tracing a chronological history. But twentieth-century novels may skip around different times and places, use flashbacks, look at events from different perspectives or through the eyes of different characters. Why the change? Because human consciousness has changed. The same differences show up in films, particularly with regard to camera angles and a shifting of scenes that may seem to break with linear logic.

With parables, the plotlines are fairly fixed. But the big difference is at the point of entry. We can conceivably begin in the middle of a parable and then rearrange episodes. A sermon on the Vineyard Laborers can begin, not with the calling of workers, but with the protest over wages paid at the end of the day:

> Well, the same pay for different hours at work may be the kingdom of God, but, bluntly, it isn't fair. Interpret the story any way you will, it still adds up to injustice. Some workers bore the weight of the day; they worked in the blazing heat from sunup to sundown, windblown and weary, for forty dollars. Others showed up at the cool end of the day, put

in a quick hour, and picked up the same forty-dollar paycheck. Look, it's wrong isn't it? Paying everyone the same, no matter how much work they do, destroys initiative. Back in the nineteen thirties, almost every union hall in America had a motto painted on the wall: "A Fair Dollar for a Fair Day's Work." But, in the parable, neither the dollar nor the day's work is fair. Forty dollars for one hour; forty dollars for twelve! No matter how you read the story it adds up to injustice. Perhaps it's an image of the kingdom of God, but to be truthful, it's bad business.

The matter of recruiting workers actually will show up toward the end of the sermon.

Another example: You will be reading a sermon on the Unmerciful Servant who was forgiven billions but refused to ease up on a fellow servant owing a few hundred (pp. 109–11). Instead of starting the sermon with the canceling of billions of debt, the sermon starts out quite differently:

> Begin with a question: What's so wrong with the agent? Isn't he simply trying to collect what is rightfully his? The agent has been generous. When one of his fellow agents is caught short, he lends the man a thousand dollars. But when it's payback time he discovers the man is a deadbeat; he can't pay back the loan. So what does the agent do? He slaps a summons on the man and has him jailed for bad debts. Is his behavior so unusual? Doesn't First American, Third National, or NationsBank go after people who default on their loans? The fact is, collecting on a debt is simply good business. If we let debtors go scot-free our whole economic system will come tumbling down; it's based on people paying their debts. And here in America, faced with the recent savings and loan scandals, we could have used a few hard-nosed agents, couldn't we? No wonder George Bernard Shaw has a character admit, "Forgiveness is a beggar's refuse. We must pay our debts." So be objective when you hear the parable. The agent may sound a little curt, but the fact is a loan is a loan and ought to be paid. So ask yourselves, What's so wrong with the servant?

Subsequently, I turned back and recalled that the man had himself been forgiven billions. Thus, in the parable on the Unmerciful Servant, we entered at the plot's second episode and then turned back to the first episode. The change allowed us to set up American business practice in contrast to God's grace! Of course, we could instead have entered the parable with the other servants who were furious because the servant, forgiven billions, had not forgiven a colleague's small debt: "Other agents, seeing what had happened, were terribly upset. Going to the boss, they told him all about everything that had happened." A sermon could then turn back to see why the other servants were furious.

How do you decide when to alter plot? The best rule is to ask where the parable invites us hearers into its plot. Often we will enter when the "surreal" detail disturbs us, as when workers are all paid the same wage, or when a servant refuses to forgive a small debt after being forgiven a whopping big debt. Sometimes you will want to enter a parable at the point where the parable represents or challenges our own social attitudes. Recall that in the parable of the Rich Farmer (pp. 191–92), we began with the farmer wanting to build bigger barns to store his goods, thus lining up his action with American entrepreneurship. Why might we wish to replot a parable? We redesign parables so they may do what they are intended to do!

Parables have reference to the mystery of God-with-us. When and how does God enter a parable? Later in these pages you may wish to compare a sermon on the parable of the Sower (pp. 66–8) with a sermon on the parable of the Prodigal Son (pp. 204–7). With the Sower, reference to God occurs in move 2, whereas in the Prodigal Son, alignment with the mystery of God occurs in the last move of the sermon. These necessities dictated a reordering of the plots in different ways.

Dramas without Catharsis

Parables, as we have seen, are peculiar stories. They are remarkable in their spareness. We are seldom told why anything happens; causes are not examined. And we are not often taken into the inner thoughts, feelings, or motivations of characters in parables. Sometimes, particularly in Luke, we overhear interior monologues, but these are never profoundly reflective; they are merely reasonings. For example, in Luke 12:18–19 the rich farmer muses: (1) I have a bumper crop. (2) What will I do? (3) I will build bigger barns. Likewise in Luke 15:17–19, the prodigal son, hungry in a far country, is desperate. He reasons: (1) I'm hungry. (2) Father's farmhands eat well. (3) I will go to my father's house. These interior monologues do not explore emotions or deep motivations.

If we do encounter emotions in parables, feelings are not described or analyzed; they are implied by dialogue. Remember how the all-day workers were angry when one-hour workers were paid the same wage as they: "Those last ones you hired worked only an hour, and you paid them what you're paying us, who've worked all day long under the hot sun" (Matt. 20:12). They are angry. So is the elder brother in the parable of the Prodigal Son: "Look, I've worked for you for years and never disobeyed one of your orders, and you never gave me so much as a goat so I could party with my friends." But feelings or motives are not described directly; we do not enter the interior world of characters to feel with them. Instead we overhear attitudes as the characters speak. The spareness of the parables, their taut design, may be deliberate, as some writers suggest:

1. Eric Auerbach argued that biblical narratives report actions and words, but do not explain. They do not fill in the gaps by investigating motives or locating causalities. Instead we must speculate. Thus biblical narrative may leave room for the mysteries of God-with-us. Auerbach contrasts biblical narrative with

Greek narrative—for example, *The Iliad*—which turns inward to explore the motivations of different characters and which is quite explicit with regard to causality.[3] Biblical stories are spare, not because they are more primitive and less sophisticated, but because they are oral, evocative, and, above all, implicitly theological.

2. Bertolt Brecht, the great German playwright, was something of a revolutionary. He wanted drama to incite thoughtful moral or political action. He argued that catharsis was the enemy of revolution. Traditionally, catharsis was viewed as a product of tragic drama. If people in an audience could feel with a tragic hero, could participate inwardly in the hero's death, then they would be purged redemptively. No, said Brecht, an audience might be emptied of feeling and yet be morally or politically untouched, like Tolstoy's rich Russian lady who wept at tragic drama but continued to underpay her coachman. So Brecht determined to block identifications, to prevent *feeling with* characters on the stage. Apparently his practice worked—his first play produced a riot in the theater. A collection of his plays is titled, *Parables for the Theatre.*[4]

What can we learn? Don't fill in the gaps with psychological excursions. Don't explain causes. Don't go beyond the parable to explore why things happen as they do in parables. Above all, don't explain away what we have termed the "surreal." Leave room for the often inexplicable movements of grace.

As for feeling, the rule is hard and fast—don't investigate psychological reactions or motivations. We are to look at parables, be puzzled by parables. Usually we are deliberately kept at a distance, looking at characters and their actions. Once in a while we are taken into a story. For example, we are meant to join the all-day workers' grievance committee. Likewise, we are meant to be outraged when a man, forgiven billions, throws another man in jail for a small debt. We join with other servants going to complain about his behavior. But notice that both parables begin with episodes that look dispassionately at what's going on. In most cases, we are to do no more than look and listen. If we explore feelings, they must be *our own reactions* to the unfolding of the parable's plot.

If, for example, we spend time in a sermon experiencing what the prodigal son must have felt when he returned to his father, we will skew the story. Instead the parable wants us to look at and be astonished by the father's bizarre behavior. You may feel compelled to deliver dialogue with passion when passion is called for, but please do not reach into the characters and describe their immediate feelings. Let biblical wisdom guide you. The Bible does not empathize, moralize, or explain motives, causes, or reasons. The Bible allows stories to be stories, not psychological novelettes. Part of the problem is that clergy are convinced that people are converted by catharsis, above all, people must be made to feel. Apparently Jesus did not agree, for his parables are told with a lean, spare language designed to force thoughtfulness. Like Brechtian drama, they almost seem to prevent emotional identifications. Perhaps they too are more interested in revolution than catharsis.

On Choosing a Target

Years ago Ernst Fuchs suggested that there are two ways to learn about a cat. One way is to dissect the cat and then to label all the animal's parts. But the other way is to put a mouse in front of a cat and see what happens. Fuchs was drawing an analogy to biblical scholarship, with particular reference to parables. All of us have been wearied by pedantry, by dissecting and labeling.

The cat and mouse image is useful: There are parables that simply will not work until they are allowed to chase something. For example, in the parable of the Leaven, where leaven leavens a whole loaf of bread, we discover that, in the Bible, leaven is always and everywhere a symbol of sinful corruption. So when Jesus is saying that the kingdom of God is like leaven taking over a whole loaf, he is aiming his parable at the idea that only the righteous, indeed, the religious righteous, will enter the kingdom of God. Therefore, if the parable of the Leaven is to work, the parable must counter the idea of a kingdom populated exclusively by the morally qualified. So a preacher will have to depict the idea of a righteous realm for the parable to shatter.

Another example: The little parable of the Mustard Seed seems to be a deliberate burlesque of the mighty cedar of Lebanon, a symbol of national power and triumph. In Ezekiel 17:22–23, the cedar is a symbol of Israel's political dream; someday Israel will be great like the cedar, and "the birds of the air" (i.e., pagan nations), will live under her branches. Instead of a mighty cedar, Jesus pictures a weed, indeed, a weed regarded as a public nuisance. For the parable to have impact it must be aimed at national or religious triumphalism. Ministers will have to evoke dreams of greatness, political and religious, that lurk in every congregation so the parable of the Mustard Seed will be able to do its work. A mouse for a cat!

Even longer parables can be aimed at particular attitudes. A number of Jesus' parables seem to oppose the idea of God as a judge who is delighted to punish the wicked and pleased to reward the religiously pure. What about the vineyard owner in the parable of the Tenants? He makes no move to punish the sharecroppers who beat up his agents. He keeps on sending more and more agents. They also are beaten up and one is killed. The owner still defers punitive action: "Well, maybe I better send my son." The parable counters the idea of God as an impatient judge, eager to destroy the wicked. With many parables we must ask what they are meant to chase; rhetorically, we must provide a mouse to animate the cat. Many parables seem to be aimed at particular attitudes.

Metaphors and Images

I have argued that parables work with metaphorical power. Parables take images from the familiar and put them side by side with a mysterious kingdom of God. In the process, something odd, something extravagant, something deliberately bizarre is added as a kind of disrupting agent. The extravagant, what we have called the "surreal," seems to shatter our cohesive sense of world, thereby opening us to a different realm. Thus parables are tricky. They are sophisticated story systems that may be designed for conversion.

To preach parables will require not only smart homiletic designing so that the parables can do what they intend to do, but also a respect for metaphor. How can we align illustrations, examples, and images we may need with the central metaphor that may be built into a particular parable? Obviously, if the parable has to do with sheep and shepherds, a preacher will want to avoid illustrations that refer to computers or factory assembly lines. Industrial illustrations would disrupt or weaken the pastoral imagery of the parable. Preachers must learn to assess the illustrations as they relate to the central metaphors involved.[5]

If such a requirement seems restrictive, we can widen associations somewhat. Take the parable of the Sower: Its metaphor, sowing seed, is related to spreading the gospel message (no wonder a fine recent commentary on Mark is entitled *Sowing the Gospel*).[6] Thus we have two metaphorical fields to work with: (1) farming, seed, and growth, 2) preaching, teaching, and speaking the gospel. Here is a list of the illustrations and images, move by move, from the sermon I have provided on the parable (pp. 66–8):[7]

Move 1:	Farmer planting fields
	Missionary preaching in Russia
	Preaching to winos and New York City subway crowds
Move 2:	God telling Moses and Ezekiel to speak
	Scandinavian Christians preaching in the streets
Move 3:	Couple in a city apartment shutting out a Jesus hymn
Move 4:	Famous preacher who stopped speaking
Move 5:	Woman in a city apartment full of plants
Move 6:	Boy poking seed into tenement window sill

Of course, in addition to the illustrations listed there are refrain systems and brief images, most of which are related to the parable—"rock, thorn, and highway"; "thirty, sixty, a hundredfold." But notice that all the images are related either to speaking the gospel or to seed and growth.

Take another example: The parable of the Vineyard Laborers again offers metaphorical fields—workers, unions, wages—aligned with God's free, undeserved grace and calling. Again the images and illustrations I have chosen fit the fields (pp. 115–18):

Move 1:	Union motto: "A fair dollar for a fair day's work"
Move 2:	Skid-row drunk with same reward as Billy Graham?
Move 3:	Father's complaint: "You God, you don't play fair!"
Move 4:	Harvard Business School on worker motivation
Move 5:	Businessmen in *High Tor* bargaining with God
Move 6:	C. S. Lewis man: "Not asking for bleeding charity"
Move 7:	"The wonders of redeeming love and my unworthiness"

In both examples, I have located two fields from which images and illustrations may be drawn. Then I have found metaphors and illustrations to fit.

Can most parables be analyzed as having metaphorical fields? Of course they can. The Good Samaritan (p. 182) offers *images*—travel, robbers, religious functionaries, medical care—and *theological ideas*—compassion and "love your neighbor." The Friend at Midnight (pp. 185–86) has *images*—food, hospitality, neighbors in need—and *theological ideas*—prayer, God's answers, God's goodness. The metaphorical fields in most parables range from weather patterns in the sky, to empty houses, to children's games, and so forth. Illustrations and examples should be aligned with metaphorical fields so as to support rather than undercut a parable's metaphorical power.

Packages of Meaning
Addressed to . . . ?

Most preachers tend to proclaim parables as if they were addressed to individuals in their personal self-awareness. Probably we interpret parables as addressed to individuals because in America we seem to be trapped in patterns of individualism, patterns that are bolstered by notions of personal salvation left over from the soul-winning revivals of the late nineteenth century. The religious personalism of the revivals was reinforced in the twentieth century first by the rise of "The New Psychology" and, subsequently, by the art and literature of the existentialist fifties. Regarding parables, many preachers were influenced by Dan Via Jr.'s groundbreaking book, *The Parables,* which, emerging from the New Hermeneutic, urged a kind of existential interpretation.[8] But parables, like their rabbinic prototypes, were spoken in and for a community. They are meant to circulate in a group that has some understanding, however vague, of God's realm. So, although anyone can read a parable personally, parables are intended for an audience, indeed, for a community of faith. After all, the image, "kingdom of God," is a sociopolitical metaphor. In a word, the parables are not self-help literature.

American religious individualism is a chronic problem for preachers and, in part, a problem perpetuated by preachers. We seem to suppose that in order to be relevant sermons must be addressed to the felt self-awareness of each individual soul. But we forget that the "you" of the Great Commandment is a corporate "you all," and that the commandment itself not only urges love for God but is riveted together with neighbor love. Questioned by Pharisees, "Teacher, which commandment in the law is the greatest?" Jesus replies,

> You shall love the Lord your God with all your heart, and with all your soul, and with all your mind. This is the first and foremost commandment. And a second is the same thing, "You shall love your neighbor as your own."[9] (Matt. 22:36–39, DGB)

We are not individuals who exist in individual self-awareness; we are always interacting, always coupled with others. Playwright Tony Kushner says it boldly:

Marx was right: The smallest divisible human unit is two people, not
one; one is a fiction. From such nets of souls societies, the social world,
human life springs.[10]

I concur: "one is a fiction." Parables are not addressed to the individual self but
always to the two or more units of interactive humanity.

The Embarrassments
of Interpretation

Now we must deal with a sticky problem. What do we do when a Gospel writer
has obviously misunderstood a parable? For example, Matthew tells the parable
of the Unmerciful Servant in which an unforgiving agent ends up in torture. Then
Matthew adds a rather nasty tag line: "So also will my heavenly Father do to you
unless everyone of you forgives your fellow human from your heart." Matthew
does not seem to understand the unlimited mercy of God, "in whom we live and
move and have our being." So when we preach, must we preach Matthew's hor-
rible error? I have picked an obvious example, but there are others, perhaps less
obvious, where a Gospel writer has clearly misunderstood a parable. Does the
story of the Unjust Judge teach us to pray all the time? Probably not. And did
Jesus intend the story of the Dishonest Steward to teach us to "make friends for
yourselves with your crooked cash so that when you go broke, you may be welcomed into eternal housing"? And what do we do with editorial additions that
Gospel writers may have made to parables? An example of this occurs when
Matthew adds to the parable of the Feast that the invited guests "seized his slaves,
humiliated and killed them. So the king was enraged. He sent his army to destroy
those murderers and burn their city" (Matt. 22:6–7). The problem occurs often
enough so that preachers must decide what to preach. Are we bound to follow
interpretations of the Gospel writers, or can we openly correct them?

The problem has been complicated by the crypto-fundamentalism of recent
Word-of-God theologies. If the whole Bible is to be revered as Word of God, how
can we venture to correct misinterpretation? Matthew's addendum to the Unmerciful Servant is simply bad theology; why can't we say so? James Barr has argued
that the Protestant Reformation "put us on the road which led toward a full biblical criticism on the one hand, and at the same time on the road which led to fundamentalism on the other."[11] The remark is quite correct. To oppose papal
authority, Reformers countered with absolute biblical authority. If the Bible is
ultimate authority, then we must study biblical texts with every useful critical
method available, but, at the same time, we must promote the divine authority
of the biblical text. Preachers are trapped. Critical study may show us that
Matthew has misunderstood the parable of the Unmerciful Servant, but if we correct Matthew openly will we not undercut the authority of scripture? And if we
undercut the authority of scripture are we not questioning our own Protestant
Christianity?

There may be no solution to the problem short of foregoing the authority of scripture as well as reforming our peculiar Protestant heritage.[12] As far as I can see, the early church managed quite well without any developed notion of the authority of scripture; good heavens, they didn't have a developed canon for years and years! We contemporary Christians appear to be much more rigid than our founders.

What to do? We preach the gospel message. The Bible contains the gospel and is therefore often labeled "Word of God." But we must not take a further step and say that the *whole* Bible, every verse, equals the gospel message. The solution to our quandary: Preach the gospel and tell the truth.

Meanwhile, preachers may solve the problem in two sensible ways: First, in reading scripture you can simply delete Matthew's additions to the parable of the Feast. You can even explain to your people that scholars are rather certain the two verses have been added to a Jesus parable. Second, if you are not going to edit a parable you can certainly say that Matthew's conclusion to the Unmerciful Servant is a theological disaster. Why not? The solution is simple—it's called telling the truth. Go back to the Reformation and in commentaries you will find both Calvin and Luther correcting scripture. Our real need is to correct the crypto-fundamentalism of current Word-of-God theologies as well as American pop religion.

Why Preach the Parables?

Three times in the twentieth century scholars have engaged in a "quest of the historical Jesus." Every time the quest has led to a renewed interest in parables. Why? Because Jesus preached a kingdom of God in parables. As preachers we should not only wish to preach about Jesus, but to preach the preaching of Jesus Christ!

Parables are exciting and, if you have any interest in homiletic craft, they are great fun to preach.

PART 2

4

Parables in Mark

The Gospel of Mark is a dramatic, apocalyptic Gospel written in a popular style. Probably the Gospel was written around the year 70 C.E. when the temple in Jerusalem was destroyed.[1] Mark believes that he and his companion Christians are living in the last act of a great drama, waiting for final apocalyptic scenes— a great tribulation, including a profound testing of the church, followed by the inauguration of God's new social order.[2]

Norman Perrin argues that Mark sets up a pattern of preaching and being "delivered up." John the Baptist preaches, and in 1:14, he is "delivered up." Then Jesus preaches and in 9:31 he is "delivered up". Finally, Christians preach and in turn can expect to be delivered up (13:9–13).[3]

As a result, Mark comes down hard against triumphalism among Christians, particularly triumphalism fostered by some sort of Petrine party within the churches.[4] Though Christ has been raised, the church should not expect triumph in the world. Just as Christ was crucified, so Christians can anticipate persecution and death. Mark pictures disciples gleefully expecting triumph (see 8:27–38; 9:2–13; 9:30–37) but rebuked by Jesus who reminds them over and over that "the Son of Man must suffer many things and die."

The most peculiar theme in Mark may be what has often been labeled the "messianic secret." Yes, Christ is Israel's true king, but his kingship is hidden because he must suffer and be rejected.[5] Yet, in his suffering, the true nature of his kingship is revealed. So climactically, when Christ cries out, "My God, my God why have you forsaken me?" a centurion declares that he is a "Son of God." With the crucifixion, Mark has the skies go dark—a terrible "day of the Lord" that judges all humanity—and then has the veil of the temple shatter as a sign of the coming new order. But all through the Gospel of Mark, Christ's kingship is withheld until, ironically, he dies, crossbound under the title, "King of the Jews."

The disciples in Mark do not fare well. They are an obtuse, power-happy crew, who, when the chips are down, will scatter, betray, and deny their Lord. The women come off a bit better, for they follow along watching Jesus' death

61

and burial. But again, in the end they too fail. They do not declare Christ's resurrection; Mark 16:8 ends in what appears to be an incomplete sentence, "They were afraid for . . . " Perhaps the only faithful disciple is the white-robed figure at the tomb announcing, "He is not here; he is risen!"

Parables in Mark are closely tied into his theological concerns. In Mark 4, the farming parables all have to do with the preaching of the gospel—we are to sow seed and then trust God's following grace. But Mark's somewhat labored allegory of the soils explains (rather moralistically) why some seed grows and other seed does not. The soils are types of people who, subsequently, show up as characters in Mark's story.[6] The agricultural parables in chapter 4 govern the first half of Mark's Gospel, seed sowing being an image for preaching the gospel.

The parables of the Returning Master and of the Tenants set up themes for the passion narrative. The Tenants (12:1–11) provides a theology and, in a way, a history, for the parable traces a rejection of God's messengers—several prophets followed by the "Son of God." Then the parable of the Returning Master (13:34–36), at the conclusion of Mark's little apocalypse, prefigures the disciples' utter failure—they sleep, they scatter, they deny their Lord. Nevertheless, the Gospel ends with a preacher at the empty tomb, perhaps draped in a white baptismal robe, commissioning the church's evangelical task—"Go tell!"

Most of the parables in Mark also show up in Matthew and in Luke—the Sower (4:3–8), the Mustard Seed (4:31–32), and the Tenants. In addition, the Returning Master has affinity with Matthew's story of the Closed Door and may relate to a passage in Luke 12:35–38. So there is only one parable not picked up by Matthew and Luke, namely, the peculiar parable in which, watched over by God, seed grows automatically, only to be hacked down in a brutal harvest (4:26–29). But the parable may be a clue to Mark's own apocalyptic theology.

Mark also uses images—lamp under a bushel, salt losing its effectiveness, new patches on old garments, new wine in old wineskins, the bridegroom and wedding party, and, of course, the fig tree. So Mark views the gospel as true light and the community of faith as something new breaking into the old age that is passing away.

PARABLES IN MARK

Sower   Mark 4:3–8   Sermon
                        Matthew 13:3b–8
                        Luke 8:5–8a
                        Thomas 9

Seed and Harvest   Mark 4:26–29
                        Thomas 21:4

Mustard Seed   Mark 4:30–32
                        Matthew 13:31–32
                        Luke 13:19
                        Thomas 20:1–2

Tenants   Mark 12:1–8   Sermon
                        Matthew 21:33–39
                        Luke 20:9–15a
                        Thomas 65:1

Returning Master   Mark 13:34–36
                        Luke 12:35–38

SOWER
(Mark 4:3–9; Matthew 13:3b–8;
Luke 8:5–8a; Thomas 9)

MARK 4:3–9

[3]"Listen: This sower, see, went out to sow. [4]As he sowed, some seed happened to fall along the road, and birds came and ate it up. [5]Other seed fell
on rocky places where there was not much soil, and it sprung up right
away; [6]but when the sun came up, it was scorched and, because it didn't
have deep soil, withered. [7]Still other seed fell among thorns, and the
thorns grew up and choked it, so it produced no grain. [8]But some seed fell
in good earth and up came grain, sprouting and growing, to yield thirty,
sixty, a hundred times." [9]He said, "Those who have ears, let them hear!"

THOMAS 9

Now the sower went out, took a handful [of seeds], and scattered them.
Some fell on the road; the birds came and gathered them up. Others fell
on rock, did not take root in the soil, and did not produce ears. And others fell on thorns; they choked the seed[s] and worms ate them. And others fell on the good soil and produced good fruit; it bore sixty per
measure and a hundred twenty per measure.

Farmers in Jesus' parables are an odd lot. Here is a farmer who carelessly tosses
most of his seed into rock piles, thorn bushes, and right down the busy lanes of a
highway! Joachim Jeremias (1963, 110–12) tried to argue that the farmer was sowing seed according to custom *before* he plowed. He cited an article on ancient farming to support his contention. But, reexamined, the article is quite unconvincing
(Drury 1985, 55–58). In first-century Palestine, seed was far too precious to be sown
carelessly. Seed was at a premium; twice in the first century Palestine had to float
loans and buy seed from neighboring peoples. Farmers, at least wise farmers, sowed
seed carefully. But not this dummy! Most of his seed goes awry—thorn bushes,
rocky places, busy pathways. You picture him sowing seed in all the wrong places
and then dusting off his hands so that some seed somehow floats into good soil.

Seedtime and harvest were common metaphors in the ancient world, often
applied to education. {The Vanderbilt University crest still has an acorn from
which, presumably, mighty oaks (i.e., accomplished students) will grow.} We
have several versions of the parable, not only in Mark, Matthew, and Luke, but
also in the *Gospel of Thomas* and in *1 Clement*. We could have a few more today
because the image fits preaching. Just as Mark was dismayed by how few listeners responded to preaching, even preaching with apocalyptic urgency, so are
we. We preach the good news as fervently as we can, but recently in the U.S.A.,
church memberships have dwindled. Thus preachers are apt to turn away from
the pulpit and invest their energies in institutional management. They go for

special services, "contemporary worship," mixed media presentations, small group spirituality, and, above all, program, program, and more program. In our churches, we echo the idiotic old NBC slogan, "Now more than ever." But our "more" is often a vacuous whirl. But, oddly enough, God has assigned preaching to the church, so our primary calling is the declaration of the gospel.

The parable speaks to us preachers as it spoke to first-century Christians. Apparently the parable did not speak directly to Mark for, of all things, he added a long allegorical interpretation to the parable (Mark 4:14–20) in which he blames his preaching problem on listeners. What's the problem? Why, bad soil! Some seed falls in the roadways where people are too busy; they hear, but the seed never roots because "down deep they're really shallow." Some seed falls in rocky places. Rocky-soil people are excited by the gospel message, but when troubles come they lose faith. Other seed falls among thorns, that is, among the rich, where "things" choke growth. The allegory may be a comfort to preachers, but there is absolutely no doubt that it is secondary. Indeed, when it comes to syntax, vocabulary choice, and the like, Mark himself was the probable author. Note that his allegorical explanation stresses the quality of different soils, whereas the parable contrasts seed scattering and harvest.

Bernard Brandon Scott [1989, 355–58] contends that the harvest is not necessarily impressive—"thirty, sixty, a hundred times." He remarks that Luke merely has a final figure, "a hundred fold" (Luke 8:8), whereas *Thomas* has a neat mathematical progression from "sixty" doubling to "a hundred and twenty." But Mark has a triad, "thirty, sixty, a hundred times." While the triadic form is an oral convention, Scott argues that the progression—30, 60, 100—is not mathematically neat like *Thomas* and, therefore, connotes a less than adequate image. Though Jeremias (1963, 150) supposes that the triad is a symbol of an eschatological fulfillment, Scott is skeptical. He knows that the day of the Lord will bring a messianic harvest, but he notes that such promises are usually unmeasured symbols of huge extravagance. Here, however, the final figure is a hundredfold, which would be a good, but not unexpected, return. In the Babylonian Talmud, the "world to come" will be filled with wonder so that each individual grape will produce twenty measures of wine! And when Heroditus describes what to him is miraculous fertility in Babylon, he speaks of "two hundredfold." Thus Scott argues that a hundredfold is no big thing.

Scott is probably right, but we are unsure. If the contrast in the parable is between a rather careless farmer scattering seed in all the wrong places and an unexpected final harvest, then "thirty, sixty, a hundred times" is a fair return. Scott argues that the closure is rhetorically inadequate because it does not follow a progression (e.g., 30, 60, 120, doubling with each increase) or end with a huge, extravagant figure. But closure is achieved by the round figure "a hundred times" instead of a progression of 30, 60, 90, which would connote an unended continuation. In the Greek, *en triakonta kai en exakonta kai en ekaton* effects rhetorical closure by offbeat rhythm: *-konta, -konta, -katon.* So, though the harvest may not be eschatologically enormous, given an incompetent sowing, it is at least a harvest and an obvious witness to grace. Grace is a grand expectation in any pulpit anywhere.

Sermon

This full-length sermon was delivered in 1981 and subsequently published in *Pulpit Digest* under the title, "A Fool Farmer and the Grace of God."

Introduction   Some years ago, an American was invited to lecture in a foreign country. He stood on a platform facing a thousand people, none of whom could speak a word of English. "I'm glad to be here," he said, whereupon an interpreter leapt up and spoke for a full minute. "But, I didn't say all that," he protested, "I didn't say all that!"

Jesus told a little parable about a farmer sowing seed. Later someone came and added a long, long explanation. You can almost hear the voice of Jesus shout across the centuries: "I didn't mean all that!" So now, let's go back and listen again to the little parable Jesus told. Said Jesus, "A farmer went out to sow. . . . "

1   "A sower went out to sow," said Jesus. You hear the story and think to yourself, what a dumb, dumb farmer! Can you imagine any farmer stupid enough to sow seed in a thornbush, a rock pile, or right down the center stripe of an interstate? The parable is laughable, almost as silly as the Christian church sowing seed of the gospel! We may not have tossed God's word into thornbushes, but we've certainly preached good news in mighty odd places—from the rocky coasts of Alaska to the jungle thickets of South Africa, all over the world. What's more, we still do. The other day an appeal came in the mail to support a preaching mission to communist Russia—there's rocky soil! In our own land, every evening lay preachers spout good news to the winos in Detroit's downtown, and every afternoon there's an evangelist soapboxing the gospel to push-and-shove crowds in the New York City subway system. Rock, thorn, and highway—if there's anything sillier than sowing seed in a rock pile, it's the Christian church spreading good news of the gospel. You hear the parable and think to yourself, what a dumb farmer!

2   Of course, if anyone's a fool in the parable, God is. God's the fool! For has not God commanded our speaking? Has God not told us to go to every nation, to cover the world with the Word? And God doesn't seem to care whether anyone listens or not. God doesn't compile lists of hot prospects, or recommend evangelizing only where there's enough cash to build a church—that's an old Presbyterian game. God says "Preach!" and the command is unconditional. So when Moses came up to complain that he, Moses, was not much into public speaking, God interrupted him, saying, "Speak!" Or Ezekiel, who reminded the Lord that when you come right down to it, dry bones are not what you'd call a responsive congregation, God said "Preach!" There's a group of Scandinavian Christians with a wonderful custom. Whenever a minister is ordained, the person leaps up, strides out of the church, and begins to preach to startled passersby. Perhaps that's what God has in mind, for God wants us out of our stained glass and into the world speaking. God has commanded us to preach good news—everywhere. So if there's a fool in the parable, the fool is God!

3 Well, be honest: Results are less than impressive. How few do respond. Here we've been preaching the gospel for twenty centuries and the world's only about twelve percent Christian. Rock, thorn, and highway—at least the parable understands the odds. Nowadays, nobody but nobody seems to want to hear the gospel, particularly in America. Maybe we aren't desperate enough, hungry, hurt, or hard up enough to hear the gospel. Twentieth-century America seems rocky soil indeed. An off-Broadway play showed a couple sitting in a big city apartment, thick pile rugs and sinky couches, when, all of a sudden, a Salvation Army band parades by the window blaring a Jesus song. The young man gets up, goes and slams the window, saying, "I really don't see what Jesus can do for us!"[7] Maybe that's our problem: We don't see what Jesus can do for us. Can he fill our tanks with cheap gas, or curb a runaway inflation, or tell us what on earth to do with our MX missile system? Jesus doesn't seem to speak to our all-American agenda, so we don't see what he can do. Rock, thorn, and highway! Be honest: we preach the gospel, but results are scarcely impressive.

4 So how easy it is to become discouraged. How easy to lose heart. When nobody's listening, who wants to speak? Perhaps that's what's happened to us mainline Protestant types; because nobody seems to listen, we've quit speaking. We turn evangelism over to the gray clapboard backstreet pentecostal churches, or to Jerry Falwell wearing a Reagan button where his cross should be! Listen, we are not talking about our denominational seminaries, or boards and agencies far away, we're talking about us right here; we have not been speaking the gospel. When was the last time you actually talked to anyone, even your own family, about the God you believe in? When? Some years ago a famous Protestant preacher lost his voice; he never spoke another public word. The condition was diagnosed as psychological, for as a friend explained, "He looked up one day and discovered nobody was listening!" Is that our problem? When the world seems tone deaf to the gospel, we turn off. Instead of scattering seed, we've kept our church lawns well-mowed. How easy, oh how easy it is to become discouraged, to lose heart.

5 But hold on. Hey, take a look at the end of the parable. Look, thirty times, sixty times, a hundred times—a harvest! God takes our foolish leftover, throwaway seeds and turns them into triumph. There's a harvest coming; someday "every knee shall bow and every tongue confess that Jesus Christ is Lord to the glory of God the Father." No idle dream; it's a promised word of the Lord and the Lord keeps promises. Someday it shall be! A cartoon showed a big-city apartment filled with plants. There was philodendron around the curtain rods, ivy on the walls; there were buckets, pots, ashtrays all filled with plants, everywhere. The place looked like a jungle. In the middle of the room a little lady was explaining to a neighbor, "Would you believe, it all began with one African violet!" We laugh, laugh for joy, for God will take

our foolish seeding of the gospel and turn it into a miracle. There is a harvest promised! Someday the fur-capped Russian and the Detroit wino and the New York subway crowd and the Indiana farmer will all come together in one glad gang before God; it shall be. Hey, look at the end of the parable. Thirty, sixty, a hundred times over—there's going to be a harvest.

6 So guess what? Agenda for the church: Speak the gospel and trust God. Trust God and speak the gospel. What else is the church for but to spread the good news? Shall we spell it out? Your church does not exist to spruce up your morals; God may not be much interested in what we call "morality." The church does not exist to teach your children religion; Christian faith may not be "religion." Your church does not exist to provide Christian fellowship; you can rub human fur against human fur almost anywhere. No, the church lives to preach the gospel! That's what a church is for, to name God in the world. And you wonder why we don't. Think back over your own life. We're all brought up badly, and we all live broken, patched-together lives, riddled by funny fears and guilts that, my God, we'd like to forget. But here we are now, with a kind of joy knowing we're forgiven, able to love a little, miraculously, once in a while. Looking back, we know it's God who's done all—set you free from yourself for love. Well, somehow you'd think we'd want to spread the news, news of God's good, undeserved grace in a world that seems grace-less. What else is a church for? There's a wonderful poster with a trite caption. The caption: "Who plants a seed trusts God"—trite. But the picture gets to you: not a picture of a farmer sowing a field, but of a grubby tenement kid poking seed into a catch of dirt in a concrete windowsill. "Who plants a seed trusts God." Image of the church in the twentieth century, trying to sow seed of the gospel in a chill, concrete world. So, agenda for the church: Trust God and speak the gospel, speak the gospel and trust God.

Conclusion   Where do we live? Well, between the stammer of our speaking and the grace of God; the stammer of our speaking and the promised grace of God. Funny, we don't talk much of God. We can talk about sex—it's interesting. And we can talk about basketball—in Indiana it's almost pathological. But talk about God? We don't. We feel foolish inside and are tongue-tied. But listen, God wants us to name God's name into our conversations so folk will know who God is and believe. Stammer, blush, but dare to speak. "Between the foolishness of speaking and the grace of God—" A good place to live, dear friends—only a step to the kingdom of God.

Discussion

Introduction   The introduction is cumbersome. It was designed to solve a problem, namely, the allegory that is attached to the parable. But if the allegory is not read as a part of the scripture lesson, some other introduction would be better. Besides, these days people are not familiar with scripture; probably they don't know the parable is followed by an allegory.

1   All the first move does is to depict the farmer as a foolish, careless seeder, and then to link the seed metaphor to the church's evangelical preaching. Notice that I define the church's task as worldwide, but then narrow down to our own land with examples from Detroit and New York. Toward the end of the move I introduce a refrain, "rock, thorn and highway," which we will hear again.

2   The second move doubles the idea of "foolish" but, of all things, applies the word to God. The move develops in three sections: (1) God commands our preaching, (2) God doesn't calculate the odds as we do, and (3) God's command is unconditional to Moses, Ezekiel, and us. God's command and our speaking is picked up in the Scandinavian Christians' ordination custom.

3   Now we turn to look at how few people do respond to our preaching. Notice the use of the refrain that was set up in the first move, "rock, thorn, and highway." The illustration from the off-Broadway show fits the context and introduces a phrase, "I really don't see what Jesus can do for us," which in turn permits, "Can he fill our tanks with cheap gas, or curb runaway inflation, or tell us what on earth to do with our MX missile system?"—all problems at the time the sermon was preached.

4   Here we work off the idea of scant results; results that prompt discouragement. Please note, I am presenting Mark's problem as our problem. Because we get little response, we become hopeless with regard to preaching. Note also the candor about "backstreet pentecostal churches" and the aside regarding Jerry Falwell. Pentecostal churches are growing now because fifty years ago they preached to the poor. Mainline denominations have been losing members in no small part because they have chosen to preach to a bourgeois middle class. I use a true illustration about a famous pulpit preacher who lost his voice. Notice how the illustration counters the Scandinavian custom of a minister, once ordained, rushing out to preach to the public. I pick up the metaphor of the parable with, "Instead of scattering seed, we've kept our church lawns well-mowed."

5   Now suddenly, we want to turn to the end of the parable in a major shift from analysis to the final promised harvest. Naturally, I introduce a rather more freewheeling style. (Note that there is a quote from scripture to back up the idea of a promise.) The rather substantial illustration (which provoked laughter) works well. Like the illustration in which the young couple closed their window on a "Jesus song," it also takes place in a big city apartment, but fills the space with growth. Subliminally a congregation overcomes discouragement with flowers and laughter. To the illustration we add a reference to the sermon's first move, "Someday the fur-capped Russian and the Detroit wino and the New York City subway crowd . . . " I add to the list an Indiana farmer because the sermon was preached in Indiana. Notice we also have a new refrain to counter "rock, thorn, and highway," namely, "thirty, sixty, a hundred times."

6   We turn now to the church as God's preachers. Because the idea of the church as a preacher may seem strange these days, I set up a forceful system: "Shall we spell it out? Your church does not exist to . . . " Then I follow with an appeal to the experience of grace in personal lives, changing the rhetorical style to do so. The illustration of the poster with the little boy planting a seed also takes place in a city apartment.

Conclusion   The conclusion begins with confession: "we don't talk much of God." Sex, yes; and basketball (big-time in Indiana), yes; but God, no. Then, admitting our embarrassment as we dare to speak, we recognize our location— "between the foolishness of speaking and the grace of God."

The parable of the Sower spoke to Mark's age and speaks to our own times as well. In a semi-secular season, when preaching is not a popular all-American activity, we need to hear good news of God's prospering grace.

SEED AND HARVEST
(Mark 4:26–29; Thomas *21:4)*

MARK 4:26–29

26The kingdom of God is as if a man were to sow seed on the ground, 27and then go to sleep and get up, night and day, and the seed sprout and grow without his knowing. 28On its own, the earth produces first the blade, then the ear, then the full grain in the ear. 29But when the grain is ready, quick, the farmer "puts in the sickle for it's harvest time!"

Here is a parable that has troubled hearers for centuries. No wonder both Matthew and Luke dropped it from their Gospels. The problem is the final verse. The words are a direct quote from a particularly nasty section of Joel 3:13. The prophet is pleased to picture a battle in which Israel's enemies will be cut down like grain at harvest. Look at the so-called "war scroll" in Joel 3:9–16:

> Proclaim this among the nations:
> Prepare war,
>   stir up the warriors.
> Let all the soldiers draw near,
>   let them come up.
> Beat your plowshares into swords,
>   and your pruning hooks into spears;
>   let the weakling say, "I am a warrior."
> Come quickly,
>   all you nations all around,
>   gather yourselves there.
> Bring down your warriors, O LORD.
> 12Let the nations rouse themselves,
>   and come up to the valley of Jehoshaphat;
> for there I will sit to judge
>   all the neighboring nations.
> Put in the sickle,
>   for the harvest is ripe.

Go in, tread,
    for the wine press is full.
The vats overflow,
    for their wickedness is great.
Multitudes, multitudes,
    in the valley of decision!
For the day of the LORD is near
    in the valley of decision.
The sun and the moon are darkened,
    and the stars withdraw their shining.
The LORD roars from Zion,
    and utters his voice from Jerusalem,
    and the heavens and the earth shake.
But the LORD is a refuge for his people,
    a stronghold for the people of Israel.

The prophet hopes that God will annihilate other nations, nations that have battered poor Israel. So Joel takes pleasure in dreaming vengeance. No more beating swords into plowshares, no more turning spears into pruning hooks, as Isaiah had prophesied. Now is the time to make farm implements back into weapons and destroy the wicked—other nations. The text may feature semi-apocalyptic images (e.g., "sun and moon are darkened and the stars withdraw their shining") often associated with the sure, if brutal, judgment of God.

So guess what? After a wondrous affirmation of God's patient grace, suddenly the militant quote from Joel is tacked onto the parable. Does the parable picture a God who will patiently bring the whole creation to fruition only to hack it down in sudden fury? Here's the problem for preachers: We can read the text as mercy *and* judgment, or, deliberately, we can face a choice. If we affirm a God whose patient grace supports our sin-struck humanity, we will erase the words from Joel, but if we cherish wrath, perhaps we will have to delete grace—an either/or choice. Here is how one preacher, Archibald Hunter, conjoined the two themes. He speaks of God as "the Father of Christ," and then proceeds:

> The seed which he gave his Son to sow in Galilee, which was watered by the bloody sweat of his cross, and which, by the resurrection and the coming of the Spirit, began to yield its own rich crop of saved men and women, is still growing secretly but surely to fruition; and as our God is a living and judging God, there will come a time when he "sets to work with the sickle" because the harvest time of the ages is come.
>
> The final question is the old one: "Who is on the Lord's side?"Christ is still calling men to enter God's kingdom and align themselves with his purpose and:
>
> > Once to every man and nation
> > Comes the moment to decide.
>
> Will we take our place in that kingdom of his Father which he offers us? Or will we simply go our own way and refuse his

invitation? Either way God's kingdom stands and grows for ever. Either way, his sovereignty will be exercised, in blessing or in judgment. It is for us to decide whether we will be found on the Lord's side in the battle.[8]

Earlier in his treatment of the parable, Hunter had spoken of "agricultural grace" and had written of the sure growth of the kingdom like seed which, though we cannot see it germinate, grows by God's grace. But notice that after he has introduced the harvest image, he ends up with "whether we will be found on the Lord's side in the battle." What began with growing seed has shifted to a battlefield. God will nourish *and* annihilate!

Bernard Brandon Scott (1989, 363–71) argues that the parable is designed to make an audience choose between the two image systems—patient growth or bloody harvest. Generations have been puzzled by the parable, but Scott offers an alternative: Perhaps the parable was designed to force an interpretive decision on hearers.

Preachers may not wish to encourage congregational self-righteousness—we are virtuous Christian people and, therefore, may anticipate with well-deserved delight annihilation of the unrighteous. Nor will we wish to preach the parable as descriptive of God's nature, an alternating current of grace and wrath. Such a God would demonstrate divine schizophrenia. Tennessee Williams has one of his characters, Shannon, an ex-priest, "a man of God on vacation," explain how he preached a final sermon to his smug congregation:

> Look here, I said, I shouted, I'm tired of conducting services in praise
> and worship of a senile delinquent—yeah, that's what I said, I shouted!
> All your Western theologies, the whole mythology of them, are based
> on the concept of God as a *senile delinquent* . . . like the sort of old man
> in a nursing home that's putting together a jigsaw puzzle and can't put
> it together and gets furious at it and kicks over the table. Yes, I tell you
> they do that, all our theologies do it—accuse God of being a cruel senile
> delinquent, blaming the world and brutally punishing all he created . . .
> I shouted after them, go on, go home and close your house windows, all
> your windows and doors, against the truth about God![9]

Though Shannon longs for the sweet silver rain of God's mercy, he cannot reconcile mercy with the hells on earth he has seen, which, to him, are signs of God's harsh judgment. If we try to hold the verses of the parable together we too are bound to end up with God as a "senile delinquent." Agricultural grace will turn into an arms race!

Take a second look at the parable. At the outset, notice that the farmer is at best incompetent. In spite of all those rather romantic affirmations of Jesus' supposed rural background, most of the farmers Jesus describes are truly dumb. In the parable, Jesus' farmer carefully plants a field and then flat-out quits working. According to Isaiah 28:24–26, farming requires long hours of labor:

Do those who plow for sowing plow continually?
 Do they continually open and harrow their ground?
When they have leveled its surface,
  do they not scatter dill, sow cummin,
and plant wheat in rows
  and barley in its proper place,
  and spelt as the border?
For they are well instructed;
  their God teaches them.

Apparently the farmer in the parable is not "well instructed," for he doesn't even know that his crop is growing night and day. He does not harrow the ground continually. Either he is lazy, or a dunce, or both. Nevertheless, according to the parable, the crop grows *automate.* The word is used in the Septuagint translation of the Hebrew scriptures to indicate God's mysterious helpfulness, what might be termed "agricultural grace." During a sabbatical season when fields lie fallow, what grows by itself, *automata,* is a God-given provision for food:

> For six years you shall sow your land and gather in its yield; but the seventh year you shall let it rest and lie fallow, so that the poor of your people may eat; and what they leave the wild animals may eat. (Ex. 23:10–11)

Though we are dealing with an irresponsible farmer, God will observe an unscheduled sabbatical and prosper growth. God's grace will provide.

What's more, God's agricultural grace is slowly productive. The process is measured: "first the blade, then the ear, then the full grain in the ear." Notice the deliberate stages of growth; God is a careful gardener. The poetry of the parable fosters trust in the sure hand of God. In some ways the parable is like an earlier parable in the same chapter where a farmer throws seed in all the wrong places—rock piles, thornbushes, and roads; nevertheless, God brings a harvest, "thirty, sixty, a hundred times." Both parables seem to celebrate God's compensating grace.

Then, abruptly, there is the cruel instruction, "Put in the sickle, for the harvest is ripe." What on earth can we do with the awful ending?

As a faithful preacher, you must decide. Is the parable an "and" or an "or"? How will you preach? The issue cannot be resolved on the basis of the Bible. You must think theologically and decide. Or, better, you must preach theologically and enable your congregation to make their decision in faith. To do so, you will want to pick up the poetry from the passage. You will use graceful, measured language to describe the slow, sure, careful ways of God. Then, by contrast, whatever your interpretation, you will counter with a sudden, brutal description of wrath—a wrath that in Joel reverses God's promises of peace. For example:

> Wait a minute! Hold on! The farmer "puts in the sickle for it's harvest time." The words are a quote, actually a particularly nasty quote from the prophet Joel. Someday, Joel hopes God will gather in all Israel's political enemies so they can be crushed like grapes in a wine press or

hacked down like grain at harvest. The images are cruel. Ask yourselves, why would God help a harvest to grow so carefully, "first the blade and then the ear and then the full grain in the ear," just for the exquisite pleasure of destroying the whole harvest? Is God two-faced? One day God helps a harvest to grow into grain and the next day, in a fit of pique, God destroys it all. If our God is so utterly capricious, one day smiling, one day stern, how can we trust God? God, the almighty indecision in the sky! Mercy to grow, then a hack-down judgment day—the parable makes no sense.

Then you will want to lead your congregation into thinking through the nature of God, a God whose love can be discovered in the image of Christ crucified. God our judge is the God who, in the symbol of Christ crucified, dies in suffering love for us all. Surely such a God cannot authorize a terrifying valley-of-decision slaughter. You will lead your congregation into a profound grasp of God's good mercy. In effect, you will help them to edit the Bible with theological thoughtfulness.

THE MUSTARD SEED
(Thomas *20:1–2*; Mark *4:30–32*; Matthew *13:31–32*; Luke *13:19*)

THOMAS *20:1–2*
The disciples said to Jesus, "Tell us what the Kingdom of Heaven is like." He said to them, "It is like a mustard seed, the smallest of all seeds. But when it falls on tilled soil, it produces a great plant and becomes a shelter for the birds of the sky."

MARK 4:30–32
30And he said, "What can we compare with the kingdom of God? What parable can we use for it? 31Like a mustard seed which, sown on the ground, is the smallest of all seeds on earth, 32but, when sown, it grows up and becomes the greatest of all shrubs, spreading big branches so the birds of the air may nest in its shade."

MATTHEW 13:31–32
31He put another parable before them saying, "The kingdom of the heavens is like a mustard seed which a man sowed in his field. 32Surely it's the smallest of all the seeds, but when it grows, it is greater than the shrubs and becomes a tree, so birds of the heavens will come and live in its branches."

LUKE 13:18–19
18So he said, "What's like the kingdom of God? With what can I compare it? 19It is like a grain of mustard seed which a man took and sowed in his

garden; it grew and became a tree, and the birds of the air made nests in its branches."

You can trace an evolving tradition in versions of the Mustard Seed parable (Crossan 1973, 45–49). Some scholars suppose the earliest text is in *Thomas*. Mark is more elaborate, stressing the contrast of smallest to greatest. By the time the parable shows up in Matthew, the mustard plant has become a tree. Luke's text is as terse as *Thomas's*, and, like *Thomas,* mentions cultivated land, a garden, but along with Matthew pictures a mustard tree. From a modest plant, the parable seems to have produced a mythological tree.

The parable has been preached for centuries in a rhetoric of growth, from the least to the greatest. The interpretation is justified, for clearly the Gospel writers are dreaming of enormous growth. Thus ministers have promised congregations success-story growth. After all, hasn't the Christian enterprise grown from a handful of disciples to a worldwide movement with millions of adherents? If ministers have not pushed the image of a triumphant church, they have hyped the power of faith. Faith may seem insubstantial, a minor-key theme in our lives, but as faith grows within us, it can empower us to "move mountains." So in Christian preaching, the mustard seed is tiny but promises a payoff! For centuries, the Christian church has harbored triumphalist fantasies.

Some years ago, biblical scholar Robert Funk wrote an article with a somewhat whimsical title, "The Looking Glass Tree Is for the Birds" (1975, 9–26). He noted that the parable plays around with images drawn from Hebrew scripture texts that promised little twig Israel would be great like a towering cedar of Lebanon. Such great-tree texts show up in Ezekiel and in Daniel. The tree is alluded to in Isaiah (10:33–11:1; 14:4–20) and Zechariah (11:1–2) as well as in some Psalms (37:35–36; 104:16–17). Evidently a vision of triumph had captivated Israel and the image would be familiar to Jesus' audience. Here are the major texts:

> Thus says the Lord GOD:
> I myself will take a sprig
>   from the lofty top of a cedar;
>   I will set it out.
> I will break off a tender one
>   from the topmost of its young twigs;
> I myself will plant it
>   on a high and lofty mountain.
> On the mountain height of Israel
>   I will plant it,
> in order that it may produce boughs and bear fruit,
>   and become a noble cedar.
> Under it every kind of bird will live;
>   in the shade of its branches will nest
> winged creatures of every kind.
>
> (Ezek. 17:22–23)

> Whom are you like in your greatness?
>> Consider Assyria, a cedar of Lebanon,
> with fair branches and forest shade,
>> and of great height,
>> its top among the clouds.
> The waters nourished it,
>> the deep made it grow tall,
> . . . .
> So it towered high
>> above all the trees of the field;
> its boughs grew large
>> and its branches long,
> . . . .
> All the birds of the air
>> made their nests in its boughs;
> . . . .
> and in its shade
>> all great nations lived.
>>   (Ezek. 31:2–6)

Notice that while Ezekiel 17 seems to be looking to the future of Israel, from the little twig to the towering tree with birds nesting under the shade of its boughs, in Ezekiel 31 the cedar is Assyria and birds will nest in branches of the tree. The great cedar seems to be a symbol of political power, and the "birds of the air" would appear to be other nations. So whether the image is a promise to little Israel or a representation of Israel's enemies, it is a trimuphalist dream, particularly if the "little twig" is included. The great tree is a vision of political power and the dependency of other nations. The image also shows up in Daniel 4:10–12:

> Upon my bed this is what I saw;
>> there was a tree at the center of the earth,
>> and its height was great.
> The tree grew great and strong,
>> its top reached to heaven,
>> and it was visible to the ends of the whole earth.
> Its foliage was beautiful,
>> its fruit abundant,
>> and it provided food for all.
> The animals of the field found shade under it,
>> the birds of the air nested in its branches,
>> and from it all living beings were fed.

In Daniel the tree stands for Nebuchadnezzar's dream of a politically powerful kingdom, a dream that God will dispel with devastating judgment (4:14):

> Cut down the tree and chop off its branches,
>> strip off its foliage and scatter its fruit.

> Let the animals flee from beneath it
> and the birds from its branches.

In every case, then, the cedar of Lebanon, "the great tree," is a symbol of a triumphant political greatness—or, as in contemporary church pews, a symbol of worldwide ecclesial triumph.

Robert Funk argues that the parable of the Mustard Seed was a "burlesque," a spoof, a satire on the cedar of Lebanon image. The parable begins small, "the smallest of seeds," and ends up not in triumph, but with a plant about as likeable as a skunk cabbage and as substantial as milkweed! Nevertheless, surprisingly, "birds of the air" nest in its shade.

Mustard plants were not popular in ancient Palestine. Though the plant supposedly had healing properties, it spread like a weed. "It grows entirely wild," says Pliny, "[and] when it has been sown it is scarcely possible to get the place rid of it." (Scott 1989, 380) As many commentators have noted, mustard seed was banned from planted gardens. The Mishnah is often cited as forbidding mustard seed in garden plots:

> No kind of seeds do they sow in a garden bed, but all kinds of vegetables do they sow in a garden bed. Mustard and smooth chick-peas [are considered] kind[s] of seeds.[10]

We seem to have an odd parable indeed. Although the seed may start small, it ends, not in triumph, but with a suspicious, often rejected weed, whose branches would scarcely support a nest for birds much less offer any significant shade. No wonder Funk uses the term "burlesque." The parable can no longer be preached with a confident note of triumph.

Preachers should realize that the Mustard Seed parable is aimed at a particular mindset, namely, a lust for big-time success. If the parable is to do what it is designed to do, preachers must invoke the dream of triumph. In a sermon introduction, we can speak of the necklace with a little marble containing a mustard seed. We can recall what it means to people—a promise of little to the large. At the outset we can remember how sermons have been preached in the past, full of hope and hype, from twelve disciples to a worldwide church, from weak faith to mountain-moving confidence.

Then, in a first move, we can admit how much we like visions of greatness, particularly at a time when membership in many American churches seems to be dwindling. Wouldn't it be sweet if the nation were swept by revival and church pews filled up again? Sweeter still if the church were socially important. Gerald L. K. Smith commissioned a seven-story statue of Christ on top of an Ozark mountain, convinced that with the statue, "The world comes to us at Eureka Springs."[11] Big dreams indeed.

Then we can see what Jesus does hand us—not triumph but a weed about as attractive as ragweed in August! A weed "despised and rejected." (Obviously the Bible doesn't promise anyone a rose garden.) No, the church will not be a winner. In our world, the body of Christ gets crucified. What else can we expect? Did not Jesus himself end "despised and rejected" on a cross? Yet through him the world may be saved. Think it out, perhaps by God's grace the world may be saved through the broken body of the church. Notice that to preach the Mustard Seed parable you must first evoke images of triumph for the parable to debunk with its hard word.

The other theme that preachers can work with is hidden in the rule against planting mustard seed in a garden. Again Jesus depicts a kingdom not of the righteous but of impudent rule-breaking sinners. The seed is forbidden and produces a suspicious, nuisance-value plant; thus the kingdom of God will be open to the undesirable.

Let us be clear: When the Gospel writers tell the parable, they are hoping for whopping future growth. They are dreaming of triumph. Matthew believes that his little congregation will grow into a new Israel, and Luke may well suppose that Christianity will spread throughout the empire. No wonder both evangelists turn Mark's shrub into a full-sized tree. But given the direct citations from Ezekiel and Daniel, the parable is best described as a burlesque. Did Jesus play around with a cedar of Lebanon satire? Probably. There is no support for triumphalism, national or ecclesial, in Jesus' teaching. Preachers will have to decide what to do. Should we follow the Gospel writers or buy into Robert Funk's interpretation of the original Jesus parable? In view of Funk's compelling biblical research, it is difficult to preach the parable as a message of triumph. If we remember the cross, triumph is even more unlikely.

The parable may be difficult to preach, something of a downer, but a lot wiser than hollow dreams of churchly conquest.

TENANTS
(Thomas 65—66; Mark 12:1–11;
Matthew 21:33–43; Luke 20:9b–18)

THOMAS 65—66

65:1There was a good man who owned a vineyard. He leased it to tenant farmers so that they might work it and he might collect the produce from them. He sent his servant so that the tenants might give him the produce of the vineyard. They seized his servant and beat him, all but killing him. The servant went back and told his master. The master said, "Perhaps (they) did not recognize (him)." He sent another servant. The tenants beat this one as well. Then the owner sent his son and said, "Perhaps they will show respect to my son." Because the tenants knew that it was he who was the heir to the vineyard, they seized him and killed him.
2Let him who has ears hear.

66:1Jesus said, "Show me the stone which the builders
have rejected. That one is the cornerstone."

MARK 12:1–11

1He began to speak to them in parables: A man planted a vineyard, put a
hedge around it, dug a winepress, and built a tower. He leased it to sharecroppers, and went away. 2In due time, he sent a slave to the sharecroppers in order to collect produce of the vineyard from them. 3Grabbing
him, they beat him up and sent him away empty-handed. 4Again, he sent
another slave to them; him, they hit in the head and humiliated. 5He
sent another; him, they killed. Many others were sent; some beaten up,
others killed. 6He had one more, a beloved son. Finally, he sent him last,
saying, "They will respect my son." 7But the sharecroppers said to one
another, "Here's the heir. Come on, let's kill him and we'll collect his
inheritance." 8Taking hold of him, they killed him and threw him outside
the vineyard.

9What will the owner [literally, *kyrie*, "Lord"] of the vineyard do? He
will come to destroy the sharecroppers and give the vineyard to others.
10Haven't you read the scripture? "A stone which builders rejected has
ended up as the cornerstone. 11The Lord has done this, and it's marvelous in our eyes."

The parable of the Tenants appears in all the Synoptic Gospels as well as the
Gospel of Thomas. While there are some scholars who suppose that the terse version found in *Thomas* indicates the shape of an original parable, most scholars
are skeptical. In the Synoptic Gospels the parable obviously has been allegorized
in view of the crucifixion: the owner = God; the abused servants = prophets; the
beloved son = Christ Jesus. The "cornerstone" verses from Psalm 118:22–23,
familiar early-church apologetic material, have been tacked on as a conclusion.

Mark seems to have begun the elaboration of the parable. He designed his
Gospel around two parables, the Sower (4:3–8) and the Tenants (12:1–11). He
recounts the Sower and then, after supplying an allegory of the different soils,
proceeds to demonstrate his allegory by introducing rocky-soil people, thorny
people, trampled people, and a few good-soil types. Then, prior to his passion
narrative, Mark introduces the parable of the Tenants, which he then proceeds to
demonstrate in his story of the trial and crucifixion of Jesus—God's beloved son
killed. Matthew picks up the text from Mark and subjects it to still further elaboration (Matt. 21:40–46). Do we have an original Jesus parable somewhere
under the allegorization? Maybe or maybe not; it is impossible to say. But
the parable has been treasured by generations of Christian preachers; it is in the
homiletical canon and we must find a way to preach the passage.

Obviously, in Mark the parable draws on the imagery of Isaiah 5:1–7, the
famous allegory of the vineyard:

My beloved had a vineyard
    on a very fertile hill.
He dug it and cleared it of stones,
    and planted it with choice vines;
he built a watchtower in the midst of it,
    and [dug] out a vine vat in it.
                    (vv. 1b–2a)

Even in Isaiah, the vineyard ends up in tragedy. For though carefully planted, the vineyard produces bad fruit: "[H]e expected it to yield grapes, but it yielded wild grapes." Thus God declares a verdict:

And now I will tell you
    what I will do to my vineyard.
I will remove its hedge,
    and it shall be devoured;
I will break down its wall,
    and it shall be trampled down.
I will make it a waste;
    it shall not be pruned or hoed,
    and it shall be overgrown with briars and thorns.
                    (vv. 5–6a)

The passage in Isaiah is an announced allegory, "For the vineyard of the LORD of hosts is the house of Israel" (v. 7a). The image of Israel as a vineyard shows up again and again in the Hebrew scriptures (e.g., Ps. 80:8; Jer. 2:21, 12:10; Ezek. 15:1–6, 19:10; Hosea 10:1). Thus, authentic or not, the parable draws on a familiar biblical tradition. Mark regards the several servants as prophets, and scholars wonder if the prophet who is "hit in the head" is a veiled reference to the beheading of John the Baptist. The question, "What will the Lord of the vineyard do?" may be original, echoing, "I will tell you what I will do," in Isaiah 5:5, but most scholars think not.

Could the situation described in the parable happen? William Herzog II (1994, 98–113), drawing on recent studies of violence in Galilee, reads the parable in the light of peasant resentments. Much farmland had been taken over by agribarons in Jerusalem, and tenant farmers were bitter over being turned into sharecroppers on what was once their own land. Thus, to Herzog, the parable describes some sort of peasant revolt.

Even if such a context is not involved, tenant farming was common and, according to Derrett (1970, 289–300), was performed under carefully delineated covenant agreements. For the first few years, tenants could subsist by growing other crops on the land while the vineyard matured, sometimes planting cash crops between the rows. Thereafter tenants split the produce fifty-fifty with the owner. But, according to Derrett, such a stated agreement would not be overturned in open revolt.

Jewish scholar David Stern argues that Jesus probably did tell the parable, but that the "son" in the original parable was John the Baptist (Thoma 1989, 48–80; Stern 1991, 185–97). He notes that the parable follows a controversy over authority: "By what authority do you do these things?" To which Jesus answers by asking a question, "Did the baptism of John come from heaven or was it of human origin?" (Mark 11:30) The "chief priests, the scribes, and the elders" refuse to respond. In turn, Jesus will not answer their original question and, instead, tells them the parable. Stern also believes that the citation from Psalm 118 was original. The Jewish narrative *mashal* often followed a discussion such as Mark records in 11:27–33 and frequently might conclude with a quotation from scripture (Thoma 1989, 27–31). Jewish scholarship is important: Stern's argument, as well as David Flusser's study of the same passage (Young 1989, 282–316), deserves attention.

Certainly preachers will not want to historicize the parable — Israel has been the wicked vinedressers and now the vineyard is turned over to us responsible Christian tenants. While Matthew obviously reads the parable as historical allegory, we need not. Such a scheme would be blatantly anti-Semitic. Besides, any preacher who supposes that "Christian nations," by contrast, welcome prophets and are faithful to God's will have failed to notice the Holocaust or the assassination of Martin Luther King Jr. No, the passage must be widened to include the whole wide world and all human beings. We are the wicked who reject God's living word. We are all vinedressers who deserve eviction.

The truly interesting character in the parable is the owner. Whereas Isaiah's "beloved" planter uprooted his vineyard in anger when it produced wild grapes, the owner in Jesus' parable displays absurd patience. He sends an agent to collect produce and the sharecroppers beat him up. He then sends another who is also beaten and "humiliated." Still another is dispatched and he is killed outright. Finally, he naively sends his own son, who is also murdered. Any notion of honor is long gone. Normally an owner would move in right away to claim his due. After a second agent is beaten, Jesus' audience would be wondering what's going on — in effect, what's the matter with this owner? Then there are more agents and more beatings as well as a few murders. The situation is absurd! When the son is sent and killed, the parable has tipped from reality into a grotesque parody of Isaiah 5. But if the parable is absurd, it is only absurd as a testimony to God's astonishing mercy. Like the father in the parable of the Prodigal Son, the owner here is patient with a "love that will not let us go."

Incidentally, the sharecroppers' notion that by killing off the son they, in turn, could inherit the land is equally odd. Herzog thinks that if the tenants were original owners whose land had been usurped by an absentee owner, then by killing the son they might hope to get their property back (Herzog 1994, 110–13). But Herzog's reconstruction seems unlikely. The tenants' plan, "Let's kill him and we'll collect his inheritance," is quite unrealistic. But, homiletically, the phrase is a fine symbol for the rebelliousness of human sin which, of course, is as foolish.

John Dominic Crossan (1973, 90) rejects the concluding line, "What will the owner of the vineyard do?" If the owner has repeatedly wimped out, why is he suddenly a threat of punishment? As for the cornerstone quote from Psalm 118, though it may have been tacked on by the early church, it is also a testimony to the resurrection. The "son" who was killed is now risen, and a community of the forgiven is built around him.

Sermon

This sermon, written in the mid-1960s, was revised and preached in 1974 at a Muhlenberg College chapel service.

Introduction   Can you picture Jesus preaching the parable? Can you imagine him speaking to a crowd of listeners in the temple court? There on the edge of the crowd are high priests and learned teachers, the religious leaders of Israel. Jesus is telling them a story about themselves. Remember how it goes? A man owned a vineyard and he sent agents to collect his share of the profits. But his vineyard workers beat them up and sent them way. Finally, he sent his own son, and they killed him. You can imagine how the story went over with the priests and leaders of Israel. No one likes to be labeled a murderer, especially in a religious building. "What will the Lord of the vineyard do with his wicked workers?" Jesus asked. The sermon was over and Jesus' congregation began to organize a lynch mob; apparently the parable got to them.

1   Well, if we're honest we'll have to admit the parable gets to us too. We understand the story. We should, for though it's a story of Israel, it's our story as well, and the story of the whole human race. We've always rejected the prophets. Trace your way back through history from Martin Luther King Jr. to Thomas More and Joan of Arc, back all the way to John the Baptist, Jeremiah, Amos, and old Elijah. We have a long, unlovely record of rejecting the prophets of God. Some we've killed, some we've stoned and some we've merely treated with silent reproach. Generation after generation, we've tried to stop prophets from speaking. There was a marvelous book published some years ago, a satire, pretending to be the history of a British village. There were pictures in the book showing what the village looked like down through the centuries—the 20th century, the 18th, the 1500s, the year 1000. But in every picture there were people throwing rocks at a speaker. That's the picture, isn't it? Our picture? Again and again, God has sent prophets to us and we've chased them away—the story of Israel, our story, the story of the whole human race.

2   Of course, when you think about it, it's easy to understand: Nobody loves a prophet. Prophets spot the gap between what we believe and how we behave, and drive the word of God in between. Prophets measure the distance between what we do and what God demands. God wills peace on earth. Then, "Why," says the prophet, why have you Americans spent billions of dollars killing more people in less time than any nation on the face of the earth? And why did you nod your approval last week when President Nixon announced millions of dollars sliced from welfare spending but not a dime from the military budget? God has given us a commandment, "You shall not kill." Why then, asks the prophet, have you been silent while more than thirty states moved to reinstate the death penalty? "Love your neighbor," God has spoken, so why do most churches still spend close to seventy percent of their cash on themselves? The prophet's word addresses the gap between what we believe and how we live, and that's painful. Did you see the cartoon that showed two ministers gazing ruefully into an all but empty collection plate—one or two coins and an "I Like Ike" button? "So much for prophecy," says one of the ministers. God has sent prophets to speak to the world, to lay claims on us, and year after year, century after century, we've brutally sent them away.

3   But then, guess what? In the parable, the lord of the vineyard sends his own son. He sent his only son and what happened? "Come on, let's kill him off and take over the property," the vineyard workers cry. The parable bumps us into the hard fact of sin—our rebellious human spirit. Our drive for power is absolute and, therefore, absolutely against the Lord God. Wasn't it Jean-Paul Sartre who used to argue that if there were no God to rebel against, humankind would not be rebellious? Solution: get rid of God and you get rid of sin as well. Sartre has almost seen his dream come true in our deGodded, secular world. And the result? The result is, we are as rebellious as ever. See it in the arrogance of the White House, in the power madness of large corporations, and, if you have the courage, in the shape of your own private dreams. Whenever God says Yes, there's something in us that says No; whenever God says No, the strident human ego shouts a defiant Yes. We are like a tribe in north China that Emily Hahn describes; they were so rebellious that if they didn't have an emperor they'd have invented one simply to rebel against him. So even if we didn't have a God, we'd rebel. "Come on," the sharecroppers cried out, "Let's kill him off and take over."

4   So they killed him. They killed off the only son. Maybe we can't see the shape of evil in our lives until there's a cross set up in the world with a "Son of God" nailed on it. There, see the shape of our rebel cruelty. An artist exhibited a contemporary painting of the crucifixion. There was the cross and all around a crowd, but with a difference. The artist had painted the faces in the crowd with familiar figures from our world. There was the president, and there a famous churchman, and a face from *Time* magazine's "Man of the Year." And the title of the painting? Three words: "Were you there . . . ?" Well, that's the picture we are meant to see during Holy Week. We can see our world around the cross—power politics, business ethics, and a "silent-majority" church— our faces bright-eyed with excitement, flushed with a strange, almost gleeful pleasure: "Come on, come on, let's kill him off and take over the world!" So we crucified God's true son.

5   What then will the lord of the vineyard do? Jesus asks the question and it's up

to us to answer. What would you do if you were God and had to put up with a rebel human race like ours? Wasn't it old Martin Luther in a bleak mood who answered the question: "If I were as our Lord God and . . . people were as disobedient as they now be, I would knock the world in pieces"?[12] Well, there is a hard line in God's will. Go home, read through a history book, and see what you find. Whenever nations have failed to obey God, they have fallen—as, incidentally, our nation shall fall. Whenever empires have risen in the arrogance of power, they have been brought low. Whenever the rich have gotten richer and the poor multiplied, God has impoverished the rich and raised up the poor. God is not mocked! Read your history book side by side with the Bible and you can't escape the conviction that there's a no-nonsense side to the will of God. If you were God and the world treated you as it has treated God, what would you do? It's a good question, but hard to answer. In answering, we condemn ourselves. The parable is over now; the conclusion is grim.

6   The parable is ended, but then, suddenly, on the Bible page, God's word continues. For Jesus turned to his stunned hearers and asked, "Haven't you read your scriptures? 'The stone which the builders rejected has become the cornerstone.'" We're baffled. The words don't seem to make sense. They don't fit the parable. Vineyard workers and building blocks—it's the worst mixed metaphor in the Bible. Look, if nothing else, it adds a different ending to the story. By our logic the story should have ended with a massacre, with the sharecroppers slaughtered and the vineyard turned over to new workers. By our logic, the parable should end violently—kill for kill, hard punishment for rebel sin. No, instead Jesus Christ was raised from the dead, and the only son whom we killed is now Lord of our lives. A few years ago there was a Broadway show acted on two stages at once. On one stage the actors acted their parts. But on a second stage, a small stage off to one side, sat an actor playing the role of the playwright. In the third act when things had gotten into an awful mess, the playwright leapt across to the larger stage and started rewriting the script. That's what happened on Easter Day. The human story should have ended with the wrath of God; instead there's resurrection. "The stone which the builders rejected has become the cornerstone." The only son we killed off has been raised up the Lord of all.

7   So now, look, we are living in a great, good second chance for the world. God has rewritten our story. Of course, it doesn't get us off the hook. The fact is we still must reckon with the Lord. Not with an absentee God, but with the Lord Christ who came among us with the word of God. We know now that though we may rage and rebel, though we may set up a cross in our own souls to crucify the Lord, God's power is greater than our rebellion. God's faithful love cannot be killed off. We're going to have to give in, to come to terms, God's terms. God's patient love will wear out all our sinful tantrums, bear all our sinful abuse, like a rock on which our lives are built. The "Son" the world rejected is now the Lord.

Conclusion   The parable of the wicked sharecroppers—it's Israel's story, the human story, it's our story. "Were you there when they crucified my Lord?" We were. But Christ is risen now and is still the Lord. Dear friends, there is nothing we can do but come to terms, saying to one another: "Come, let's live for the Lord and honor his earth." Come on now, let's live for the Lord.

Discussion

Introduction   The introduction is much too long. But in general I suspect congregations do not listen to scripture readings well, so a quick plot reprise may be useful. The review of the story is set within an image of opposition, "Jesus' congregation began to organize a lynch mob."

1   Immediately we move the parable out of the Bible and into our world. Stepping aside to avoid the anti-Semitism, we affirm that "it's our story. . . *We've* always rejected the prophets." Notice the mix of modern, historical, and biblical prophets that are listed, from the contemporary back to the Hebrew Bible. The move concludes with the refrain, "the story of Israel, our story, the story of the whole human race."

2   Now we probe why we reject prophets. Again we avoid reading biblical history and, instead, refer to America. The examples should be three but, foolishly, I bordered on four. Why is three the preference? Because studies seem to indicate that an audience can grasp three, but when a fourth is added the audience can be confused and the examples weakened. I yielded to the temptation and tried to sneak in a subordinate example; it was not helpful. But, please note, though the revised sermon was written in the 1970s, we are still cutting welfare and pumping billions into military spending. I added the cartoon to bring the section back to the subject of prophetic preaching, as well as to relax the audience a bit before moving on to a still more intense section. Danger! The audience probably laughed away earlier material.

3   Here we move to the Son of God analogy. In the phrase, "Come on, let's kill him off," we can see the hurt of our own sinful rebellion. We pick up the argument from Sartre (who himself was drawing on Nietzsche) and see how his logic ends, namely, in our huge rebelliousness. I don't know why I added Emily Hahn's quote; it was a mistake. I don't need to refer to another name in the move when I could have said much the same thing in my own language. The move ends in dialogue from the text, but today I would add a nondialogic concluding sentence. Beginning or ending a move in dialogue weakens the necessary breaks between ideas.

4   Once more we mention the parable's plot, but instantly turn to our present world. We are the crucifiers—"We were there." The illustration of the painting offers a visual image. The move probably needed further development, although "our faces bright-eyed with excitement, flushed with a strange, almost gleeful pleasure: 'Come on, come on, let's kill him off,'" works pretty well.

5   Notice that throughout the sermon, I am pretty much following the plot of the parable. The parable asks, "What will the lord of the vineyard do?" We add, "Suddenly it's up to us to answer," and at once we are out of the parable and into the contemporary. Luther's quote answers the question and enables us to affirm God's hard line. Then we draw on examples from history (deliberately not personal examples), to establish that "God is not mocked." After returning to the question we must answer, I deliberately risk stopping the sermon: "The parable is over."

6   Scholarship says that the parable ended, but then an early church added the quotation about the rejected stone. So I risked imitating the scholarly sequence. I seemed to conclude the parable. Then I added, "God's word continues." The new ending to the parable has been written out of resurrection faith. Thus the move begins in bafflement: "The words don't seem to make sense." Puzzling over the mixed metaphor, vineyards and building blocks, we finally remember the resurrection. Then I add a slightly off-target illustration about a Broadway play, *Knickerbocker Holiday,* acted on two stages.

7   The final move is necessary. If we simply conclude with the resurrection message we will be guilty of handing out cheap grace. Christ is risen, but through him we are still confronted by the demands of God. Though the move is theologically correct, it is not developed very well. We need to echo some of God's demands with regard to peace and concern for neighbors.

Conclusion   The conclusion draws together phrases that were heard previously in the sermon—"Israel's story, the human story, it's our story," "Were you there . . . ?", " . . . come to terms." Then I tried to rewrite the rebel phrase; instead of "Come on, let's kill," I substituted, "Come on now, let's live for the Lord." I am not sure that the rephrasing would work unless delivery were faultless.

The problems for preachers are (1) how to interpret without tumbling into rank allegorization, and (2) how to avoid historicizing so as to move the parable into the contemporary world. The answer is in a theological reading of the parable: We are the tenants and our human nature is in rebellion.

RETURNING MASTER
(Mark 13:33–37; Luke 12:35–38; see also Matthew 25:1–12)

MARK 13:33–37

33Take care, watch and pray; for you don't know when the time will be. 34Just like a man who is going out of the country—when he leaves home, he puts his slaves in charge, assigning each work to do. And he orders the doorkeeper to keep watch. 35So be on watch, for you don't know when the master of the house will come—in the evening, at midnight, at cockcrow, or in the morning. 36You don't want him to come and find you sleeping. 37What I say to you, I say to all—Watch!

LUKE 12:35–38

35Be dressed for action and have your lamps lit. 36Be like people waiting for their Lord who is returning from the wedding banquet so when he comes and knocks, they can let him in at once. 37Blessed are those slaves whom the Lord finds on the alert when he comes. Truly, I'm telling you, he will dress himself, have them relax at table, and then come to wait on them. 38If he comes at midnight or the dawn and finds them [alert], blessed are those slaves.

Did Jesus tell the parable of the Returning Master? Probably not. Most of the second-coming parables are products of an early church which, in worship, would cry out, "Lord, come!" The parable shows up in Mark's "little apocalypse." In Mark the parable functions as a somewhat stock warning to Christians to be alert and busy doing the Lord's work when he comes. But more, in Mark's version the parable has been tailored to fit the design of his Gospel: "[Y]ou don't know when the master of the house will come — in the evening, at midnight, at cockcrow, or in the morning. You don't want him to come and find you sleeping." Remember, Peter would soon deny Christ at cockcrow. Then, later, the disciples would fall asleep while Christ passionately prayed, and be caught napping when soldiers came to arrest their Lord.

So Mark offers two different ways of preaching the parable. Preached one way, you can ask your congregation to be "alert," indeed to "watch and pray" lest a moment arrive when they will be called upon to testify to their faith or, dramatically, to live out the gospel in their own lives. Such moments are often missed because they arise in conversations. When someone makes a racial slur, do we stop the conversation, not self-righteously, but firmly, to express Christian concern? Or when someone hands out a jingoistic military "solution" for national enemies, do we counter with a concern for peace? In every case, do we dare connect our own positions with a reference to God? Again and again, we face times of testing.

You can preach a different sermon, however, by picking up the phrase, "he puts his slaves in charge, assigning each work to do." Here is a chance to speak of Christian responsibility in daily work and, more, the sense of our work being an assignment from God. Of course, the real work we have been assigned is defined not merely by workplace positions, but by our responsibility to the gospel and our service to God and neighbors.

Mark is an apocalyptic theologian, so the passage has cosmic meaning. Mark believes that it is only a matter of time before God sweeps away all worldly powers and establishes a new social order. Thus, for him, the second coming is both a conclusion and a beginning. The old order will be judged and replaced by a new order that displays righteousness and peace. Mark's apocalyptic vision may seem difficult to preach. Yet, at present, our world is being shaken, and an old-order world is being replaced. In such moments, we must look to the promised pattern of the kingdom and be alert to new possibilities amid a crumbling social order.

We are to watch for signs of God's new order forming among us. Mark is apocalyptic, but we can interpret his urgency for our own times.

Incidentally, notice that Matthew has enlarged the image into the parable of the Closed Door, about a bridegroom and ten waiting bridesmaids (Bultmann 1968, 118). Matthew imagines bridesmaids, five of whom were prepared, and five of whom lacked oil for their lamps, thus missing out on a party (see p. 166).

In Luke there is a disparate group of sayings having to do with the second coming. Luke 12:39–40 is a stock warning about the unpredictable thief who can break into your house when you are not watching.[13] Then in Luke 12:41–48, there is a rather turgid teaching from Q (also found in Matthew 24:45–51): "Blessed" is a servant at work when his master arrives, while, beware, a lazy servant who takes advantage of the master's delay is hacked to pieces. A reference to "delayed in coming" ties the teaching to a fading hope of second coming.

Before these sayings, Luke tells us his version of the Returning Master. If the parable in Luke 12:35–38 is from Mark, it has been rewritten radically. Luke turns Mark's parable into a celebrative wedding party and then adds an astonishing verse:

> Blessed are those slaves whom the Lord finds on the alert when he comes. Truly, I'm telling you, he will dress himself, have them relax at table, and then come to wait on them.   (v. 37)

Luke has transformed the vision. No longer need we cringe in fear of moral failure or maintain a vigil of prayer lest our faith falter. No, we are promised a great banquet, a celebrative wedding party. What's more, Luke adds an astonishing line; the master "will dress himself, have them relax at table, and then come to wait on them." The possibility of a host waiting on table is so bizarre that Luke's audience would have been jarred by the very idea. Yet a serving master is what we encounter in John's famous foot-washing scene. And a serving master is also the theme of Philippians' equally famous hymn celebrating Christ,

> who, though he was in the form of God,
>   did not regard equality with God
>   as something to be exploited,
> but emptied himself,
>   taking the form of a slave,
>   being born in human likeness.
>   (Phil. 2:6–7)

Think of a master who serves!

Luke's version of the parable will be fun to preach. Whenever preachers say "watch out" there seems to be an element of fear. But Luke's passage has reversed the pattern. When the gospel message says "Watch!" we are to live on tiptoe, looking out for a party, a grand celebration we would not want to miss. God is coming out of the future, not merely to begin partying with us, but to wait on us. A servant God for a servant people! All fears of failure and of judgment have been transformed by the figure of Jesus Christ. We can break bread in advance because we know that the world will ultimately end up not with a bang or a whimper, but in a party. Think of a party with God!

Notice how the second coming tradition is being rewritten. In Mark we read an apocalyptic text: Be alert, be watchful, we live in a time of testing before the coming of the Lord. In Matthew we encounter the same theme, but now we are waiting for a bridegroom's banquet we wouldn't want to miss. By the time Luke rewrites the tradition, the banquet host will not only welcome us to table, but will wait on us himself.

The transformation of apocalyptic warnings began early. Written before 48 C.E., 1 Thessalonians is the earliest of Paul's letters. At the beginning of 1 Thessalonians 5, there is a stock apocalyptic warning, "the day of the Lord will come like a thief in the night. Whenever they say, 'peace and security' then sudden destruction will come like birth pains to a pregnant woman—there is no escape!" We are told to be awake, "alert and sober"—or else! Then, quite unexpectedly, the warnings are shattered:

> God has not destined us for punishment, but for gaining salvation through our Lord Jesus Christ, who died for us, so that whether we are alert or asleep, we will live together with him. (1 Thess. 5:9)

Early Christianity may have been swept by apocalyptic fervor, expecting a terrifying "day of the Lord." First Thessalonians and Mark are early and both appear to be apocalyptic. But from the start, the idea was being modified because the crucified "Lord" has died for us and, in resurrection wonder, has come to us with mercy. So, "whether we are alert or asleep, we will live together with him."

Preachers who preach apocalyptic passages about the second coming should participate in the same process of transformation, turning apocalyptic into partying.

5

Parables in Matthew

Matthew contains a large number of parables. Nine are from Q and therefore also appear in Luke. Four are from Mark. At least eight others seem to be unique to Matthew, nine if we count the Wedding Garment added to the parable of the Feast. Material found only in Matthew is often tagged "M" by scholars.

In general, Matthew's parables are somewhat less humorous than those he shares with Mark and Luke. For Matthew, the figure of Jesus has created a crisis in Israel and stakes are high — life or death, inclusion or harsh exclusion where there will be "weeping and gnashing of teeth." Israel must choose in view of a coming judgment. Anticipation of judgment seems to loom in the background of many Matthean parables.

John Donahue picks up another characteristic of Matthew:

> Matthew loves the grand scale. Mark's shrub (Mark 4:32) becomes a tree (Matt. 13:32); the treasure and the pearl exceed all value (Matt. 13:44–46); the debt of the servant exceeds the taxes from Syria, Phoenicia, Judea, and Samaria (Matt. 18:24); ten bridesmaids are the retinue for a rich man's daughter (Matt. 25:1–13); and the talents given to the servants equal wages for thirty, sixty, or 150 years (Matt. 25:15).[1]

Exaggeration suggests importance to Matthew rather than a cause for laughter.

Years ago, Jack Kingsbury (1969, 130–37) noticed that the parables bunched in chapter 13 of the Gospel of Matthew were, in effect, a hinge. In chapters 1–10, Jesus, a new Moses, preaches and teaches Israel, as well as demonstrates his healing power, but in chapters 11–12 Israel rejects him. At the start of chapter 11, he tells the parable of the Children in the Marketplace and then, toward the end of chapter 12, he tells the parable of the Empty House, both of which are critical of Israel. Chapter 13 begins with parables told to the crowds, so "they will indeed listen, but never understand." Then in the middle of chapter 13, Jesus turns away from recalcitrant Israel and begins to instruct his disciples privately. He tells his "new Israel" parables full of promise. They are given images of the "kingdom" that shall be. Scholars believe Matthew's Christian/ Jewish community is being persecuted by a neighboring synagogue.[2] Thus chapter 13 may be Matthew's own turning from a Jewish mission to a wider Gentile audience.

In the first half of the Gospel, most of the parables are brief similes or images. There are many such images in the Sermon on the Mount, most of which seem to have been drawn from Q. Of course, parables at the beginning of chapter 13 are the agricultural parables from Mark 4, which the crowd does not grasp. But in verse 13:36, Jesus "left the crowds and went into the house," to address his disciples. Then Matthew draws on his own special source, M, for an allegorical reading of the parable of the Planted Weeds, followed by the Treasure, the Pearl, and the Fishnet. In chapters 20 and 21, there are three "vineyard" parables: The Vineyard Laborers starts chapter 20, and the Two Children along with the allegorical parable of the Tenants (from Mark) end chapter 21. In chapters 24—25, there are three parables of judgment in a row, following Matthew's version of the "little apocalypse" and his discourse about faithful and unfaithful servants (24:45–51): the Closed Door (25:1–13), the Entrusted Money (25:14–30), and the Last Judgment (25:31–46). Then, on a strong note of judgment, Matthew tells the passion narrative.

A number of scholars have pointed out that Matthew has turned several parables into historical allegories, particularly the parables in chapters 15—22. Clearly Matthew views old Israel as being replaced by his new Israel community. Thus in the parable of the Vineyard Laborers, the contrast between old and new Israel shows up as all-day workers become disturbed by the boss's generosity toward latecomers, as two sons obey and disobey their father in the parable of the Two Children, and as wicked Tenants abuse servants, finally killing off the owner's son, and thus must be replaced by new, responsible tenants.

Matthew is also concerned with the moral obedience of his own community's members, a theme that he develops first in chapter 18 with the Lost Sheep and the Unforgiving Servant but that emerges with full force in the final four eschatological parables in chapters 24—25. The church has replaced Israel, but now the church must be ethically obedient to God's wise laws.

Be warned. Matthew's understanding of parables could trap preachers into blatant anti-Semitism. And his harsh judgment parables, separating good and evil, could lead interpreters to preach a moralistic God who labels human children, directing some to a heavenly banquet while consigning others to a teeth-grinding garbage dump. Preachers will have to correct Matthew's rather singular understanding of the longer parables with theological awareness.

Matthew instructs our faith, calling us to radical obedience. His teaching urges charity, mercy, and love. Matthew's moral earnestness is worth declaring in our own easy-going, therapeutic culture. We are related to God, love for love, but love means going along with God ethically.

PARABLES IN MATTHEW

Planted Weeds	Matthew 13:24–30 *Thomas* 57	Sermon
Treasure	Matthew 13:44 *Thomas* 109	
Pearl	Matthew 13:45 *Thomas* 76:1	
Fishnet	Matthew 13:47–48 *Thomas* 8:1	
Unmerciful Servant	Matthew 18:23–34	Sermon
Vineyard Laborers	Matthew 20:1–15	Sermon
Two Children	Matthew 21:28–32	Sermon
Last Judgment	Matthew 25:31–46	Sermon

PLANTED WEEDS
(Thomas 57; Matthew 13:24–30)

THOMAS 57

The kingdom of the Father is like a man who had [good] seed. His enemy came by night and sowed weeds among the good seed. The man did not allow them to pull up the weeds; he said to them, "I am afraid that you will go intending to pull up the weeds and pull up the wheat along with them." For on the day of the harvest the weeds will be plainly visible, and they will be pulled up and burned.

MATTHEW 13:24–30

[24]He put another parable to them, saying: The kingdom of the heavens is like a man sowing good seed in his field. [25]While people slept, an enemy came, sowed weeds in among the wheat, and stole away. [26]When the crop came up and produced grain, the weeds showed up as well. [27]The owner's field hands came up to him and said, "Boss, didn't you sow good seed in your field? How come there are weeds?" [28]He said to them, "An enemy did this!" So his field hands asked him, "Do you want us to go and pull them up?" [29]But he said, "No, for in gathering the weeds you might root up the wheat. [30]Let them both grow together until the harvest. At harvest time I will tell the reapers, 'Gather the weeds first, tie them in bundles to burn, but gather the wheat into my barn.' "

All you have to do is to keep reading, for Matthew adds a rather labored allegorical interpretation to the parable:

> The one who sows the good seed is the Son of Man; the field is the world, and the good seed means the sons of the kingdom; the weeds are the sons of the evil one, and the enemy who sowed them is the devil; the harvest is the close of the age, and the reapers are angels.   (Matt. 13:37–40)

Everything in the parable is tagged and labeled. The result, of course, is a somewhat tedious allegory. Jesus was not an allegorist, though his followers frequently have been.

Most recent parable scholars label the story a product of the early church, even though, in abbreviated form, it is found also in the *Gospel of Thomas*. Here is a judgment call from the Jesus Seminar:

> The parable reflects the concern of a young Christian community to define itself over against an evil world, a concern not characteristic of Jesus. Letting the wheat and weeds grow up together suggests the final

judgment rather than agricultural practice. In the judgment of a major-
ity [of the Seminar], the Planted Weeds is only distantly related to words
of Jesus, if at all.   (Funk, Scott, and Butts 1988, 65)

Of course, even if the parable is not authentic Jesus material, it shows up in
our Christian writings and does address a concern of the church: How can
the church be morally pure and yet live in the worldly world? If we try for
purity, we lose our evangelical touch with the world. If we give ourselves to
attracting the worldly, we can become morally lax and lose our souls. A peren-
nial problem.

If we preach the parable, there are two cautions:

1. We can address the recurring concern for the church's faithfulness without having to preach a corrupting Devil. Trevor Ling argues convincingly that
the early Christians were already beginning to demythologize the Devil.[3] We can
continue their good work. While evil in our world often seems organized and,
obviously, has invaded all our social structures, we need not dodge human
responsibility by positing a satanic figure. If evil is systemic, its systemic power
has been created by human societies. But, though the world may be systemically
corrupted, the calling of the church is *always* in the world. Our problem is to
acknowledge complicity—we are often worldly, contentious, and sinful, yet we
seek to serve God with both resistance and faith.

2. We must be careful not to divide humanity into good and evil even though
the parable seems to do so. The problem for human beings is our chronic ambiguity. We are a mixed breed, both good and evil; even our prayers are not exactly
free of sin, or our charities or our broken loves. We are creatures of singular wonder and occasional heroism who also are capable of designing gas chambers for
the Holocaust! Therefore, though the parable ends up burning the weeds while
letting pure wheat grow in God's sunshine, preachers will seek to be better theologians than Matthew.

There is another genuine concern that underlies the parable: How can we,
mere mortals, make ultimate judgments over other human beings? Our moral
eyesight is none too good. As one of Jean-Paul Sartre's characters exclaims, "I
am no longer sure of anything. . . . Night is falling; at twilight a man needs good
eyesight to distinguish the good Lord from the Devil."[4] The problem: We human
beings are chronically astigmatic! Our moral judgment is skewed, particularly
when we weigh our neighbor's conduct.

So we all live in the mercy of God—a wide, wide mercy indeed. If churches
are holy, it is not by moral endeavor or exclusiveness; holiness is conferred by
God, like a crisp bright baptismal robe flung over besmirched sinners. We cannot, indeed must not, judge one another. Again and again, Christian writings
quote Jesus' injunction, "Judge not!" (Matt. 7:1; Luke 6:37; Rom. 2:1; Phil. 2:3;
James 4:11–12). Rather, in covenant we can seek a common holiness within the
mercy of God.

Preachers will want to begin with the problem: How can our church be pure? Do we judge? Do we expel? What do we do? A wise preacher will confess the ambiguities of our shared human nature. We live in a world that systemically corrupts us. Yet we cannot leave the world. We cannot reject the world glibly by pretending we are "Resident Aliens," for, according to the gospel message, God loves the world—yes, even our thoroughly secular world! The preacher may even wish to warn against making moral judgments, a practice that inevitably leads to corrosive self-righteousness on the part of those in power. No wonder Jesus lays down the sharp command, "Judge not!" The solution is to live together in God's Mercy, forgiving one another and blessing one another, while we wait the weighing of all lives by the God of love.

The parable of the Planted Weeds is exceedingly difficult. Give a congregation allegory and they are apt to hold tight. How comforting it is to feel we are the righteous remnant, the good wheat, and that our freewheeling neighbors are headed for a bonfire. Such literalism simply runs counter to the gospel of God's astonishing grace. So if we preach the parable, we must preach with both intelligence and large charity.

Sermon

Here is an old sermon delivered in 1960. The sermon is a bit wordy, with a static structure and an embarrassing number of alliterations:

Introduction　　There is a famous painting by Pieter Breughel. At first glance you see a farmer sowing seed in a furrowed field. But look again and you notice there are stars in the sky; the man is furtively sowing seed at midnight. The title of the painting—"The Parable of the Tares." Remember the story? When seed began to grow there were weeds sown in among the wheat. "An enemy has done this," cursed the landowner. He ordered field hands to leave the field alone: "Let both grow together until harvest time." The parable is puzzling—the mystery of good and evil. When the plants came up the weeds appeared also. How shall we interpret the parable of the Tares?

1　　"When the plants came up the weeds appeared also." Good and evil grow together in life, or so the parable says. You cannot separate right from wrong, innocence from iniquity, in our kind of world. You cannot survey the whole of life and say with certainty, "This is good, that is evil," for they are always intertwined. Alex Miller claims that the reason many Americans enjoy watching television Westerns is because they are uncomplicated. There are good guys and bad guys and, at a glance, you can tell a hero from the villains. Evil is obvious on the frontier; virtue is at home on the range. How wonderful, says Miller, "to face real and unqualified evil, plug it and see it drop."[5] In real life, evil is never unqualified; goodness never stands alone. There's the problem—weeds among the wheat!

2 "When the plants came up the weeds appeared also." See how good and evil
grow together in our world. You cannot separate the nations into heroes and
villains. Not a chance! We have supported Chiang Kai-shek's government in
China, forgetting that under Chiang Kai-shek corruption was commonplace.
Now we damn communist Red China as the devil's spawn, but overlook the
land reforms, the flood control, the huge gains in public education. We try to
oversimplify our world, dividing everything up into sides, good and evil, but
it won't work. There is benefit in every blight, in every blessing a shadow.
The poet John Milton, writing more than three hundred years ago, saw the
truth: "Good and evil, we know in the field of this world, grow up together."[6]
Look at the world; see for yourselves.

3 The same truth is obvious in our own personal lives. You only need to glance
next door or, better, look into your own muddied soul. Our lives are a mosaic
of good and evil; in our virtues hide our darkest sins, strange hybrid creatures
that we are. Adolf Hitler, despite his power lust and perverse prides, had
an unfailing appreciation for beauty in art. And George Washington, our
honored forefather, kept a mulatto concubine on his property. Human nature
cannot be catalogued; it is a complex of virtue and vice. Austin Pardue visited a children's art class, watching as youngsters fashioned figures out of
clay. On a table in the classroom stood an angel shaped with wings outspread;
beside it a cruel devil's head. To his surprise, Pardue discovered the statues
had been shaped by the same small child. In each of us an angel soul and
a scheming devil—the human problem! "When the plants came up the
weeds appeared also." Good and evil, evil and good, they grow together in
human soil.

4 Said the landowner to his field hands: "Let both grow together lest in gathering the weeds you uproot the wheat." It may not be sane policy for a farmer,
but when it comes to human nature, it makes sense. "Let both grow together."

Why? Because more often than not our attempts to eradicate evil become
an evil in themselves. Whenever we Christians try to eradicate evil we end up
being self-righteous and cruel. How many heretics found flames in the name
of our religious purity? Governments are no better. Whenever governments
try to stamp out evil they end up in a witch-hunt, witness the late and unla-
mented Senator Joe McCarthy. Whenever human justice threatens evil with a
human punishment it becomes unjust—exhibit A: capital punishment. The
hatred of evil can be an evil. Have you read Nathanial Hawthorne's short story
called "The Birthmark"? There was a beautiful woman whose beauty was
marred by a red mark across her cheek. Her husband was determined to
remove the birthmark so her beauty would be perfect. With creams and cos-
metic treatments he finally did remove the blotch, but killed his wife at the
same time. When will we understand; we are not God to judge, not God to
purge, not God to redeem the earth. We have weeds sown in our souls, and
we stand in need of mercy.

5   So what then? Shall we tolerate evil? No, for the toleration of evil is in itself evil. God intends us to be patient, but not coy with evil. One of James Thurber's characters speaks our modern attitude: "We all have flaws," he says, "Mine is being wicked."[7] So we treat wickedness as a personality quirk, and sin as cultural immaturity, and write off evil as a guilt complex. But the Bible is blunt: a weed is a weed, and evil is evil to be watched with care in the field of our lives. Did you see that George Price cartoon? It showed a man being chased around his house by a giant creeping vine while his wife leaned out a window shouting, "Look out, George, here it comes again!" When we become overtolerant of evil it can threaten to destroy us. Yes there are times when evil must be hacked down if virtue is to survive. Nevertheless, we weed at our own risk with fear and trembling, lest in gathering the weeds we root up the wheat. Said the landowner in the parable, "Let them grow together until the harvest."

6   "Until the harvest"—God alone is the God of the harvest. God alone is wise enough to separate wheat from weeds, good from evil. Only in light of God's truth can we see good and evil clearly. British botanist Julian Huxley carried around a huge magnifying glass whenever he went out walking. He could spot a weed in a well-cultivated garden, or a flower growing up in the midst of weeds. So with Jesus Christ. He looked deep into the human soul and saw clearly. In Zacchaeus, a man condemned by the crowd around him, Jesus spotted a latent generosity. In Peter, a brave disciple, he saw a coward's heart. He saw cruelty in a high priest's faith and extravagant love in a street-worn prostitute. And he still does. In the Spirit of Christ, we can sense the villainy in virtue and the wonder that sometimes shines through wickedness. The truth is in God, for God alone is Lord of the Harvest.

7   In God's power there will be a harvesttime. God's scythe will be thrust into human history; evil will be cut down so that goodness may flourish. The words of Froude ring true: "The world is built on moral foundations: In the long run it is well with good; in the long run it is ill with the wicked."[8] The cross of Christ is witness to the truth. Evil had done its worst. Evil had set up a cross and torn down a corpse, crucifying all that was good and true and beautiful. But God was still God, and in God's power Christ Jesus was raised up again. So we know that though evil may seem to crowd out all that's worthy in the world, crush beauty, and twist truth, nevertheless the harvest is in God's hands and we can trust God with our lives. After the League of Nations had been voted down, William Taft stood with a friend on a Washington street corner and said bluntly, "You ought to know that in our world the best things get crucified," then added passionately, "but they rise again."[9] Yes, by God, they do rise again. In Christ we know that goodness will rise again in an eternal harvesttime.

8   Meanwhile what is our duty? Our duty is to grow in God's grace. Listen, you can't separate good and evil, not in yourself, not in the world. Try it and

you risk destruction. But you can live under God's grace and trust God to bring the seed of love within your lives to a flowering. And you can do little else but enjoy the sunshine of God's care and dew of God's continual mercy. Look, the parable of the Wheat and the Tares should be a comfort. By midsummer most of us are weary of lawn care, and we may be willing to let both grow together. Though most of us have fertilizers, weed killers, sprays, and all the rest, weeds seem to come up anyway. But take heart, there's a new product called Lawn Builder. Somehow or other it feeds the grass and at the same time feeds the weeds so they enlarge and wither away in the sun. Perhaps God's grace does much the same. Grace nourishes goodness but puffs up evil so it perishes, for God brings all our lives to a harvest.

Conclusion   Is there any parable as puzzling as the parable of the Wheat and the Tares? The parable acknowledges the inexplicable presence of evil on the earth. "Let both grow together," said the landowner. The parable challenges our glib moral judgments; it urges a deep trust of God. All we can do is to close our Bibles on the parable and command our ambiguous lives to God. We can do so now.

Discussion

The sermon does wrestle with the problem of good and evil, but, written when I was only a few years out of seminary, it does not have much theological depth. Look over the patterns move by move:

Introduction   The introduction works pretty well. There are no more than ten sentences and it pictures the parable, along with a little dialogue. Then it brings up the mystery of good and evil.

1   The first move simply sets the problem before us—the intermixing of good and evil; evil is never unqualified, goodness never stands alone. The Miller quote works nicely. Thereafter the sermon design goes categorical—evil in the world and evil in our personal lives.

2   The move is a little brief and features no more than a single example, China, plus a brief quote. The Cold War was beginning and the China example lets us question political stereotypes. I don't know why I cited John Milton, since a preacher could say the same sort of thing without quoting anyone. Notice the self-aware alliterative language: "benefit in every blight, in every blessing." The alliteration is a product of my immaturity, and I find it annoying now.

3   Here's the second categorical move, evil in "your own muddied soul." Again development is simple: two contrasting examples, Hitler and George Washington, followed by the art class illustration. The move, though again brief, may be strong enough to register, but does it touch *our* lives?

4   Here is a troubled move. The first three sentences seem to be a general introduction to the problem—weeds must grow with the wheat—and then, abruptly, there is the question "Why?" So the start of the move is awfully choppy.

Note that by now the audience will be rather tired of chained examples in every move. Here we chain church, government, and justice, and then follow with a rather good illustration. The listing of examples may be getting much too familiar, however.

5   In move 5, I made a large mistake. The Thurber quote works pretty well. The congregation might giggle over "Mine is being wicked," and, therefore, sense how we varnish over evil. But my error is adding more laughter with the George Price cartoon. Although I am urging a congregation to quit tolerating evil, I make evil amusingly tolerable. The perfect single illustration would be the plant in the Broadway show, *Little Shop of Horrors*. The plant is tolerated, fed regularly, but grows out of control and finally eats up its owner. But the sermon was preached before the show opened.

6   The sermon shifts again. In the first three moves we looked at good and evil in life. Then in the next two moves we were trying to take action. Now we turn to God. There is a mistake: Move 5 ends with a quote, and move 6 begins with a repetition of the same quote. The moves will mush together, obscuring the new idea. Move 6 is not nearly strong enough. Again, I am dismayed by some stagy alliteration—"villainy in virtue," "wonder . . . through wickedness." Style should serve meaning, and will serve best when it doesn't call attention to itself.

7   In move 7, I am trying to affirm that God watches over good and evil and, with the same power that raised up the crucified Christ, will bring goodness to harvest. But the move is not well constructed because it contains two quotes. The Taft quote might work, and could have been developed, but I do not need the Froude quote. Instead I should have developed the idea contained in the Froude quote in my own words. Two quotes in one brief move never work. The move is gospel and should have been developed with much more care and forcefulness.

8   The final move contains a pretty good illustration, "Lawn Builder." The parable could encourage preachers to picture God burning up the wicked at harvesttime, which, probably, was what Matthew had in mind. Here the idea is that God gives growth, and that evil will self-destruct by excessive growth. I wish I had worked off the illustration with greater precision.

Conclusion   The conclusion starts out all right, but the last three sentences are weak. In actual delivery, I hope I improvised a better conclusion.

The parable of the Planted Weeds is an allegory in Matthew. Preachers must refuse the temptation and bypass allegorization. We must refuse to divide humanity into good and evil people. Instead we must help our congregations to consider the ambiguity of good and evil. Lately, pop moralism encourages the idea that we are basically virtuous people and, with a little concerted effort, can remake the moral world. Lots of luck! The world is mysterious and, with new "hybrid weeds," much more complex than we may suppose. The parable was not an original Jesus story, but nonetheless is a subject of Christian concern.

TREASURE
(Matthew 13:44; Thomas *109)*

MATTHEW 13:44
Again the kingdom of the heavens is like treasure hidden in a field, which, finding, a man rehides, and in his joy goes and sells everything he has and buys the field.

THOMAS *109*
The Kingdom is like a man who had a [hidden] treasure in his field without knowing it. And [after] he died, he left it to his son. The son did not know [about the treasure]. He inherited the field and sold [it]. And the one who bought it went plowing and found the treasure. He began to lend money at interest to whomever he wished.

In Matthew, two parables, the Treasure and the Pearl, appear in sequence. Matthew believes they are essentially duplicates. But the key words following "the kingdom of the heavens" are different; in the one parable, it is "treasure"; in the other, "merchant." Though Matthew tends to be a buncher, gathering like things together, the two parables are *not* alike.

Traditionally, preachers have emphasized the joy of finding and the necessity of self-sacrifice: We must be willing to give up everything for the sake of God's joyful realm. Indeed Matthew himself, in coupling the Treasure and the Pearl, had some such message in mind. The two coupled parables appear in Matthew's crucial chapter 13 after Jesus has turned from preaching to the Jewish crowds and has begun to instruct his disciples privately. Matthew is calling disciples to be willing to give up all for the sake of the kingdom of heaven. Recent scholarship has raised serious questions about such an interpretation.

John Dominic Crossan has written a small book on the Treasure parable, *Finding Is the First Act* (1979). Although the parable has usually been preached by urging congregations to give up everything to gain spiritual treasure, Crossan and others suggest a different set of meanings. Crossan argues that the first word in the parable, "treasure," is a surprise. He has studied treasure stories in different cultures and has discovered that treasure is never the first word; instead, treasure is almost always a conclusion. Treasure is something we find at the end of a story. He then looks at the Jewish tradition and finds the same pattern. Treasure comes at the end of a plot as a reward for obeying God's law or for observing a devout life of prayer. For example, many commentators quote a rabbinic parable in which a man, Abba Judah by name, was charitable (Scott 1989, 396). But one day when he was broke, he saw rabbis he knew he should support, and "his face was filled with suffering." What could he do? His wife, equally devout, told him to sell half of the field, the only property they had left, and give to the rabbis. In return, the rabbis prayed for him to be blessed. Sure enough, when plowing the remaining half of the field, his cow fell and broke a leg. When he bent down to help her, "the Holy One, blessed be He, opened his eyes, and he found a jewel."[10] Treasure is the last word, a reward for sacrifice.

But in Jesus' parable, "treasure" is the first word. Crossan argues that a Jewish audience would be surprised. The man in the parable had done nothing to earn the treasure—no piety, no devout obedience, no charity—he merely stubbed his toe on treasure left in a field.

Finding treasure hidden in a field was not unusual. In the absence of any First National Bank, people buried their money in the earth for safekeeping. See how the plot of the parable moves along: (1) A man finds treasure hidden in a field. (2) He is elated ("Whooooo boy, found me a treasure!"). (3) Then greed kicks in, so he reburies the treasure. (4) He then goes out and sells everything he owns to buy the field for himself.

All of a sudden, with the last phrase, we realize that the man has found treasure in *someone else's field*. He wants to possess someone else's treasure. Another Jewish parable tells of a rabbi who, after buying a donkey, discovers a valuable pearl tangled in its mane. Though his students cheer his good fortune, he says, "I paid for a donkey, not a pearl" and returns the pearl to the original seller. Moral: "[A] deed which causes God's name to be magnified is greater than the sum of all worldly riches."[11] By contrast, the treasure finder wants to possess the treasure for himself. Once more, Jesus is telling a parable about a rascal.

The parable in the *Gospel of Thomas* is also about a dishonest man. The treasure finder in *Thomas*'s version of the parable ends up with money he loans out at interest in absolute violation of Jewish law against loaning money with interest (see Ex. 22:25; Lev. 25:36–37; Deut. 23:19–20). Seemingly, the lust to possess is corrupting.

A Jewish audience would scold *Thomas*'s rogue, but would be doubled up with laughter on hearing Jesus' parable. The treasure finder who bought the field was a certifiable dummy! According to Jewish law, a law with which everyone was familiar, if you find treasure in a field you have bought, it reverts to the original owner, twice over (Derrett 1970, 6–13). The man has been a spectacular fool. If he starts spending the cash shortly after buying a field, people will ask where it came from and he will be suspect. If he holds onto the cash from fear of exposure, it will do him no good. Treasure finding filled the man with joy, but the desire to possess corrupted him, turning his calculating shrewdness into utter stupidity. He bought a field to possess a treasure that he can never use.

Now think back to the usual way in which the parable is preached: We must give up everything in order to secure for ourselves the kingdom of God. Think it out theologically: Can God's kingdom be possessed? No. We can live as citizens in God's kingdom, but it is God's, not ours, to own or order. If "treasure" is wisdom, as in Proverbs 8–9, it is a free gift from God and nothing we ourselves can secure:

> Take my instruction instead of silver,
>   and knowledge rather than choice gold;
> for wisdom is better than jewels,
>   and all that you may desire cannot compare with her.
>   (Prov. 8:10–11)

Wisdom is treasure, like gold and jewels, but it cannot be earned. Wisdom, *"sophia,"* is a free gift.

> [Wisdom] has sent out her servant girls, she calls
>   from the highest places in the town,
> "You that are simple, turn in here!"
>   To those without sense she says,
> "Come, eat of my bread
>   and drink of the wine I have mixed.
>   (Prov. 9:3–5)

Real "treasure," then, may be to live as citizens beneath God's rule and receive all things by grace alone. Certainly we cannot possess the kingdom; it is not ours to control. Entrance into the kingdom is by a free invitation. If we try to earn our way in, we will lose our way completely!

Preachers must choose. Matthew has lined up three parables—the Treasure, the Pearl, the Fishnet. He is clearly holding out a promise of reward to those who must sacrifice. Do we preach Matthew's promise of reward? Or do we preach the parable with its original reversal? We may wish to go along with Matthew; there are scholars who would so argue (Hedrick 1994, 120–32). But if we preach the reversal, the parable will be exciting. You will move from the "free-grace" finding of treasure, to the joy of discovery, to the sudden desire for possession, to laughter—the kingdom is not possessed, but lived in!

Which is gospel? Sacrifice for a payoff, or the laughter of grace discovered?

PEARL
(Matthew 13:45; Thomas 76:1–2)

MATTHEW 13:45
Again, the kingdom of the heavens is like a man, a merchant, in search of fine pearls, who found one very valuable pearl, and went away and sold everything he had and bought it.

THOMAS 76:1–2
[1]The Kingdom of the Father is like a merchant who had a consignment of merchandise and who discovered a pearl. That merchant was shrewd. He sold the merchandise and bought the pearl alone for himself.

[2]You too, seek his unfailing and enduring treasure where no moth comes near to devour and no worm destroys.

Matthew has put two parables next to each other, the Treasure and the Pearl. In each parable something is found, and, at great sacrifice, possessed. Matthew believes the two parables are alike. But are they? In writing the parables, Matthew has ordered them in a similar way. Along with the Fishnet that follows them, each parable begins, "The kingdom of the heavens is like . . . ," then each names an object, then a relative pronoun ("which" or "who") followed by a participle ("finding") and then an action ("rehid," "bought," "sorted"). Matthew has created a stylistic bond conjoining the three parables.

Nevertheless, the parables may be quite different. Scholar Otto Glombitza lists the differences.[12] Here are a few: (1) In one the kingdom is *treasure,* in the other a *merchant* (an object and a person); (2) the treasure is hidden, but the pearl is evident and sought after; (3) verbs in the Treasure are in the present tense, but in the Pearl they are generally past tense; (4) the man who stumbles on treasure buys the field by assembling what little he possesses, but the merchant is a rich speculator. The parables seem to be structured in a similar way only because of Matthew's stylistic editing.

We could notice still another contrast: The man who finds the treasure is devious. He plans to deceive the man from whom he buys the field. The rich pearl merchant, in contrast, is in the business of buying and selling pearls. He is not dishonest but, evidently, has an eye for value.

Here's the catch: The merchant turned *all* his assets into cash to buy the one beautiful pearl. What will he live on? The pearl is only valuable when bought or sold. So the man has bought a pearl, but what has he purchased? An emptiness, for in order to survive he will have to sell the pearl anyway. Is the parable a warning against our lust for possessions? Perhaps. But then, how do we line up the pearl parable with the phrase "the kingdom of the heavens is like . . . "?

Compare Jesus' parable with the version we find in the *Gospel of Thomas: Thomas*'s version appeals to our all-American profit motive. The man is shrewd and sells merchandise for the pearl. Because *Thomas* is a Gnostic work, presumably the "pearl" is secret knowledge that an initiate may possess, while others, not so shrewd, lose out. But images of selling and buying and shrewdness surely contradict the Christian notion of "saved by grace alone."

Again we must ask the blunt question: How can entree into God's kingdom be purchased? How can it be possessed by anyone? The image, "kingdom of God," is a realm governed by God in which citizens may live obediently. It is not an *objet d'art* to be admired, or a commercial venture, or something we can control via ownership. The sermon, "We must give up everything to possess the kingdom of God," is a theological disaster. In the Bible, ownership is often suspect, as it probably should be. After all, "the earth is the Lord's and all that is in it" (Ps. 24:1).

Preaching a parable that contains an inner contradiction is not easy, particularly when, as even in Matthew, the assumption is to sacrifice in order to gain an ultimate reward. So the problem for preaching is how to set up the parable, lure a congregation into an initial affirmation, and then swing the parable around to discover we have earned nothing. Preachers, then, must offer life in God's free-grace kingdom as a joyful alternative to religious free enterprise, namely, a works/possession theology.

Was the Pearl originally a Jesus parable? The Jesus Seminar voted Yes, but I confess to being skeptical. The Treasure parable could well be original Jesus material, for the man is a bit devious and Jesus frequently tells parables that feature rascals. But the Pearl seems to celebrate possession per se; it leads to the sort of Gnostic elaboration found in the *Thomas* version. Though Matthew brackets the two parables together, nevertheless, we can be somewhat skeptical.

We are to "ask, seek, and find," the Bible advises, but without any pride in our shrewdness or our piety or our religious fervor. As Luther observed, "We are beggars all." Our "asking, seeking, and finding" are scarcely a saving work. Beggars reach out but are totally dependent on generosity. Matthew's parables, the Treasure and the Pearl, could lead to "payoff preaching"—if you are willing to sacrifice, you will get happiness, God's presence, and, quite likely, prosperity. But rightly the two parables are stories of foolish miscalculation on the part of those who suppose they can control God Almighty or possess a happiness that is only given free.

Preaching the Pearl requires a careful homiletic strategy. Certainly we can talk of an attractiveness in things of God, hints of beauty or wonder or free-from-self happiness we want to enjoy full-time. Like Dante, we can discover a kind of lure in the mystery of God, like the attraction of the pearl. The trouble is, we want what is promised in the gospel, but without the annoying presence of God. Possession is a pernicious dream. Possession, even the possession of beauty, may turn into nothingness.

The only genuine pleasure is a life full of give and take with God.

FISHNET

(*Matthew 13:47–50;* Thomas *8:1–2*)

MATTHEW 13:47–50

47Again, the kingdom of the heavens is like a fishnet cast into the sea, gathering every kind of fish together. 48When it is drawn up on the shore filled, people sit down and collect the good into containers and throw out the bad.
49Thus it will be at the end of the aeon. The angels will go out and separate the wicked from the righteous, 50casting them into the fiery furnace. There will be weeping and gnashing of teeth.

THOMAS *8:1–2*

[1]And he said, "The man is like a wise fisherman who cast his net into the sea and drew it up from the sea full of small fish. Among them the wise fisherman found a fine large fish. He threw all the small fish back into the sea and chose the large fish without difficulty.

[2]Whoever has ears to hear, let him hear.

The parable ends with Matthew's favorite phrase: "There will be weeping and gnashing of teeth." Matthew's images of judgment are frequently harsh. God will judge the whole human enterprise on the basis of morals, particularly charity, and the wicked will be punished. Perhaps Matthew's stern images were a product of persecution he experienced, although the Hebrew scriptures certainly look to a day of the Lord when YHWH will come to judge the world.

The image of a fishnet shows up often in the ancient world. It is employed by Herodotus in the fifth century B.C.E. and is found in the collection of fables attributed to Aesop (Scott 1989, 315). Here is how the image appears in the Aesop tradition:

> A fisherman drew in the net that he had cast a short time before and, as luck would have it, it was full of all kinds of delectable fish. But the little ones fled to the bottom of the net and slipped out through its many meshes, whereas the big one was caught and lay stretched out in the boat.[13]

In the *Gospel of Thomas* the version is quite similar. A "wise" fisherman draws in a net and finds it filled with small fish. Among them is one "fine large fish." The fisherman keeps the fine fish and throws the little ones back into the sea. *Thomas* is a Gnostic Gospel, and the big fish probably represents true redemptive knowledge that makes other matters minor, indeed, makes "small fish" not worth keeping.

In Matthew's understanding, the "fable" is changed; angels gather in the righteous "fish" and consign the wicked ones to a "fiery furnace." Matthew has allegorized the parable in a manner to match his interpretation of the Planted Weeds (Young 1989, 220–21). The two parables are, however, quite different. The Planted Weeds is an appeal for a patient postponing of judgment because in our world, with limited moral insight, it is impossible to separate the righteous from the wicked. The parable of the Fishnet, however, depicts the day of the Lord as a moment of ultimate judgment when only "keepers" will be saved. Actually, as some scholars have noticed, the little fish escape with their lives, whereas presumably the big fish gets eaten up (Via 1967, 117)—not an appealing prospect.

Is the Fishnet a parable of Jesus? Most scholars are skeptical. The fish story appears to be a tradition circulating in the ancient world that eventually was collected by Aesop (Hedrick 1994, 126). In turn, Matthew picked up the fable and used it climactically as the conclusion to a series of parables he has Jesus preach to the disciples in chapter 13. Was the focus of the story originally on the value of fish to a fisherman as is found in both Aesop and Thomas? Perhaps Matthew has transformed the story into a warning of judgment. The parable seems to run counter to many of the Jesus parables in which mercy is urged and patience with evil encouraged.

If preachers must preach the parable, how can they handle its image of judgment? The theme of judgment is clearly biblical; God is our judge. We should not write off judgment as primitive religious superstition to be dropped by our wised-up, more modern age. Clearly, the Bible calls for righteousness in our common lives and condemns the amoral as well as the immoral. The Ten Commandments appear to be a kind of "bottom-line" ethic. Human beings cannot live in God's love and commit murder or covet another person's spouse. They cannot steal another's property or be lying witnesses against a neighbor. They may not disown their parents or force workers into a seven-day week. Above all, they may not be dedicated to false gods; idolatry is ultimately self-destructive. These are firm commands and, presumably, there will be judgment in view of such commands. Nevertheless, commands are a secondary legal structure written over God's primary covenant of love to which we respond in ethical living.

More than commands, the Bible paints images of the kind of social order God proposes. Though the Declaration of Independence calls for individual rights— "life, liberty, and the pursuit of happiness"—the Bible pictures a social order where all God's children live together with God, interacting with justice and love. The biblical dream may be wiser, for my liberty to engage in the pursuit of my happiness is almost certain to collide with a neighbor's similar aim. Visions of God's covenant community are the stuff of ethical consideration quite beyond the bottom-line constrictions of the commandments. We are to love God and to love our neighbors as our own kin, which in God's world they truly are. Thus we will be judged (1) as we respond to God's free covenant love, and (2) as we may or may not join with neighbors in the kingdom of God.

Sometimes ministers can enjoy preaching judgment, as perhaps Matthew may have done. But watch out! We must not define God's judgment by our own personal condemnations, but only by the character of God, a God who is on display in the crucifixion and resurrection of Jesus of Nazareth. If God is a lover who will die, accepting the rejections of the human world and, rising, still faithfully love, then God's judgment will be love as well. To be judged by God's love is not a matter of fiery furnaces. Punishments can be designed to break the will, as law-and-order people seem to suppose, but love can break the heart.

To preach the parable means that you will be critical of Matthew's notion of God's judgment: "weeping and gnashing of teeth." To call the Bible "Word of God" does not mean Matthew cannot be as wrong as any interpreter, including us. The Bible is a gift because it contains good news, the liberating gospel message, and not because every single word ought to be uncritically accepted as authority. Fundamentalism is a heresy we can easily avoid, and should!

If we do preach the Fishnet, we can simply drop verses 49–50. The basic parable, speaking as it does of everyone being "caught" into the kingdom of God, is preachable. Did not Jesus use the image of fishing for evangelism? Moreover, the notion that God's rule has a firm ethical demand—we are called to be holy as God is holy, and to be just as God is just—is also a message to be declared. But the idea implied in verse 48, that God could "throw away" the "bad fish" is not consistent with the gospel message. God has given us life. According to the faith, God loves human children. Would any loving parent paste "good" and "bad" labels on children, and then throw away those tagged "bad?" We will be judged by God's love and, what's more, we will be judged on the basis of "works." But to preach that God, whose nature is self-giving love, will destroy the wicked in a fit of divine petulance is an impossible theological contradiction. The cross is witness to God's ever faithful self-giving love and yet, oddly enough, the cross itself is our judgment. Perhaps the cross is a clue to the preaching (and *correcting*) of the Fishnet parable.

UNMERCIFUL SERVANT

MATTHEW 18:21–35

21Coming up, Peter said to him, "Lord, how many times will I forgive my fellow humans when they do me wrong? Seven times?" 22Jesus said to him, "No, I'm telling you, not seven times, but seventy times seven!"

23The kingdom of the heavens is like a man, a king, who wanted to settle accounts with his agents. 24The first one brought before him owed ten billion dollars. 25Because he didn't have enough to pay, the boss ordered him to be sold, along with his wife and children and everything he possessed, so as to collect. 26Falling down before him, the agent said, "Hold off, and I'll pay you everything." 27Filled with pity, the boss let that agent go and forgave his debt.

28But, going out, the agent found one of his fellow agents who owed him a thousand dollars and, grabbing him by the throat, said, "Pay up what you owe!" 29Falling down before him, his fellow agent said, "Hold off, and I'll pay you." 30But, he wasn't interested; he went and had him thrown into prison until the whole debt could be paid.

31Other agents, seeing what had happened, were terribly upset. Going to the boss, they told him all about everything that had happened.

32So, calling in the agent, his boss said to him, "You wicked agent, I forgave all you owed when you pleaded with me. 33Should not you have been moved to take pity on your fellow agent as I pitied you?" 34Furious, the boss handed him over to torturers until he paid him back everything he owed.

35So also will my heavenly Father do to you unless every one of you forgives your fellow human from your heart.

At the outset, let's admit that Matthew, hipped on judgment, doesn't quite grasp the parable he is telling. His "preface" is an imagined scene in which Peter asks a question, "Lord, how many times will I forgive my fellow human beings when they do me wrong? Seven times?" Matthew has just concluded a discussion of church discipline, so the question, though put on Peter's lips, seems to refer to another church member. How often do we forgive? Jesus' answer is emphatic: not merely seven times, a good sacred number, but seventy times seven, which is a Jewish colloquial way of saying, "to infinity." We are to forgive forever!

Then, of all things, in an epilogue Matthew pictures God with a somewhat short fuse. According to Matthew, God will punish us, indeed torture us forever, if we don't "forgive freely from the heart." Somehow Matthew's understanding of the parable has become skewed.

The parable itself has an odd shift. At the beginning it refers to a "king," but then the language shifts to *kyrie,* often translated "Lord" or "Master." Here as with other parables I have used the word "boss." Many Jewish parables feature royalty (Stern 1991, 19–21). Although "king" may fit the situation—only kings could play around with billions of dollars—I suspect the parable was originally about a boss and his agents. The amount of money involved is staggering. Ten thousand talents would not be small change. If a talent was worth six thousand denarii, and a denarius might be nearly forty-eight dollars, then a talent figures to be around three hundred thousand dollars. The loan in the parable was roughly three billion dollars, nowadays a much, much larger figure. Even if we acknowledge that amounts of money in biblical days do not translate into our contemporary economic system, we still are dealing with a big, big bundle of cash. As John Donahue (1988, 63) calculates, the amount "exceeds the taxes from Syria, Phoenicia, Judea, and Samaria." So the agent's reply, in effect, "Just give me a little time and I'll pay it all," is ludicrous.

The parable lends itself to preaching. Its movement triggers responses that prompt theological meaning. Doesn't the huge debt fit the notion of all we owe God our creator? A God who has given us all good things. A God whose love is beyond all calculation. A God who has called us to be partner people.

And what of the unforgiving agent? Do we not judge our neighbors harshly, demanding of them what we do not require of ourselves? We want what's coming to us, every penny, every gesture, total respect.

Our congregations, appalled by the behavior of the unforgiving agent, will join all the other agents and, in effect, go before the boss in order to accuse. The boss gives us exactly what we ask for—he castigates the unforgiving agent, revokes the forgiven debt, and then orders the man to be jailed and tortured forever! Tortured forever is a bit much, isn't it? Shocked, we examine our attitude toward the agent only to discover there is another unforgiving agent in the parable—us. The parable is a trap for our own self-righteousness.

Bernard Brandon Scott (1989, 271) suggests that the parable might have functioned in a Jewish/Gentile setting. When Jewish listeners heard how much money was involved, they would assume the parable was about Gentiles. Herod's annual budget for Israel was around six hundred talents, a good deal less than ten thousand talents in the parable. But then, when the man's huge debt is forgiven, the audience would revise their opinion; surely the boss was a Jew, for only a Jew could so freely forgive. When the agent (actually, *doulos,* "slave" in Greek) goes after a colleague who owes a small debt, the audience would wonder what could motivate such a demand. They would be outraged by his behavior, and join with the "other agents" in condemning his behavior. Then they would be utterly abashed when, at their behest, the man is condemned to torture. Torture was absolutely unthinkable to a Jew.

The problem for preachers is how to design a sermon so that the parable may do what it wants to do *to us.*

Sermon

The following sermon was preached in 1993 at a ministers' conference in Williamsburg, Virginia, sponsored by *Lectionary Homiletics.*

Introduction   A few years ago, there was a book that catalogued the parables of Jesus. The book listed parables as "comedies" or "tragedies," according to how they ended. Well, the parable of the Unforgiving Agent is a clear-cut tragedy. Remember how the story ends? "You wicked agent," the boss shouts, and turns the man over to be tortured forever. Of course, Matthew goes the parable one better (or is it worse?), for he tacks on a nasty postscript: "So also will my heavenly Father do to you unless every one of you forgives." The parable of the Unforgiving Agent is not what you would call "user-friendly," is it? What on earth are we to do with such a terrible parable?

1   Begin with a question: What's so wrong with the agent? Isn't he simply trying to collect what is rightfully his? The agent has been generous. When one of his fellow agents is caught short, he loans the man a thousand dollars. But when it's payback time he discovers the man is a deadbeat; he can't pay back the loan. So what does the agent do? He slaps a summons on the man and has him jailed for bad debts. Is his behavior so unusual? Doesn't First American, Third National, or NationsBank go after people who default on their loans? The fact is, collecting on a debt is simply good business. If we let debtors go scot-free our whole economic system will come tumbling down; it's based on people paying their debts. And here in America, faced with the recent savings and loan scandals, we could have used a few hard-nosed agents, couldn't we? No wonder George Bernard Shaw has a character admit, "Forgiveness is a beggar's refuge. We must pay our debts."[14] So be objective when you hear the parable. The agent may sound a little curt, but the fact is a loan is a loan and ought to be paid. So ask yourselves, What's so wrong with the servant?

2   Answer: Ten billion dollars, that's what's wrong! The agent had just been forgiven billions of dollars! "Hold off, give me a little more time" he had
shouted, and then, unexpectedly, the debt was simply canceled. Notice that
the loan was not extended or renegotiated, Donald Trump style. No, the debt
was outright canceled. Ten billion dollars waved away in an instant. If the
parable has anything to do with God, the figure is too small. God has given
us everything—life and breath and love, the good earth and the high stars—
everything to us ungrateful sinners. We who default praise and offer God
nothing more than our waywardness. Yet God forgives us; every day of our
broken lives God forgives. So the debt we owe God is beyond calculation. Old
James Denny, a preacher, trying to get through to his congregation news of
God's prodigious mercy, imagined hauling a huge life-sized cross up the pulpit steps, standing it there, and shouting, "All this God has done for you!"[15]
Ten billion dollars is too small a figure; God's mercy is beyond all our human
calculation—"Love so amazing, so divine, demands my life, my soul, my
all."[16] In the parable, when the agent begged for mercy, the boss forgave his
whole huge debt.

3   Well, no wonder the other agents were outraged; we are outraged too. Here is
a man forgiven billions, and what does he do? He goes out and jails a neighbor over small change! We are furious, aren't we? The man is downright
unforgivable. Doesn't God's mercy get to him at all? Is he crass, like the voice
of the crook in W. H. Auden's "Christmas Oratorio"? "I like committing
crimes," he says, "God likes forgiving them. Really the world is admirably
arranged!"[17] Or is it a kind of self-righteous blindness? Does he see himself
as a daring entrepreneur, whereas his fellow worker was nothing more than
an unreliable deadbeat? Self-righteousness, we do it all the time, don't we?
Saddam Hussein—we call him the Hitler of the Middle East, and in doing so
wrap our own nation in patriotic righteousness. Of course, we forget that we
sold Hussein his tanks when we were backing him against Iran a few years
ago. And we conveniently forget that all along we've been supporting Kuwait,
an undemocracy famous for violations of freedom and justice. But if we see
ourselves as righteous, then our debtors are bound to be deadbeats. Here's a
man forgiven billions and what does he do? He throws a neighbor in jail for
a thousand. Of course the other servants were outraged. And, yes, we'll join
their protest, for to tell the truth, we are furious too.

4   So what happens in the story? When we complain, the boss hears us out and
agrees. "You rotten agent," he scolds, and tosses the man in jail to be tortured
forever and ever. And guess what? We have become unforgiving servants too,
no better than the unforgiving man himself. Though forgiven much, he
refused to forgive. We, though forgiven by Jesus Christ, haven't forgiven
either. Did you see that wonderful Bill Moyers' program on public TV—a
one-hour special all about the hymn "Amazing Grace"? Moyers interviewed
singers, Johnny Cash and Judy Collins among them, asking how the words of
the hymn got to them: "Amazing grace, how sweet the sound, that saved a

wretch like me," that was the phrase—"a wretch like me." And when Moyers asked why they were "wretches," most people went silent and you could see them staring into memory. Maybe the parable gets to us the same way, for suddenly we see our own endless failure to forgive, to forgive our families, our neighbors, yes, even ourselves. "You rotten servant," the boss explodes, and turns the man over to the torturers. We got what we wanted. We didn't forgive. We turned him in and in doing so we are convicted. We are unforgiving servants all.

5 So, what's the answer? The answer is to live full-time in the mercy of God. Listen, mercy is not something you get and you give, like cash in a business transaction. We don't dole out mercy like cookies to good little children. No, way back a cross was set up outside the city of Jerusalem, and back then we were forgiven once and for all, back when the whole human world was forgiven by God. Ever since we live in The Mercy—the air we breathe, the grace we trust, the life we live—all mercy. We have been forgiven, past tense, forgiven once and for all. As a young man, Walter Horton worked on an ambulance crew. One night they picked up a knifed prostitute who'd been slashed in a fight. She was dying. "Do you think God forgives anyone bad as me?" she asked. A nurse gave the right answer: "God cares about you," she said, "God forgives you."[18] Because God has already forgiven our terrible human race, we forgive all our neighbors, even those we think are quite unforgivable. We live, all of us, in the mercy of God. Poor sinners all, bowing to one another in The Mercy.

Conclusion What are we going to do with old Matthew? He told the parable, but he just didn't get it—"So will my heavenly Father do to you if you don't forgive." How could Matthew miscalculate? Remember the start of the parable, how Peter came hustling up to Jesus: "How many times do I forgive? Seven?" To which Jesus answered, using a Jewish phrase for mathematical infinity: "No," said Jesus, "seventy times seven," which is to say, forever. Guess what? The way God forgives is forever. Forever.

Discussion

The last move, move 5, is not within the parable. Yet the parable obviously calls us to be merciful toward one another. I have deliberately left Matthew's calculating language behind—mercy is not a transaction. No, we live in the mercy, for God, "in whom we live and move and have our being," *is* mercy. Could God's love be anything less? If we hold back and in self-castigation refuse to forgive ourselves, we are usurping God's role as our merciful judge and installing ourselves. Likewise, if we refuse to forgive a neighbor, we are violating the merciful context of our lives; we are condemning another human being whom God has forgiven. We are not overlooking judgment, because the word forgiveness implies the recognition of sin. But we sinners, who live in The Mercy, can embrace all other poor sinners. They also live in The Mercy. Let's step right out of the transactional formula. Thus we will read the famous text, "If we confess our sins, God is merciful," not as a requisite earning of mercy by confession, but as, "if we should confess sins, we can be sure that . . . " And we can say the Lord's Prayer, but not as a bargain: "Look Lord, we forgive our trespassers, now come through according to contract and forgive us." No, in Christ the robe of mercy has already been cast across all our lives.

Let's review the sermon:

Introduction   Notice that at the outset we have labeled the parable; it is not "user-friendly." What's more, we have identified the addendum, "So also will my heavenly Father do to you unless every one of you forgives your fellow human from your heart," as a Matthean addition to the parable. The last sentence calls us to reconsider the parable.

1   Deliberately, we have entered the parable in its second episode, asking the congregation, "What's so wrong with the agent?" Isn't he merely collecting what is rightly his? By reversing the pattern of the parable, we can make the second move even more dramatic. Linking the agent's loan to banking and our economic system will tend to justify the man's actions, but only for a while. Of course, subtly, we may question our usual economic practices.

2   The second move answers the first. What's wrong? Ten billion dollars worth of mercy, that's what's wrong! The problem with the move is a lack of theological clarity. Are we in God's debt because of God's good gifts or because of God's mercy? The move is not clear. The Denny quote, an old legendary illustration, begins to focus the issue on God's mercy. But the pattern could be clearer; we owe a debt of gratitude and are, nonetheless, forgiven.

3   Here we react, along with the "other servants" in the parable. Outraged, we will go off to complain to the boss. In the move, we explore the source of outrage. Was the man merely shallow, or was he self-righteous? The sermon was preached during escalating fury with Iraq, so the Saddam Hussein example was chosen deliberately. Forgiveness and self-righteousness are not merely personal matters; they are political as well.

4   The move begins well, but the Moyers illustration is diffused and not as effective as it might be. What's the big problem with the move? It doesn't really do what the parable is designed to do, namely, trap us in the midst of our unwillingness to forgive. We should be aghast at the sentence of torture and forced to reconsider.

5   The final move also lacks clarity. What am I trying to say here? That mercy is not transactional because we *live in* mercy, or that forgiveness is a past-tense action on God's part? The themes are intermixed and, therefore, unclear. The illustration of the dying prostitute, a bit schmaltzy, illustrates the second option, but the move itself speaks the first option.

Conclusion   The conclusion goes back and connects with the introduction; we must deal with Matthew's misinterpretation. Thus we set Jesus' supposed words over against Matthew's rather rigid postscript and discover God's forever mercy!

What about criticizing Matthew, a Gospel writer? Unless you are totally dedicated to worshiping every word in the Bible—a dubious proposition at best, there is no need to ignore theological errors that may occur in scripture. The Bible does not display theological uniformity. If the Bible can be labeled "Word of God," it is not because every clause is inerrant or that in every writing there is a consistent "Christian" message. Such a position is just plain bad theology, if not lunacy. The Bible is "Word of God" because it declares the liberating message of God's redeeming love. The message was preached by early Christians who were as inept, foolish, and sinful as we are. Can we preach gospel from the parable and, at the same time, be critical of Matthew's conclusion to the parable? Of course we can, and should!

VINEYARD LABORERS

MATTHEW 20: 1–15

[1]The kingdom of the heavens is like a man, a boss, who went out in the morning to hire workers for his vineyard. [2]Having bargained with the workers for forty dollars a day, he sent them into his vineyard. [3]Going out again about nine o'clock, he saw others standing around doing nothing in the marketplace. [4]He said to them, "You go on out to my vineyard too, and I'll pay you whatever's fair." So they went.

[5]Going out at noon and at three, he did the same thing. [6]About five o'clock he found others standing around and he said to them, "Why are you standing around doing nothing?" [7]They said to him, "Because no one has hired us." So he said to them, "You too, go out to my vineyard."

[8]When evening came, the boss said to his foreman, "Call the workers in and pay them their wages, from the last hired to the first." [9]And those hired around five o'clock each got forty dollars. [10]Now the first hired thought they'd get more, but they each got forty dollars. [11]Picking up their pay, they started grumbling at the boss, [12]saying, "Those last ones you hired worked only an hour, and you paid them what you're paying us, who've worked all day long under the hot sun!" [13]But he answered them, "Friend, I do you no wrong. Didn't you bargain with me for forty dollars a day? [14]Take what's coming to you and get out! Suppose I do decide to pay the last the same as you; [15]can't I do what I want with my own? Is your nose out of joint because I am generous? (literally, "Is your eye evil because I am generous?")

Here's a parable that has troubled congregations for centuries. We meet a boss who pays inept, last-minute workers forty dollars, but then pays all-day workers the same amount. No wonder he has a grievance committee protesting his pay scales. The American labor movement championed the slogan: "A Fair Dollar for a Fair Day's Work," but here's a boss who seems to be handing out a decidedly unfair dollar for an unequal day's work. When workers voice protest, he answers angrily, "Can't I do what I want with my own?" sounding like a champion of nineteenth-century laissez-faire economics taken to an extreme. What a troubling parable!

At the outset, let's clear up some confusion. In first-century Palestine the work day was sunup to sundown, a twelve-hour schedule. (Under pressure of harvest such long days are not unusual even in our own land.) Workers were paid a denarius a day. The only value for a denarius given in the Bible is here in the parable—a denarius is what farmworkers are paid for a day's work. So I guessed a figure of forty dollars because there is some evidence that the vineyard owner is paying below scale.

A little more background: The boss goes to the marketplace where workers stand around waiting to be hired. At 6:00 A.M. he dickers with an initial group and they agree on forty dollars. The Greek word is *symphonesis,* "agree," but it implies agreement *after* bargaining. Thus I have translated it, "Having bargained with his workers . . ." because later in the story the boss asks, "Didn't you bargain with me for forty dollars?" The word emphasizes the workers' involvement in the deal. Of course, those in the 5:00 P.M. crowd are merely asked, "Why are you standing around doing nothing?" They answer, "Because no one has hired us." Instantly we know who they are. They are the undesirables—the boozers, the goof-offs, the careless, the disabled, the dumb—in a word, the unreliable. They are people no one wanted to hire. Of course, in our racist society, they could also be minorities.

The parable sets up an audience brilliantly. With the first group of workers at 6:00 A.M., we learn they have bargained a wage of forty dollars. With the 9:00 A.M. group, the boss says, "You go on out to my vineyard too, and I'll pay you whatever's fair." Now we have a figure in mind defined as a fair wage. So a notion of fairness is introduced into the parable. The 5:00 P.M. bottom-of-the-barrel workers are merely sent out to work; they will put in less than an hour in the cool of the evening.

Congregations take in the facts and, at the payoff when the foreman hands out the same paycheck for all, inevitably, they will agree with the grumbling all-day laborers: "Those last ones you hired worked only an hour, and you paid them what you're paying us, who've worked all day long under the hot sun!" Of course, the all-day workers grumbled; the payoff is blatantly unfair. Your congregation will agree and, in effect, join the grievance committee.

Congregations will be doubly shocked by the boss's attitude. When workers protest, he becomes furious. How can we translate his rage? Perhaps, "Take what's coming to you and scram!" So the rank unfairness is multiplied by the boss's fury. The boss seems to be both unjust and arrogant. Although some scholars suspect that, "Can't I do what I want with my own?" is a later addition, it scarcely justifies the boss's pay scale. Workers who put in part of an hour in the cool of the day should not be paid the same as all-day laborers, indeed, more reliable workers, who have put in twelve hours under the hot sun. To accuse the grievance committee of jealousy, "Is your nose out of joint because I am generous?" simply aggravates the sense of unfairness.

What makes the parable shocking is the introduction: "The kingdom of the heavens is like a man, a boss . . ." How can we line up gross unfairness and unjustified rancor with God? No wonder a later rabbinic version of the story shows up with a moral lesson attached, explaining that a last-minute employee deserved equal pay because he was a better worker—"He has done more in two hours than what you did for the entire day" (Young 1989, 261). But Jesus does not add little moral explanations to his parables, particularly explanations that are completely unconvincing. No, the parable is troubling, and particularly troubling because a congregation is bound to join the grievance committee, inwardly crying, "Unfair!"

Of course, we should remember that all the workers are "called." Stories of vineyards trade on a tradition found in the Hebrew Bible where vineyard is a symbol for Israel. Did Matthew pick up the tradition and suggest that his congregation of Jewish "Jesus-people," though called by God more recently, would be given a full share of heavenly reward? Perhaps. But to speculate on the different calls at six, nine, twelve, three, and five o'clock, trying to line them up with different groups or epochs in human history as did Origen (Jeremias 1963, 33–34), is to allegorize and deform the parable. The theological crux is simple: *all* the workers are called. Thus the call of God is for all humanity. What's more, God's generosity is toward all who are called. God is a covenant-keeping God, and the covenant is love.

Sermon

This sermon was preached in 1974 to a Southern Baptist congregation:

Introduction   Old Henry Ford was an opinionated man. He handed out opinions on almost any subject—automobiles, politics, religion. Here's one of his favorites: according to Henry Ford, "Whatever is good business, is good religion!"[19] You hear the parable of the Vineyard Workers and you wonder. Here is an employer handing out the same paycheck for one hour's work as for twelve. Nowadays any employer who pulled that stunt would have a picket line around his vineyard and a grievance committee knocking on his door. The fact is, as policy, it was bad business, very bad business. Yet what did Jesus say? "Like the kingdom of heaven," he said, "like the kingdom of heaven."

1   Well, the same pay for different hours at work may be the kingdom of God, but bluntly it isn't fair. Interpret the story any way you will, it still adds up to injustice. Some workers bore the weight of the day; they worked in the blazing heat from sunup to sundown, windblown and weary, for forty dollars. Others showed up at the cool end of the day, put in a quick hour, and picked up the same forty-dollar paycheck. Look, it's wrong, isn't it? Paying everyone the same, no matter how much work they do, destroys initiative. Back in the nineteen thirties, almost every union hall in America had a motto painted on the wall, "A Fair Dollar for a Fair Day's Work." But in the parable, neither the dollar nor the day's work is fair. Forty dollars for one hour; forty dollars for twelve! No matter how you read the story it adds up to injustice. Perhaps it's an image of the kingdom of God, but to be truthful, it's bad business.

2   Of course, if the parable is about the kingdom of God, then it's bad religion as well — very bad religion. Is there to be no reward for faithful service when God opens the Book of Life and totes up the accounts? Some of us were born into the church, were publicly baptized, and ever since have been trying our best to live out the Christian life. Are we to get nothing more than part-time Christians who show up once a year on Easter Sunday? Is God going to show some skid-row drunk who's never cracked a Bible the same reward being reserved for Dr. Billy Graham? If so, then there's something rotten in heaven, isn't there? When you do more, you have a right to expect more. What's the use of being Christian all our grinding lives if it doesn't get us anywhere? "A Fair Heavenly Wage for a Fair Life's Work," that's our motto. You hear the parable and you're bound to conclude, it's not only bad business, it's bad religion as well.

3   Do you dare take the ultimate step? If the parable has anything to do with God, then, yes, God is unfair! It's all very well to have the boss in the parable make up the rules as he goes along — "Can't I do what I want with my own?" — but if God is like that, life is chancey. Is God a sovereign force you can't predict, given to impulse, with a divine finger on the scales of justice? Perhaps God's ways are not our ways, but at least they ought to be fair ways. There's an old Jewish story about a rabbi's father who became so upset with injustice that he exclaimed, "When I get to heaven, I'm going to march straight up to God, grab hold of his beard . . . and shout into his ears, 'Why do you let this happen?'"[20] When you hear the parable, you do feel outraged: Are some of us rewarded for what we do, and others for what they don't do? Forty dollars for one hour; forty dollars for twelve! Our rage is justified. God, you don't play fair!

4   How does God answer? What does God say? God says, "Take your pay and get out of my church!" That's what the boss said in the parable: "Take yours and get out of here!" We're shocked. Here is God rejecting us, God's own faithful people. Didn't God call us into the church and promise us the kingdom for doing right? And we've tried, God knows we've tried, Sunday after Sunday, singing praise, saying prayers, paying our cash in the collection plates. We have a right to expect a nod of approval, or at least a kind word. Back in the nineteen fifties, Harvard Business School did a study on worker motivation. Do workers work for money or is there some other reward they are after? According to the study, the lure wasn't pay, it was recognition. That's it! We are not asking for a starry crown or a gown of angel gauze. And we are not expecting a double share of happiness. All we want is a little heav-

enly recognition. Instead God spits out a sharp rebuke: "Take your pay and get out!" Get out of my church! We hear the words but we don't understand.

5 Then, suddenly, we begin to catch on. The boss in the parable speaks: "Friend," says the boss, grinding out the word. "Friend, didn't I give you what you bargained for?" Bargained? All along have we been thinking of faith as a bargain with God? We are baptized, we get saved, we do good, and heaven's gate should swing open. We confess our sins and come forward during revival time and we ought to be handed inner peace in return. A bargain. In Maxwell Anderson's play *High Tor,* three vaguely Christian businessmen find themselves in a storm, about to be swept away. "O God," one of them shouts, "I'll be a better man. I'll put candles on the altar, yes, and I'll get that Spring Valley Church fixed up. . . . I can do a lot for you."[21] We are not so crass, but live a bargain nonetheless. Counting our virtues with one hand and, with the other, reaching for blessings. All we want is what's coming to us. "Friend," the boss speaks, "I do you no wrong. Haven't I given you what you bargained for?" Religion as a bargain.

6 Well, no wonder we have resented our neighbors. If we have turned our faith into a bargain with God, we want God to keep the same deal with everyone else. We're in favor of religious free enterprise—everyone for themselves in the sight of God, and we'll keep track of the hours, ours and our neighbors. The tip off? That wonderful comparative phrase, "at least I." "At least I spend some time with my family." "At least I'm sober." "At least I'm not a white racist like my neighbor." If we earn our salvation, we certainly don't want our neighbors to get saved for free! C. S. Lewis imagines a man waiting at the gate of heaven only to discover that a known murderer has been welcomed in while he has not yet been admitted. "If they choose to let in a bloody murderer all because he makes a poor mouth at the last moment, that's their lookout." He can't see himself going into heaven with a murderer. "Why should I?" he asks, "I'm not asking for anybody's bleeding charity. . . . I'm a decent man."[22] Like the all-day workers, he's resentful: "Look, we've worked all day in the hot sun," while the others, they show up late and do nothing. The workers in the parable did a little comparative labor analysis. We want fair pay, they argue, not bleeding charity.

7 Look, in God's world everything is grace, amazing grace. You can't earn grace, you can't deserve grace, you can't be moral enough to merit grace. Grace is handed out free to sinners, while the self-righteous who won't accept "bleeding charity" take their pay and go. Listen, do you earn God's love? Did you deserve the cross? Did God say, "Why they've been so good, those church people, so religious that I'll die for their sins!" No, life is nothing but cross-bound "bleeding charity," God's free grace. In God's world everything is gift, and yes, always undeserved. In God's kingdom, you work with joy, with wide wondering eyes, saying, "I don't deserve. I don't deserve." How does the old hymn go, a hymn we sing in church? "Two wonders I confess, the wonders

of redeeming love and my unworthiness."[23] In God's world everything is a free-grace gift.

Conclusion Well now, what's the good of being Christian? We can't let go, can we? A fair heavenly payoff for a fair life's work, that's our bargain. If we insist on what's coming to us, we can take our pay and go. Otherwise, we can bow before God's bleeding charity and delight in grace undeserved. Said the vineyard owner in the parable, speaking for God, "I am good," he said. Yes, fortunately, God is good.

Discussion

The sermon is a little wordy. Let us review the moves:

Introduction   The introduction works fairly well. It allows us to enter the parable at payoff time, rather than rehearsing the hiring. We enter the parable at a point of contact, when any congregation is bound to join in protest—"unfair." Mention of Henry Ford introduces the parable into a more modern context.

1 Basically the first move underscores the sense of "Unfair!" But it also hands out a little biblical background—a twelve-hour workday versus one-hour working in the cool of the evening. Notice that you can give biblical background without stepping out of an established point of view—"Scholars tells us that . . . " In addition, the move links injustice with a slogan from the American labor movement so as to vindicate the idea of a "grievance committee."

2 The second move turns and looks at the same pay scale applied to religion. Notice that the first two moves match, but reverse Henry Ford's slogan—bad business, bad religion. The move argues that full-time Christians deserve something more than Easter Day "irregulars." Then it compares a "skid-row drunk" with Billy Graham, a comparison designed especially for the Southern Baptist congregation.

3 Move three is something of a problem as it stands; it begins as a third categorical move, each of which has said, "Unfair!"—business, religion, and God. The construction is somewhat static and the tone of the moves both strident and too similar. There are preachers who have grabbed the phrase, "Can't I do what I want with my own?" and argued that God is God and in sovereign freedom can do what God pleases. The notion of God as an arbitrary ruler does not help. God's omnipotence is not carte blanche for injustice; God will act only in accord with God's nature, namely, love. The Jewish story works pretty well, but the speech is a bit long and probably should be broken up with a "he said." The conclusion to the move is deliberately intense.

4 The move begins abruptly with God speaking: "Get out of my church!" (When the sermon was preached, all of a sudden the congregation became very still.) Then the move enters into the congregational mind, asking, How come? We have been God's active people—don't we deserve some recognition? The Harvard Business School illustration fits the worker/boss metaphor of the parable. Whenever a passage has a ruling image—for example, workers in a vineyard—illustrations should fit in the picture.

5   Suddenly, as we hear the word "bargain," we begin to understand. Have we turned religion into a bargain? The illustration from *High Tor*, demonstrating bargaining with God, involves three businessmen and, therefore, fits the metaphor of the sermon. But I don't think the move is well developed. I should have described our subtle sense of being religious in order to earn something—happiness, or a trouble-free life, or heaven. The sermon also may have too many moves that feature internal reactions.

6   Here is a key move. Why do we resent our neighbors? I represent how we compare ourselves with neighbors in the gambit about, "At least I'm not . . ." Subsequently I tell the C. S. Lewis illustration about the self-righteous man. I guess the move works, but the illustration is a bit complex.

7   The final move talks of the kingdom as a sphere of free grace where nobody deserves but everybody receives God's "bleeding charity." The phrase "bleeding charity" is part of an illustration from the previous move. Such a strategy is unwise because it tends to join moves so that their separate ideas may not register. The "call" theme should have been brought out more strongly.

Conclusion   The conclusion starts out nicely, but then ends badly because, suddenly, I introduce a new theme—God's goodness. Instead I should help the congregation to step into a new world, a kingdom of God where everything is grace.

The parable of the Vineyard Laborers is fun to preach. It features a double shock. Although the parable begins in our world, a world where migrant workers do work in fields for hourly wages, it ends in a double surprise. First, all the workers are paid the same. Second, when the workers complain they are condemned and thrown out of the vineyard. We can preach the parable by exploring the two disruptions and, thereby, find our way into a new world of grace.

TWO CHILDREN

MATTHEW 21:23–32

23He was in the temple, and as he was teaching, the chief priests and elders of the people came up to him, saying, "By what authority are you doing these things? Who gave you the authority?" 24Answering, Jesus said to them, "I will ask you one question which, if you tell me an answer, I will tell you by what authority I do things: 25John's baptism, was it from heaven or from humanity?" They debated among themselves: "If we say, 'from heaven,' he will say to us, 'Then why didn't you believe him?' 26but if we say 'from humanity,' we fear the crowd for they regard John as a prophet." 27So answering Jesus, they said, "We don't know." He replied, "Neither will I tell you by what authority I act."

28What do you think? A man had two children. Coming up to the first, he said, "Child, go to work in my vineyard today." 29In reply, he said, "I will not," but afterwards he changed his mind and went. 30When he came up to the second, he said the same thing. He replied, "Sir, I go," but he didn't go. 31Which of the two did the father's will? They said to him, "The first." Then Jesus spoke to them, "I'm telling you the truth, tax collectors and whores are going into the kingdom of God ahead of you. 32For John came to you in the way of righteousness and you didn't believe him, but the tax collectors and the whores believed him. But even after seeing this you did not repent and believe him."

The parable of the Two Children is trickier than it may seem. At the outset there are three manuscript versions of the parable. I have translated the first of these. The second is essentially the same, except that the two boys appear in reverse order. The third version is puzzling. There are two boys saying and doing as in the other versions, but when the chief priests and elders answer Jesus, they choose the boy who said, "I will," even though he did not go to work.

What about the third odd version of the parable? Could it have been the original scenario? Probably not, but it does underscore a fact of first-century life. Our age is permissive. We may be used to adolescent sass, but in a patriarchal society, defiant children were absolutely unacceptable. A son or daughter who point-blank said, "No" to a father would be considered scandalous. The parable sets up a conflict of choices, disobedience or parental dishonor.

Jesus' parables seldom seem to worry over honor. Remember the father with the prodigal son; he gives the boy cash though the young man seems rudely impatient for his dad's death. Then, later, he welcomes him home without even a nod toward moral chiding. There is also the story of the man whose honor is slighted when guests snub his dinner invitations; he fills his banquet hall with bums. Again, think of a landowner whose tenants break their contract with him, beating up his agents again and again with impunity. None of these characters seem to stand up and defend their honor. Nowadays they may seem to be "wimps" to us. But then, think of Jesus; when the crowd around the cross catcalled, "If you are the Christ, save yourself," according to the spiritual, he "never said a mumblin' word." Could such patience be an image of the living God?

The text in the NRSV is a choice of three, but it is powerful. An audience in Jesus' day would have had a hard time deciding between honor and obedience. The problem for preachers today is how to recover any sense of meaningful choice. Kids who say, "I will," but don't are all but normal in our therapeutic society. Kids who defiantly refuse but later come through (if grudgingly) are also quite normal. Obedience is seldom a big thing with us. These days the whole idea of parental honor has dissolved. As a result, the parable is very difficult to preach.

Matthew has set the parable as a conclusion to a peculiar passage in which Jesus is questioned about authority. The passage seems to be a controversy-pronouncement story, similar in design to the controversy over divorce or the controversy over taxes paid to Caesar. In each story there is (1) a tricky question, (2) a counterquestion from Jesus that seems to expose the mind of his questioners, and (3) a pronouncement. The pronouncements are epigrammatic punch lines; they are nonlegal phrases that point toward the purposes of God—for example, "Give to Caesar, Caesar's and to God, God's," or "The Sabbath is made for humans, not humans for the Sabbath."

Here the chief priests and elders show up to question Jesus. They ask, "By what authority do you act?" Jesus asks a counterquestion: "Was John's baptizing from heaven or humanity?" If they say "humanity," the people will be shocked. If they say "heaven," then they must explain why then they refused to follow John. They do not answer. Therefore, Jesus gives no punch-line conclusion to the controversy. Instead he hands them the parable of the Two Children.

Sermon

This sermon, "I Will and I Won't," was preached in 1965. Later it was abbreviated for single-page publication in *Presbyterian Life:*

Introduction   The parable of the Two Children is short and simple. A father had two sons. He ordered them to work in his vineyard. One son said he would, but did not. The other son was balky: "I won't," he said, but later went to work. It does not take much thought to muddle meaning from the parable. The balky boy, the disobedient son, was actually the one who did his father's will. Simple isn't it? But now, take a second look at the parable, not as it stands on a page in the Bible, but as it is *lived* in our world today.

1   One son said, "I won't"; nevertheless he did as his father commanded. There are people who care for justice, who are concerned with human need, but who have no time for talk of God the Father. Look at the college students who have journeyed south to serve the cause of civil rights, many of whom will have nothing to do with the Christian church, or the Christian God for that matter. Many, many people today are trying to be "saints without God." Like the lad in the parable, they say no to God, but, strangely, seem to be doing God's will.

2   And we are disturbed. We have been brought up to believe that the good life is a by-product of faith in God, that if you want to love your neighbor you must first love God. Perhaps we have it wrong. An indifferent architect in one of Graham Greene's novels seems to speak directly to us: "You try to draw everything into the net of your faith. . . . Gentleness isn't Christian, self-sacrifice isn't Christian, charity isn't, remorse isn't."[24] He has a point. Were there not people who sought to love their neighbors before Christ walked the earth, who fought for justice, were kind and gentle, before he came? Can we net all the virtues when there are those who flatly refuse the will of God and yet, apparently, do it?

3 Does the parable trouble you? Surely it troubled the Pharisees who heard it first from Jesus' lips, for no one was more despised in their patriarchal world than a rebel child, nor any sin more dreadful than sullen disobedience. The Pharisees were shocked by the parable, and so are we. To us a profession of faith is all important and nothing quite so ghastly as defiant disbelief. We are proud and somewhat relieved when our children stand before a congregation to declare their faith, promising to serve the Lord, saying, "I will." And do we not remember that same solemn moment in our own lives when we took our vow and said to God, "I will"—and meant it?

4 Well, the parable stabs us with a sharp question: Do we? Do we do God's will? Or is our faith kept from the world where people hunger and hurt, fail, and suffer silent, wailing guilt? Is faith, our faith, as removed from life as a cloistered chapel—all candlelight and altars? Some years ago there was a film that showed a statue of Christ being towed through the air by helicopter. The gilded Christ floated above slums, over city litter and lost city faces to perch on a polished church tower. Is that what we have done with our faith in Christ? One son said, "I will," but he did not. "Which," asked Jesus, "did as his father wished?" Well, what do you say. "Which?"

5 Hold on. The parable is not as simple as that. It is not merely a matter of words versus deeds. The parable calls us to repentance. Said Jesus, "The tax collectors and the harlots go into the kingdom of God before you." Tax gatherers and harlots heard the preaching of John the Baptist: "He who has two coats, let him share with him who has none; and he who has food, let him do likewise." They heard and they responded. Oh, their "repentance" was not particularly religious—no rush of remorse, no salty tears streaming down to the tink of a gospel hymn. But they did hear and heed John's call for moral concern, and they remembered they had neighbors on the earth.

6 With us, however, it is much more than mere moral demand. We have Christ to deal with. Can we cast out of mind his life of wondrous love, or blink away the image of that ugly cross on which he died an ugly death for us? The poet Rilke once stood before an ancient statue and was moved. He thought to himself, "You must change your life!"[25] No pedestaled Christ from the past have we, but a risen Christ to command us. To serve him we must change our lives. A murmured prayer or a passing sense of shame will not turn the trick. What is demanded is a deliberate, responsible right-about-face in our way of living. The parable speaks clearly; it says, "Repent!" Repentance involves that extra shirt and surplus food and, of course, our neighbors.

Conclusion The parable of the Two Children is short and simple. I will and I won't; I won't and I will. Anyone can understand it. The parable is so short it demands an epilogue. How would it go? Well, the father would glance at his sons with glad surprise, saying: "See my children. They will and they do."

Discussion

Introduction   The introduction needs no explanation. My rule is never to exceed ten sentences for an introduction. I usually end up with seven or eight.

1   Here I link the balky son with earnest humanists who want no part of religion but, particularly in the 1960s, were vocal for civil rights or world peace. They were people of genuine courage and conviction who were often put off by the church. In Camus's famous phrase, they were trying to be "saints without God."

2   In move 2 I have made a bad start. Never begin a move with the word "and." Moves must be defined separately ("and" blurs the separation), yet joined by clear logic. I should have begun with, "Well, we are disturbed." The rest of the move chases a familiar pulpit cliché, namely, the notion that faith alone generates virtue: If we love God earnestly, then, presto, we will be kind, generous, and loving toward neighbors, but without faith such niceness is unlikely. But, no, the witness of virtuous pagans contradicts the conviction. Most early church leaders admitted as much, as did the Reformers. The Graham Greene quote works well, for it has an agnostic debunking the Christian claim.

3   I begin with our reaction: "Does the parable trouble you?" I mention the Pharisees who were troubled too (though there is no reference to Pharisees in the text until after the parable). But I give some biblical background on the importance of an obedient demeanor in Jesus' world. I draw an analogy to our confessions of faith offered in Confirmation or Baptism. To us, announcing publicly that "Jesus Christ is our Lord and Savior" seems to be all important. I have made a mistake in moves 2 and 3 by ending each move with a question. Since the sermon was preached, I have learned that ending moves with a question tends to weaken the start of a following move. Besides, in move 4 I will break the rule and deliberately end with a question. By previously using questions, I have weakened the impact of move 4.

4   Here I begin with a direct question: "Do we?" No, I argue, we have professed faith but then avoided the ethical obligation that faith entails. We have kept our faith in church: "a cloistered chapel—all candlelight and altars." I then follow with an image from the Italian film, *La Dolce Vita,* in which a statue of Christ, designed for a church steeple, floats high above a city's slums. The move ends, as it must, echoing the sharp question.

5   Now I stop the action with, "Hold on," and introduce a deeper level to the sermon. I pick up material from verses 31–32. I am not sure I would now use "tax collectors and harlots," which came from the translation I was using. I probably would use "racketeers and whores." Modern congregations do not know what tax collectors meant in Jesus' day. We view the IRS as a necessary if painful institution. As for "harlots," the term is anachronistic. Nowadays we say "whores" or "prostitutes" but seldom "harlots." I have made sure that a congregation does not confuse the tax collectors' repentance with anything like an altar call in church:

"no rush of remorse, no salty tears streaming down to the tink of a gospel hymn." In the Bible, repentance is not so much a feeling as deliberate ethical reversal.

6   By contrast, we who are trying to live our lives before God must *truly* repent and amend our lives. The Rilke material, though moving in an original context, simply doesn't work here; it is not strong enough. The rest of the move works fairly well.

Conclusion   The conclusion turns around to a positive implication of the parable: We should be people who say, "I will" and do so! Unfortunately, I started the conclusion by echoing language from the introduction, thus completing an emotional circle and insuring that the congregation will feel no ethical urgency at all. Round-out conclusions make people feel good, but they destroy responsive action.

The parable seems so short that many ministers may feel it is unpreachable. Moreover, because we are no longer a patriarchal society, some dimensions of the parable may not be effective. Nevertheless, the parable is compelling.

LAST JUDGMENT

MATTHEW 25:31–46

31When the Son of Man comes in his glory, and all the angels with him, then he will sit on his glorious throne, 32and all the nations will be gathered before him, and he will separate them one from another, as a shepherd separates sheep from goats, 33and he will put sheep on his right, and goats on his left. 34Then the king will say to those on his right, "Come, blessed of my Father, receive the kingdom prepared for you from the founding of the world, 35for I was hungry, and you gave me food; I was thirsty, and you gave me drink, I was an alien, and you welcomed me; 36I was naked, and you clothed me; I was sick, and you visited me; I was in jail, and you came to me." 37Then the righteous will answer him, saying, "Lord, when did we see you hungry and brought food, or thirsty and gave you drink? 38And when did we see you an alien and welcomed you, or naked and clothed you? 39And when did we see you sick or in jail and came to you?" 40Answering, the king will say to them: "Truly I tell you, inasmuch as you did it to one of the least of my family [literally, "my brothers"], you did it to me." 41Then he will say to those on his left, "Get away from me! You have been condemned to the eternal fire that is waiting for the Devil and his angels. 42For I was hungry, and you gave me nothing to eat; I was thirsty, and you gave me nothing to drink; 43I was an alien, and you didn't welcome me; I was naked, and you didn't clothe me; sick and in jail, and you didn't visit me." 44Then they also will answer, saying, "Lord, when did we see you hungry or thirsty or an alien or naked or sick or in jail and we didn't serve you?" ⁴⁵Then he will answer them, saying, "Truly, I tell you, inasmuch as you did nothing for the least of my family, you did nothing for me." ⁴⁶And they will go away into eternal punishment, but the righteous to life eternal.

Strictly speaking, the so-called parable of the Last Judgment isn't a parable at all. Some scholars label it an "eschatological vision." Such enthroned scenes of judgment, featuring dialogue between the judge and the judged, were not uncommon in apocalyptic literature (e.g., Dan. 7:9–27; *1 Enoch* 62 and 90; Rev. 20:11–15; *2 Baruch* 72–74). Here the vision also may be drawing on a metaphor from Ezekiel 34:17: "As for you, my flock, thus says the Lord GOD: I shall judge between sheep and sheep, between rams and goats." All through his Gospel, Matthew has warned against a final judgment when the Son of Man returns. Then, just before he begins his passion story, Matthew pictures the Last Judgment. Actually, Matthew may be accused of overkill, for he tells four parables of judgment all in a row: the Unfaithful Slave, who is punished when his master returns (24:45–51); the Closed Door (25:1–13), in which five bridesmaids miss out on a wedding reception; the Entrusted Money (25:14–30), where one servant is castigated for playing safe with money; and, finally, the Last Judgment. After the Last Judgment, Matthew tells the terrible story of Christ's trial and crucifixion. Christ is himself judged, imprisoned, beaten up, stripped naked, and, bawling for a drink, killed off.

The vision of the Last Judgment seems somewhat confused. It begins with the "Son of Man" judging the nations as nations. Then the parable drifts a bit and we hear of a king judging groups of people, separating them like sheep and goats. You wonder if Matthew borrowed a Jewish vision in which an enthroned God judges the nations. The theme of God judging the nations repeats in prophetic literature. In intertestamental literature, some unknown author may well have painted a full-scale picture. Matthew, much concerned with the ethical behavior of his members, seems to have focused on acts of kindness—feeding the hungry, giving drink to the thirsty, clothing the naked, comforting the lonely, visiting the prisoner.

Although it is most unlikely that Jesus ever spun out the vision, thank heavens the Last Judgment is in scripture. We are justified by grace through faith, Protestants insist, but often forget what Catholic brothers and sisters know—namely, that we will be judged not on the basis of justifying faith but by works of love. Ever since many of us stood in church on trembling preadolescent legs and rattled off our credo, "I believe in Jesus Christ as my Lord and Savior," we suppose that having confessed our faith we've got it made; our salvation is guaranteed. But what about love? Do we reach out to feed the hungry and embrace the hurt; do we check into jails to visit prisoners? Obviously, the judge in the vision is not much interested in religious "Who's Who" entries. Faith may form character and character produce works of love, but our lives will be judged not by church membership but by love of neighbor.

The vision of the Last Judgment is not quite as blatant as it seems. Notice its wonderful subtlety. Did you consider the word "Lord." Presumably these people all recognize the Son of Man; they are, in effect, church people. But one group flunks its morality test, crying, "Lord, when did we see *you* hungry?" In other words, they are saying, "Lord, if we'd known it was you, we'd have fed you. We'd have planned a special Family Night supper in the fellowship hall to honor you. You're our Lord and Savior. Of course, we'd have fed you, comforted you, clothed you, visited you—if only we'd known it was you, Lord!"

Many preachers have spotted the word "Lord" and have preached on seeing the anonymous, hidden Christ in the faces of hungry, dispossessed people. They have told us to serve our hurt neighbors as if they were Christ the Lord. While such a message may be inspiring, the vision of the Last Judgment doesn't end up with an anonymous Christ hidden in every needy soul. No, the people who did do acts of charity, the "sheep," are as surprised as the banished goats: "Lord, when did we see you hungry?" There is no Christ mysticism here. These people did not see Christ's face in hungry or thirsty or naked or lonely people. They emphatically did not visit jails anticipating a Jesus *incognito*. All they saw when they spotted a hungry person was a hungry person. The so-called sheep acknowledged their Lord, but when it came to neighbors, all they saw were neighbors in need. ˙

All of which adds up to a peculiar irreligious selflessness. The charitable people, beloved by their Lord, were not driven by religious motives and they certainly were not pandering for religious rewards. The problem with a piety that sees Christ hidden in every neighbor is that it is detached spiritually and does not focus on actual neighbors. Our religion must let us see and serve the neighbor, warts and all.

Another subtlety: In the Last Judgment, there is no check on religious affiliation. Both the "sheep" and the "goats" acknowledge the Lord, but the criterion seems to be doing the will of the Lord rather than any recorded church membership. Could a happy humanist make the grade? Why not, as long as the humanist selflessly feeds the hungry when they are hungry or visits the prisoner in prison? Perhaps the Lord knows his own by their style. And maybe, just maybe, their style is love.

There is scholarly debate over the phrase, "the least of my family." Is Matthew referring to Christian disciples or to all humanity? Interpreters line up on both sides of the question. No less than Origen, Augustine, Aquinas, Zwingli, Luther, and Calvin argue that the phrase (literally, "the least of these my brothers") refers to Christians. On the other side, insisting that "the least" are human beings in need, are many modern scholars—Jeremias, E. Schweizer, Schnackenburg, Patte, W. D. Davies and Dale Allison Jr.—plus such worthy ancients as Gregory of Nyssa and John Chrysostom. We will argue that here, "my family" refers to all humanity and "the least" singles out those in need.

The passage often is preached on the last Sunday of the church year, which in some traditions celebrates Christ the King.

Sermon

Here is a sermon written in 1965 and subsequently shortened for publication in *Presbyterian Life:*

Introduction   The parable of the Last Judgment appalls us. We do not like it at all. If only we could tear it from the Bible, or erase the words. "When the Son of Man comes in his glory . . . he will sit on his glorious throne. Before him will be gathered all the nations, and he will separate them one from another, as a shepherd separates the sheep from the goats."

1   What an awesome picture! Take it seriously, and you will shiver even in your sleep. That's how it was in a tale told about young Martin Luther. In a school book he saw a picture of Christ perched on a rainbow, consigning the wicked to torment and the righteous to bliss with a flick of his finger. And Luther trembled. Can you blame him? Call it poetry, or myth, or a nightmare left over from an excitable age, and you still can't laugh it away. Perhaps within each one of us there lives an inarticulate dread, the feeling that someday, somewhere, somehow there will be a final accounting. No wonder the parable of the Last Judgment troubles us.

2   Fortunately, there is a better picture to frame in our minds, a brighter picture to hold in view. Not a picture of Christ judicially enthroned, but of Jesus living life lowly with the likes of us. See him heal a leper with a touch or call to an outcast sinner. See him comfort the fearful, feed the hungry, forgive poor unforgivable folk. And see him on the cross turn to toss paradise to a dying thief and bend with mercy over that blood-crying crowd. That is a better, brighter portrait to post in our minds, isn't it?

3   Or is it? This is the Christ who does judge us, the Christ who died for you and for me. "Christ!" cries one of Samuel Beckett's two theatrical tramps, "You're not going to compare yourself to Christ!" "All my life," the other answers, "I've compared myself to him."[26] In that comparison we all are condemned. Dare we set our pale "pass-it-off" attitudes beside his prodigious mercy, or stand our tottering affections against his love? Perhaps this is what the parable is trying to tell us. We will not be judged by a rule book banked in heaven, kept to the last, and unlocked for a list of our sins, but by Christ's own call to love, to show mercy, to care not a little but a lot. How does the parable go? "For I was hungry and you gave me no food, I was thirsty and you gave me no drink, I was a stranger and you did not welcome me, naked and you did not clothe me, sick and in prison and you did not visit me." That is what the judge said to the wicked.

4   Do you wonder that they were surprised? "Lord, when did we see you hungry or thirsty or a stranger or naked or ill or in prison?" We can understand their question. We think of ourselves as Christ's loyal people, and suppose that we would leap to his need if he needed us. If what happened once on Calvary were to happen here again, we would be there to give him a drink if he

called. But would we? "Truly, I say to you, as you did it not to one of the least
of these, you did it not to me." Look. He is pointing to people you pass every
day—to hungry folk with huge, hurt eyes; to guilty folk with lowered eyes; to
lonely folk who, if they could, would call across their loneliness your name.
He is pointing to people you live with and work with and walk with every day
of your life. O God have mercy! No wonder the wicked were surprised.

5   But hold on and notice this: the righteous *were just as surprised.* "Lord, when
did we see you hungry and feed you, or thirsty and give you drink?" Good
heavens. These innocent creatures—they did not even know they had served
the Lord. Apparently the last time they had heard a sermon on seeing Christ's
face in the face of their neighbors they had failed to listen, for all they saw
was their neighbor. For them, no sticky religious motives were involved, no
chasing for reward. If they fed a hungry man, it was because he was hungry.
If they visited a lonely man, it was because he was lonely. The parable seems
to be calling us to a simple "secular" love of our neighbors—which means, I
suppose, that America should spend money on foreign aid because there are
nations in need *and for no other reason.* We are to love our neighbors because
they are neighbors. Catholic social worker Dorothy Day tells of sighting by
her home a man asleep in the street, drunk. Before she could reach the man,
a little Italian lady caught her arm and pointing to the man, cried out, "Jesus
Christ . . . my heart is broken."[27] Actually she may have been profane, but at
least she was accurate. The man in that place was Jesus Christ for her, lying
there in need—only she did not know it.

Conclusion   The parable of the Last Judgment appalls us: a terrifying picture.
It is all the more terrifying because we know that, truly, we do not love, we
do not care. O Lord Jesus, last Judge, but first, our Savior; help us to care.
Help us to care.

Discussion

Introduction   The biggest change in the sermon occurs here. The sermon
was abbreviated to fit on a single magazine page; therefore I had to compress the
introduction, joining it to a first move. After I quoted from the text, there were
two or three sentences, firmly stopping the introduction. Then the original first
move began.

    1   The original first move used the example of Luther, harkening back to a
time when people were terrified of judgment. But most people today do not
believe that Jesus will return as a cloud-borne Son of Man, or that he will sit on
a throne to judge the nations. They regard the image as a product of a fevered
primitive religious imagination. I grant the contemporary reaction. But in the
original move, I developed the lurking inward sense that somehow our lives will
be judged.

    2   Basically I set up the first move on an "inarticulate dread" of judgment.
Now I turn sharply to look at a "better," "brighter" picture, namely, the life of

Christ. Even in a truncated version of a sermon you can see a contrast in style between the earlier descriptions of rule-book judgment that scared Luther and the semipoetic descriptions of Christ's own concern for others—"living life lowly with the likes of us," "forgive poor unforgivable folk," "toss paradise to a dying thief." You might want to underline all the verbs in the sermon to see how verb color helps preaching.

3 The first full sentence after "Or is it?" is weak—sentences beginning with the word "this" tend to dissolve in consciousness. I am trying to argue that we will be judged by Christ, that is, by a Christ whose own life was filled with compassion and mercy and care for hurting neighbors. I pick up the Samuel Beckett scene from *Waiting for Godot* so a congregation can hear someone say, "All my life, I've compared myself to him." The move ends by returning to the passage.

4 I begin in the passage, but at once I add a sentence: "We can understand their question." Thus I can preach in a contemporary mode. As a rule I avoid Bible background sections in sermons, and I seldom cite the text itself. Biblical preaching is not preaching about the Bible; it is a preaching of the biblical message interpreted by theological and rhetorical savvy! Always, preaching must be present-tense contemporary. In the move I put us in the position of those who would have served the Lord if they had known it was he. And I have used some poetic phrases—"huge, hurt eyes," "call across their loneliness"—so as to link the move to the previous description of Christ's compassion.

5 Here I set up an abrupt first sentence: "But hold on and notice this: the righteous *were just as surprised.* . . . Good heavens. These innocent creatures did not even know they had served the Lord." I also took time to talk of American foreign aid, a public issue at the time. Remember, the context is a judgment of nations. The Dorothy Day illustration fit nicely, with the Italian woman rushing to help the drunken man ahead of Day herself.

Conclusion I reprise a phrase from the introduction, "The parable of the Last Judgment appalls us," a tactic that is normally too dangerous to use because a rounded-out discourse can be easily dismissed. I do it because I am dealing with a vision, and the reprise will tend to frame and project the material in a visionary way. But I turn the conclusion into a direct confessional plea with a repeated slight phrase, "Help us to care." A double repetition will effect conclusion.

The sermon has some nice language here and there, but is somewhat clumsy in traveling back and forth between the parable and the contemporary scene. The parable is a vision. We must preach God our Judge, but cautiously, without specific where or when literal detail. Our sermons on judgment must be impressionistic pictures.

6

Parables in *Thomas*

The *Gospel of Thomas* is often described as a second-century Gnostic "Gospel." But today scholars suppose that, in an earlier form, *Thomas* was a collection of sayings and parables that circulated during the sixties. Thus, both *Thomas* and Q may be collections of Jesus' sayings that predate our written Gospels. Q was amplified in the direction of apocalyptic, whereas *Thomas* moved toward Gnosticism.[1]

Scholars have known about *Thomas* for a long time. In 1945 a Coptic Gnostic "library" was discovered at Nag Hammadi in Egypt. One component was a collection of teachings at the conclusion of which was a title, "The Gospel According to Thomas." Actually we already possessed fragments of the same "Gospel"; three papyri containing some sayings of Jesus in Greek had been discovered around the turn of the century. We now suppose that *Thomas* was a Greek Gospel that circulated widely during the second century and was highly regarded by many early Christian leaders.[2]

The Gospel begins with the words, "These are the secret sayings which the living Jesus spoke and which Didymos Judas Thomas wrote down." One hundred fourteen teachings follow, all beginning with the words, "Jesus said." Why is *Thomas* important? Because it provides still another version of many teachings found in our Synoptic Gospels, sometimes in what may be an earlier form. More important, *Thomas* provides materials that duplicate some of what we have labeled "M" and "L"—extra sources for several texts in Matthew and one in Luke.

Previously, we noted that Q seems to have been put together in stages: Q[1], a collection of sayings; Q[2], an addition featuring end-term judgment sayings as well as teachings about "this generation"; Q[3], some narrative texts including John the Baptist material and the temptation story. For example, scholars have assigned the Beatitudes to Q[1] except for, "Blessed are those who are persecuted for righteousness' sake," which they assign to Q[2] because Christians, living a radical lifestyle, began to be rejected by their culture.

130

Was *Thomas* assembled in a similar fashion? Perhaps. The earliest stratum was apparently a collection of sayings, some of which match sayings in Q[1]. The second layer seems to have been Gnostic material and/or Gnostic redactions. The Gnostics are difficult to describe. They were world-renouncing Christians who believed they were fortunate to have a special revealed wisdom. For those "in the know," the secret teachings would (1) set them apart from all worldly wisdom, (2) perhaps set them apart from ordinary Christians, and (3) assure them of immortality: "Whoever finds the interpretation of these sayings will not experience death."[3]

The community that produced the final versions of *Thomas* was an elitist community that regarded itself as having a mysterious "spiritual" wisdom, *gnosis*, that the worldly would never know. Many of the sayings in the collection have been edited in the direction of Gnosticism, but some have not. By lining up the several versions, scholars may be able to reconstruct probable earlier versions.

Q and *Thomas* are particularly important in parable study. *Thomas* contains fifteen parables; a dozen are versions of parables found in our Gospels. Three are singular to *Thomas*.[4]

In the case of Q, we can isolate material by matching up Matthew and Luke. With *Thomas* we have a full Coptic manuscript, but it is not always possible to get at the original sayings embedded within the gnosticized texts. While we cannot establish that our Gospels drew on an early version of *Thomas,* nevertheless, the Gospel is extremely valuable in comparison:

1. Four parables are found both in Q and *Thomas:* the Mustard Seed, the Leaven, the Lost Sheep, and the Feast.
2. Two parables, the Tenants and the Sower, are found in *Thomas* and in the Synoptic Gospels, but not in Q.
3. One parable, Seed and Harvest, is found in *Thomas* and Mark alone.
4. Four parables from *Thomas* are in Matthew alone: the Treasure, the Pearl, the Planted Weeds, and the Fishnet.
5. The Rich Farmer is in *Thomas* and Luke alone.
6. The Returning Master is in *Thomas,* Mark, and Luke.

Research in the *Gospel of Thomas* has only just begun, but already there is controversy. Did the author know the Synoptic Gospels but rewrite their parables, or does *Thomas* contain a different version of the parables? Lately scholars seem to be arguing that *Thomas* is a separate collection of parables that, in an earlier form, circulated at the same time as Q. *Thomas* may contain a few original Jesus sayings not found in our Gospels and, possibly, an extra parable.

7

Parables from Q
in Matthew and Luke

If Mark, our earliest Gospel, was written around the year 70 C.E., what filled the gap between its appearance and the time of the crucifixion about forty years earlier? Was there nothing but oral tradition, a word of mouth circulation of Jesus' material? Paul wrote in the fifties and there are a few words of Jesus quoted in his letters. But before Paul, evidently there were collections of sayings that circulated in the forties.[1]

The most famous of these collections is a matter of speculation. Scholars label the collection "Q" (from the German *Quelle,* "source").[2] Though no one has a copy of Q, we know it existed because it is used by both Matthew and Luke. In other words, shared material in Matthew and Luke that is not from Mark, is apt to be from Q. Thus we are able to figure out most of what Q contained. Some scholars suppose that Q was a product of Galilean Christian communities and was compiled during three decades after the crucifixion, reaching the form in which it was circulated sometime before 50 C.E. Thus Q probably predates both Paul's letters and Mark.

What does Q contain? Basically Q was an organized list of sayings. Probably the sayings were grouped according to key words or topics—prayer, preaching, discipleship, kingdom of God, and so forth. For example, Q provided sayings that Matthew organized into the Sermon on the Mount and that Luke presented as the Sermon on the Plain. Q also provided a few parables not found in Mark but presented by both Matthew and Luke. In effect, Q is a collection of "the wisdom of Jesus."

These days scholars have studied Q material carefully. As a result, they now speak of Q^1, Q^2, and Q^3, describing the way in which the collection was compiled and enlarged. The ethical teachings are Q^1, to which a semiapocalyptic section, Q^2, was added. Finally, material relating to Jesus' temptation in the wilderness and his relation to John the Baptist comprises Q^3.

The first strata, Q^1, is a collection of teachings for those who would live in the kingdom of God—love your enemies, turn the other cheek, give to those who beg, judge not, let the dead bury the dead, go as lambs among wolves, carry no money, ask and you will receive, don't worry about your food and clothing. Obviously, a group of people so living would end up on a collision course with their culture.

If being a disciple led to family conflict and social persecution, it was inevitable that the faith would be radicalized. To disciples, the age was evil and discipleship costly indeed, but the kingdom was sure to come, with judgment on the casual world and reward for the faithful. Because the cultural situation was filled with conflict, with either/or decisions, the apocalyptic urgency of Q^2 was added and interwoven with original teachings. Some scholars have described the result as "Radical Wisdom."[3] For example, the Beatitudes that come from Q are in the style of wisdom, but are radical insofar as they counter conventional wisdom and look for social reversals coming in the kingdom of God—"Blessed are the poor; the earth will be theirs," but "Woe to you who are rich!" Most of the teachings are ethical, like the Q^1 sayings that fill the Sermon on the Mount. But parables from Q^2 are often critical of the generation in which Jesus spoke: "This generation" refuses to dance or mourn like children, this generation is like an emptied house and thus subject to visiting demons, this generation cannot read signs of the times, this generation has refused God's invitation and may be replaced at the messianic banquet. Parables warn the careless of God's inevitable judgment.

Many of the shorter teachings feature contrasts: wise/foolish, good/evil, light/dark, faithful/unfaithful, sheep/wolves, a house on rock/a house on sand, piping/weeping. Discipleship seems to mean decisive countercultural behavior.

Significantly, Matthew interprets Q teachings quite differently than Luke. Matthew wrote for an embattled Christian/Jewish community, and Luke wrote for an expanding Gentile audience.

PARABLES FROM Q
IN MATTHEW AND LUKE

House Builders	Matthew 7:24–27 Luke 6:47–49	
Children in the Marketplace	Matthew 11:16–19 Luke 7:31–35	Sermon
Empty House	Matthew 12:43–45 Luke 11:24–26	
Leaven	Matthew 13:33 Luke 13:20 *Thomas* 96:1	
Weather Report	Matthew 16:1–4 Luke 12:54–56	
Lost Sheep	Matthew 18:12–13 Luke 15:4–6 *Thomas* 107	
Feast	Matthew 22:1–14 Luke 14:16–24 *Thomas* 64	Sermon
Closed Door	Matthew 25:1–12 Luke 13:25	Sermon
Entrusted Money	Matthew 25:14–28 Luke 19:12–24	Sermon

HOUSE BUILDERS
(Matthew 7:24–27; Luke 6:47–49)

MATTHEW 7:24–27

24Everyone who hears these words of mine and does them is like a wise man who built his house on the rock. 25The rain came down, and the streams, and the winds blew against that house and it didn't fall; for it was founded on rock. 26Everyone who hears these words of mine and doesn't do them is like a foolish man who built his house on the sand. 27Then the rain came down, and the streams, and the winds blew and beat on that house, and it fell down, and its collapse was devastating.

LUKE 6:46–49

46Why do you call me "Lord, Lord" and don't do what I say? 47Everyone who comes to me, hears my words, and does them; I'll show you what they're like. 48They are like a man building a house who dug deep and laid a foundation on rock. When the flood came, the stream burst on the house and couldn't shake it, for it was built on rock. 49But whoever hears and doesn't do is like a man who has built a house on the earth, without a foundation, so when the stream burst, it fell down immediately, and great was its devastation.

Both Matthew and Luke use this little parable to conclude a major collection of Jesus' teaching—in Matthew, the Sermon on the Mount, in Luke, the Sermon on the Plain. Immediately after the parable, both Matthew and Luke announce a conclusion: "When Jesus had finished saying these things . . ." The use of an image as powerful as the destruction of a house was not uncommon at the conclusion of religious teaching. People must be warned to take teachings seriously.

The two versions are quite similar, but Matthew has added the adjectives "wise" and "foolish." Moreover, he has amplified the forces of nature—rain, streams, winds. Use of the word "stream" may be a tip-off. Anyone who has visited the Southwest, perhaps Arizona or New Mexico, knows about arroyos, the wide, dry gulches that cross the land. With spring rains the arroyos become raging rivers, smashing anything that may be in the way. Palestine in the time of Jesus also was a dry land, with similar arroyos called "wadis." The parable actually is quite humorous. Who would be so spectacularly dumb as to build a house, without foundation, in the middle of a wadi? An audience would howl with laughter at the idea.

Although Matthew has set up a somewhat pedantic moral contrast—"wise" versus "foolish," as in many rabbinic stories—the parable still contains the wonderful exaggeration of a house built in a wadi. The picture of a rushing flood may trade on an apocalyptic idea; just as Noah and the flood happened early in the human story, when the world winds down, perhaps the pattern will reverse and a greater deluge occur. But who is so blockheaded as to build a house in a flood course? Maybe someone who hears the words of Christ and ignores them.

The image of the foundation builder is not uncommon. We have the children's story of the three little pigs who built houses of brick and sticks and straw. When the big bad wolf came huffing and puffing, only the wise pig's brick house withstood assault. There is also a rabbinic parable:

> R. Elisha b. Avuyah said: A man who has good deeds to his credit and has also studied much Torah, to what is he like? To one who builds, stones below and bricks above, so that however much water may collect at the side it will not wash it away. But the man who has no good deeds to his credit, though he has studied Torah, to what is he like? To one who builds, brick first and then stones above, so that even if only a little water collects it at once undermines it.[4]

Of course, the theological concern for meritorious works is somewhat different, and the architectural advice, first the stone then the adobe bricks, is a bit more staid. But almost every culture has picked up the foundation builder image (Young 1989, 251–59).

As with the parables of the Two Children and the Closed Door, the long-standing debate about studying Torah and doing Torah may be involved as background to the story of the two house builders. If Jesus did tell such a parable (a big *if*), he might have chosen the ridiculous image of someone building a house in the middle of an arroyo. More likely, early Christianity developed the parable as a conclusion to collections of Jesus' teachings.

Preachers will want to understand that whenever the Bible talks of hearing, "hear" has the connotation of "obey." In other words, as my wife patiently explains, "hear" should mean "heed." If we do not do the words of Christ, obviously we have not truly heard him. Christianity is not Gnosticism ("gnosis" = know), a knowledge to possess for personal enhancement or even for salvation. We are not meant to "be in the know" over against those who do not know; Christian wisdom is for ethical action. Jesus' words are to do. Does not the Gospel of John speak of "doing the truth?" We think in terms of hearing and knowing and then doing as separate aspects of behavior, but in biblical thought real hearing is doing.

The parable is so brief there may not seem to be enough substance to preach. But both Luke and Matthew have set the parable in the context of a confession of faith. Read Matthew's warning, which immediately precedes the parable:

> Not everyone who says to me, "Lord, Lord," will enter into the kingdom of the heavens, but whoever does the will of my Father who is in the heavens. Many will say to me on that day, "Lord, Lord, didn't we prophesy in your name, and cast out demons in your name, and do many powerful works in your name?" And I will say to them, "I never knew you. Get away from me, you're out of control." (Matt. 7:21–23, DGB)

By picking up the context, namely, a confession of faith ("Lord, Lord"), preachers can address a particular Protestant proclivity. We seem to have the idea that as long as we believe in Jesus we've got it made; we can live secure with salvation guaranteed. But there can be no gap between believing and doing; faith is something we do. Why as Christian people do we serve God and neighbors? We serve not to merit anything, but because we are thankful for God's saving grace freely given.

The motive for a free, gleeful Christian life is the grateful laughter of those who have discovered everything is grace.

CHILDREN IN THE MARKETPLACE
(Matthew 11:16–19; Luke 7:31–35)

MATTHEW 11:16–19

¹⁶To what shall I compare this generation? It's like children sitting in the marketplaces calling out to others, saying,

> ¹⁷We piped to you, and you didn't dance;
> We wailed, and you didn't mourn.

¹⁸For John came neither eating nor drinking, and they say, "He has a demon." ¹⁹The Son of Man came eating and drinking and they say, "Look, a glutton and a drunkard, a friend of tax collectors and sinners." Yet wisdom is justified by her actions.

LUKE 7:31–35

³¹To what shall I compare the people of this generation? What are they like? ³²They are like children sitting in the marketplace and calling to one another,

> We piped to you, and you didn't dance;
> We wailed, and you didn't weep.

³³For John the Baptist came eating no bread and drinking no wine; and you say, "He has a demon!" ³⁴The Son of Man has come eating and drinking; and you say, "Look, a glutton and a drunkard, a friend of tax collectors and sinners." ³⁵Yet wisdom is justified by all her children.

Matthew's tag line, "Wisdom is justified by her actions," is different from Luke's, "Wisdom is justified by all her children," but otherwise the two versions are quite similar. In Matthew as in Luke, the saying shows up after a discourse on John the Baptist. Matthew's version of the saying is followed by Jesus' castigation of three cities—"Woe to you, Chorazin! Woe to you, Bethsaida! . . . And you, Capernaum. . . ." But Luke has the saying followed by the story of a woman anointing Jesus' feet. When host Simon the Leper complains that the woman is a notorious sinner, Jesus tells a little parable about two debtors, arguing that a person forgiven much loves much. These different follow-ups to the saying seem to shape interpretation. But there is no doubt the saying is from Q and probably came attached to a discussion of John the Baptist.

The problem: What exactly does the image mean? Jeremias (1963, 160–62) sites a source that explains a game among teasing children. The girls apparently want the boys dancing as if at a wedding, while the boys blame the girls for failing to do "women's work," namely, mourning at a funeral. The taunts seem to have crystallized into a jingle, which Jesus quotes:

> We piped to you, and you didn't dance;
> We wailed, and you didn't weep.

The Q source has attached the jingle to a speech about John the Baptist and Jesus. Douglas R. A. Hare lines out three possible interpretations of the passage.[5] (1) The passage can be allegorized. Jesus is joyful, and thus represents the wedding celebration, whereas John was dour, and reflects a funeral procession. (2) The children calling out are those who wanted John to celebrate and Jesus to be properly dour. John is too stern for religious people, and Jesus too easy. Neither is judged adequately "religious," and both are rejected. (3) The children who won't play the games are "this generation" who will not respond to the word of God, but sit on the sidelines, detached and uninvolved. If we reject the allegory, then perhaps preachers will want to package options 2 and 3 together.

Of course, it is interesting that the children are playing in the marketplace. A culture such as ours is centered commercially; we are marketplace people, preoccupied with sales and profits. No wonder we have no time to dance to love's sweet song or weep for the fact of our dying. More deeply, no wonder we have no time for God—unless there's money to be made from religion. But here, in the midst of a marketplace world, are children practicing the essentials of human life, marriage and dying.

What about the tag line? It appears to be another familiar saying. Probably Luke's version reflects the original Q saying, for Matthew seems to be echoing an earlier verse (Matt. 11:2): "John, hearing in prison of the *actions* of Christ . . ." If we follow Luke, wisdom (*sophia*) is demonstrated by all her children. Though *sophia* is feminine ("her children"), we are not plunged into Sophia Christology or pneumatology. A folksaying is a folksaying and should not be turned into theology. All the tag line means is that wisdom is proved by the behavior it produces.

Notice that I have avoided calling the jingle a "parable." Probably both the jingle and the tag line are familiar folksayings. Perhaps Jesus did say the words, for the image of scornful children refusing to participate may well describe his generation and ours. We are an uncommitted people watching on the sidelines of life, carping at the foolishness of committed Christian faith. If preachers speak of sin, then their faith is not "positive" enough. If preachers seem to be too friendly with obvious sinners, they are unsuitable representatives of our "spiritual" religion. But the carping may be merely a way to remain uncommitted, critical but uncommitted.

Sermon

Here is a sermon preached more than forty years ago in Fredonia, New York.

Introduction How different is the world today from the world when Jesus walked the earth. The mixmaster has replaced the grinding wheel, the drinking fountain the village well. A Chevrolet is swifter than a camel—if a little more expensive. The world has changed, but not the world of childhood. In Jesus' day youngsters played hide-and-seek, hopscotch, had dolls and dice and even checkers. Just as children today will parade in high heels and a bath towel pretending to be a bride at a wedding, long ago children would prance in silks and bangles in the same games of "make believe." "To what shall I liken this generation?" spoke Jesus as he watched the young playing at weddings and funerals. "To what shall I liken this generation?"—to children who stand apart, refusing to play "let's pretend." "We piped and you did not dance; we wailed, and you did not weep." Could we hear his voice above our artificial age, would we not be condemned by the same simile? Are we petulant children unwilling to lose ourselves in the moving moods of life?

1 Life is like a child's game. Have you noticed how children at play will move from inane laughter to sudden tears? Life is a complex of joy and sorrow, pain, pleasure, trial and ease, all wrapped up in a span of years. Look back at your own life and see what it has been. Remember the shyness of courtship, the urgency of love, and the triumph of childbirth, the exhilaration of troubles borne, the glory of forgiveness. Remember family jokes shared in joy or the choke of loss when tears spilled salty on the soul. Life is not a summer day, blue and bright; it is more akin to a tropical storm, unpredictable and changing. A young soldier who lay dying in a base hospital received word of the birth of a son and could both laugh and cry saying: "O God, isn't that just like life." It is. Life like child's play is made of many moods.

2 "We piped and you didn't dance." The truth is, we do not respond to life, the tragic fails to trouble us, and of joy we are suspicious. Seldom are we involved in life; more often we are remote, even detached. We live as if in a dream, seeing ourselves and all others passively, scarcely awake to life's full meaning. Perhaps it is because we experience so much of modern life secondhand, in the newspapers or paraded across a television screen. Ours is a world in which an aviator can drop a bomb and be well away before he hears the dying shriek or the orphaned wail. Ours is a world in which a scientist can examine cancerous tissue and never know the soul for whom it spells slow pain. On our earth a man may be hired and fired without so much as a handshake, hello and goodbye. We sense, but are we sensitive? Christopher Isherwood begins one of his astonishing short novels with the personal pronoun: "I. I am a camera with its shutter open, quite passive, recording, not thinking. Recording the man shaving at the window opposite and the woman in the kimono washing her hair."[6] Is that it? Have we become human cameras and no longer living souls?

3 Or is it pride that prevents our entering into life and living it with passion? Have you noticed how a girl of eight or ten, when playing at dolls with younger children, will straighten up and stand away when an adult enters the room? Self-consciousness is present; self-esteem is at stake. So we hold aloof from life lest our tears be a noticed weakness or our laughter be labeled idiocy. We are afraid to forget ourselves, our prides, in honest passion. Listen and be wary! Profound joy or profound sorrow will sweep clean the soul of self-concern and link us with others. A social worker, lecturing to her class of students, advised: "I try never to get too close to people. I avoid emotional entanglements. They take too much out of me." She is right. We are afraid to be taken out of ourselves and into the lives of others. "We piped, and you did not dance; we wailed, and you did not weep." "This generation," said Jesus; he might have been speaking to us.

4 There's the trouble: We can't be rid of Jesus. He haunts the subconscious of the race. His simplicity stuns our sophistication. His compassion condemns our hardness of heart. We are forever bothered by this passionate Christ, who wept when Lazarus died, whose tears slipped to the earth without shame. He laughed at weddings and waded in the flowered fields. He suffered as everyone suffers, and knew despair, and cried as an animal in pain, and was human. And that is precisely what troubles us: *he was too human.* How much better for us had he been less emotional. How much easier to revere an unruffled savior, cocksure and serene. But he was human, and in his sight we see ourselves as less than human. Epictetus, the Stoic, pleaded that the best way of life was never to care for anything or anyone: "If you are kissing your child or wife," said he, "say that it is a human being whom you are kissing, for when the wife or child dies you will not be disturbed."[7] Jesus dared to exchange a kiss with Judas, and how great the hurt of Jesus. Jesus cared. Jesus loved. And so, inevitably, Jesus suffered.

5 In him we see God, not a God remote in some resplendent heaven, but a God who enters human life to share in human sorrow and human joy. Here is a God who feels! Does that sound scandalous? We had sooner speak of a God far distant, of a force "X to the nth." To think of a God who feels, rejoices, mourns, angers, offends the intellect. Yet what else do we see in Christ and the cross he so bravely bore? In the last act of Marc Connelly's *The Green Pastures,* God is portrayed as an old man looking down at earth and wondering how to help human children. God hears the prophet Hosea explain how he has found love through suffering. God goes back to heaven and starts brooding. "What is it, Lawd?" cries the angel Gabriel. "It's awful impo'tant," God speaks slowly—the words seem to stumble—"Did he mean dat even God must suffer?"[8] Our faith proclaims that in Jesus Christ even God suffers, lives, dies as we. This is not dusty doctrine dispensed by a dutiful church; this is real. The pain you know, God knows. The fears you feel, God shares. Your tears are God's sorrow. Your laughter is echoed in eternal mirth. In Jesus Christ, God enters life and lives.

6 "We piped, and you did not dance; we wailed, and you did not weep." Now here's the question for us: How can we be human as Jesus was human? Nothing is more deceptive than to manufacture an emotion you do not truly feel. Sorrow and joy, unless they are spontaneous are as grotesque as the dramatic masks—a mouth turned up and a mouth turned down. How can we be intensely human?

We begin to be human when we acknowledge our relatedness and join the human race. If, in a newspaper, I read of an accident on the highway, or a revolution in Hungary, or starvation in Bombay, I am unmoved. The names I find are unfamiliar, the people strangers. But what if I should read that the revolution was on my street, that the starvation took the life of my child, what then? Wrote Albert Schweitzer, "No man is ever completely and permanently a stranger to his fellow-man. Man belongs to man."9 Life lived in the Spirit of Christ becomes personal. Every place on the face of the earth is our town and every human being a member of our immediate family. Under God we all are related. The little girl that dies in the dust of Bombay, she is yours. And the old man, a leper in the African marsh, he is yours. So Turgenev, when he had no money to give a beggar, held out a hand to clasp "the filthy, shaking hand" of the beggar and spoke, "I have nothing, brother."10 Being human is being related one to another.

7 How can we be human as God is human? We cannot, except as the love of God lives within us. Sensitivity is born of love, else it is stillborn and shrivels in the soul. You cannot be part of anything you do not love. Can you enter into the mystery of music unless you love music? Can you grasp the glory of art unless you adore beauty? So, only as you love God can you sense and share God's love. And only as you love your neighbors are you able to enter into their "person." And it is the love of the self, in the finest sense, that grants us an awareness of our deepest feelings, the sorrows and the joys unspoken. Paul Carroll pictures a servant girl, Bridget, who speaks warmly of the priest for whom she works: "You see him when he's proud, but I see him when he's praying in his little place and the tears on his cheeks; . .

you see him when his head is up fiery like a lion, but I see his head when it's down low and his words won't come. . . . It's because . . . I love him."11 It is love that opens unto us the tragic and the comic in life and lets us weep with them that weep and rejoice with them that rejoice. Love is, after all, the gift of God.

Conclusion   "To what shall I liken this generation?" asked Jesus—to children playing their games of "let's pretend." "We piped, and you did not dance; we wailed, and you did not weep." To what," Christ looks on us, "shall I liken *this* generation?" Will you yield yourself to him and dare to bear within your heart the weight of the world's tears and laughter? Will you dare to live as he dared to live? Listen! "To what shall I liken a Christian?" "We piped, and he did dance; we wailed, and he wept in sorrow." "To what shall I liken a Christian?" To Christ, to Christ the Lord.

Discussion

Introduction   The introduction is too long. Probably I could delete the second and third sentences and the start would be better. Actually the first three sentences are contradicted by sentence four, so they are in effect a "throwaway" start. Instead a single sentence, such as "Children have been playing games since the world began" could precede "In Jesus' day . . ." Shorter would be better.

1   The move is a little brief, but fairly good. The big problem is that the move has lists, five or six items in each case. The first list—joy, sorrow, pain, pleasure, trial, ease—is okay because it merely conveys a sense of many moods. But the second list, beginning, "the shyness of courtship," may be a problem. If I want my audience to remember any of the images, the list is too long. Reducing the sentence to no more than three would be better. But the listing sentences, both in a single move, will set up a repetitive rhythm. The illustration of the young soldier works well.

2   The second move also does fairly well. The move begins by recalling the verse from Luke 7:32, which subsequently will become something of a refrain in the sermon. The quote from Christopher Isherwood fits nicely, but notice that we have now two moves with examples followed by a brief quote. The moves may sound too much alike.

3   The start of the move is too abrupt and begins with an "or" and an "is it." The "or" will join itself to the previous move, so that the start is neither strong enough nor independent enough to orient an audience. As for the "it," an audience may not know what "it" is. What's more, before the first sentence has time to sink in, I am off talking about children playing with dolls. In the move, once again, I have examples and, once more, a quote toward the end of the move. Subliminally, an audience will recognize the repeated pattern of development.

4   See, I am doing it again! I feature a list of events in Christ's life, a parallel pair of sentences ("How much . . . How much . . . ") and then another quote with the words from Epictetus. I also pull off a few too many alliterative phrases—"His simplicity stuns our sophistication. His compassion condemns our hardness of heart"—a young preacher's temptation.

5   Speaking of alliteration, blame lack of self-discipline for not avoiding something as obvious as, "dusty doctrine dispensed by a dutiful church." Otherwise the move starts out pretty well, includes a contrapuntal idea—we prefer "X to the nth," an impersonal God—and then concludes with the Marc Connelly illustration. I am not sure Connelly's scene gets across. Is the black rural dialect something to be used with a white congregation? Perhaps when Connelly's play was known and celebrated such a quote could be used, but probably not now.

6   I begin the next move by echoing the text: "We piped, and you didn't dance; we wailed, and you didn't weep." I use a brief paragraph to raise the question, "How can we be human as he was human?" Brief general paragraphs, followed by categorically developed ideas do not work well. But outlines in those days tended to feature general statements followed by "points." The move is well developed, but the Schweitzer quote is not a good choice and the cornball beggar scene by Turgenev is problematic. The sermon was written in 1958 and did not show sensitivity to noninclusive language in the Schweitzer quote. Overall, if we dump the Schweitzer material the move still works fairly well.

7   I am not sure that the seventh move is clear. Am I saying we need God to give us love in order to be human, or am I saying we must love God (like loving music) to be human? The ideas are foggy. The Paul Carroll illustration, which is a bit too romantic, seems to say we must love in order to care. The move does not offer a strong finish to the sermon.

Conclusion   The conclusion may be okay, but it may have too many moving parts, each beginning with "To what shall I liken . . .". Good conclusions do not exceed a simple one or two-part design.

As I look back at an early sermon, I am not sure I have interpreted the parable properly. Douglas Hare is correct when he suggests the parable is open to several different readings, but I think I should have chased the idea of Christian faith being either too glad or too dour for the religious. In other words, I detached the saying from context. Instead I should have picked up more of the John/Jesus contrast. But in Luke the jingle preceded the story of Simon the Leper, who backed away from a woman drying Jesus' feet with her hair, quite unmoved by her passionate gratitude. Maybe the Children in the Marketplace is more open to interpretation than we may suppose.

EMPTY HOUSE
(Matthew 12:43–45; Luke 11:24–26)

MATTHEW 12:43–45

38Some of the scribes and Pharisees said, "Teacher, we want to see a sign from you." 39Answering, he said to them, "A wicked and adulterous generation wants a sign, but no sign will be given except the sign of Jonah the prophet. 40For just as Jonah was in the belly of the big fish three days and three nights, so the Son of Man shall be in the heart of the earth three days and three nights. 41People of Nineveh shall rise up at the judgment with this generation, and shall condemn it; for at the preaching of Jonah, they repented— Look, more than Jonah is here. 42A queen of the South shall rise up at the judgment with this generation and shall condemn it; for from the ends of the earth she came to hear the wisdom of Solomon— Look, there is more than Solomon here.

43"When the unclean spirit goes out of a man, he goes through waterless places, seeking rest, but finds none. 44Then he says, 'I will return to the house where I came from.' When he comes back, he finds it unoccupied, swept and bare. ⁴⁵So then he goes and brings along seven other spirits more wicked than himself, and entering, they live there. The last state of the man is worse than the first. So it shall be with this wicked generation."

LUKE 11:24–26

²⁴"When the unclean spirit goes out of a man, he goes through waterless places, seeking rest; and finding none, he says, 'I will go back to the house I came from.' ²⁵Coming back, he finds it swept out and redecorated. ²⁶Then he goes and gets seven other spirits more wicked than himself, and entering, they live there. So the last of the man becomes worse than the first."

²⁷It so happened that as he spoke about these things, a woman in the crowd lifted her voice and said to him, "Blessed the womb that bore you and the breasts which you sucked!" ²⁸But he said, "Yes, but rather, blessed are they who hear the word of God and keep it."

The parable of the Empty House is almost identical in Matthew and Luke, but their contexts are very different. Look at the two sequences:

MATTHEW 12	LUKE 11
22–32 The Beelzebub controversy	14–23 The Beelzebub controversy
33–37 Good tree/good fruit	24–26 Empty House parable
Bad tree/bad fruit	
38–42 Sign of Jonah tirade	27–28 "Blessed the womb . . ."
43–45 Empty House parable	29–32 Sign of Jonah tirade
46–50 Jesus' true relatives	33–36 Healthy eye/full of light
	Unhealthy eye/darkness

The patterns are different and yet similar. Instead of the good tree/good fruit passage, Luke has a healthy eye/unhealthy eye passage, and instead of Jesus' mother and brothers showing up, Luke features "a woman in the crowd," celebrating Jesus' mother. But in each case the episode ends with a call to ethical obedience. Presumably the material derives from Q and has been rearranged by each author.

The similarity of materials helps us to see what may be going on in the parable. The Beelzebub controversy picks up the theme of exorcism; does Jesus cast out demons by Beelzebub, the ruler of demons? The controversy ends with Jesus saying, "Whoever is not with me is against me, and whoever does not gather with me scatters." In Matthew there follows the "good tree/bad tree" exhortation. Then Matthew adds the tirade on the sign of Jonah. If you compare Luke and Matthew on the sign of Jonah, you see that Matthew has added a reference to the resurrection that is not in Luke and, almost certainly, was not in Q: "For just as Jonah was in the belly of the big fish three days and three nights, so the Son of Man shall be in the heart of the earth three days and three nights." Otherwise, both Matthew and Luke imagine the citizens of Nineveh and the "queen from the South" condemning "this generation" for their rejection of Jesus.

The little passage about Jesus' mother (in Luke, "Blessed is the womb . . .") turns the entire section from the negative to the positive: Jesus' true family consists of those who do God's will obediently.

In our contemporary world, the parable addresses cultural emptiness. Didn't T. S. Eliot label us "the hollow men"?

> We are the hollow men
> We are the stuffed men
> Leaning together
> Headpiece filled with straw. Alas!
> Our dried voices, when
> We whisper together
> Are quiet and meaningless
> As wind in dry grass. . . . [12]

The key word is "meaningless."

During the same time that Eliot wrote the poem, sculptor Henry Moore started shaping human figures with big empty holes where their human hearts should be. Watch out for emptiness. We may banish a few demons but cultural emptiness is an open invitation to be invaded by greater wickedness.

Yes, we ousted the demon of superstition, but the empty house of modern thought has been invaded by "isms and ologies," and all sorts of "things that go bump in the night." Notice the return of horror movies featuring, of all things, otherworldly angels and demons once expelled by "the age of reason." And we pared down ecclesial landholdings that had guaranteed the church's wealth during medieval years; such properties became *séculariser*. But now, in a secular society, look at the properties held by unchecked corporate powers. Capitalism's free enterprise is seldom free for the poor. We got rid of the practice of bloodletting, and now have modern medicine, thank God. But along with modern medicine we have price gouging by drug companies and competing HMOs that, like most insurance companies, are happy to drop the poor, the ill, and the chronically infirm. Maybe we have more than "seven demons" in competitive health care.

The Enlightenment got rid of religion—always cataloged under the catchall label "superstition"—but now we are haunted by a kind of emptiness, a nothingness that almost has the power of a presence.

What's the answer? The only way to protect an empty house from its emptiness is to fill it with life. Houses are meant for living people. The only way to save a society from its emptiness is to fill it with living people of faith. Conviction is the only cure for vacuity.

What is the church's calling? These days we preach in an empty hauntedhouse world. On the one hand, we must exorcise the demons that are with us now; in a secular age, they seem to have multiplied. Secular demons are camping out in our sophisticated world like tramps in a deserted house. On the other hand, we must declare the mystery of God in such a way as, once more, to make faith a live option. Perhaps, then, the rooms of our contemporary world will be decorated, not with Halloween symbols of haunting, but with the flowers of an Easter celebration, Christ risen, and the glitter of Christmas, God-with-us.

The context in Matthew can help a sermon. The tirade against scribes and Pharisees may indicate that Matthew regards Jesus as God's exorcist, but if the religious leaders will not believe in him, their house will be empty and, therefore, vulnerable. What comes after the little parable? Of all things, it is the story of Jesus' mother and brothers coming to speak with him. Did they think he was possessed? Jesus answers, "Whoever does the will of my Father in heaven is my brother and sister and mother." The cure for emptiness is not mere believing, but ethically concerned, active believing.

Should the passage be allegorized? Should the demons be named? Perhaps. The parable has a simple thesis: (1) We swept demons out of our world, (2) but we have left the modern world with a God-shaped emptiness, (3) so the demons have returned to haunt "our generation"; (4) maybe it's time to welcome the Christ who will exorcise our demons, fill our world with graceful faith, and instruct our behavior.

Luke picks up the same theme, for he follows the parable with an episode in which someone from the crowd cries, "Blessed the womb that bore you and the breasts which you sucked!" To which Jesus replies, "Blessed are they who hear the word of God and keep it."

Both Matthew and Luke correct a too simple reading of the parable. Our need is not mere belief, but rather active people, going in and out of the house, doing the will of God!

LEAVEN
(Matthew 13:33; Luke 13:20; Thomas 96:1)

MATTHEW 13:33b
The kingdom of the heavens is like leaven which a woman took and hid in three measures of flour until the whole was leavened.

THOMAS 96:1
[1]Jesus [said], The kingdom of the Father is like a certain woman. She took a little leaven, [concealed] it in some dough, and made it into large loaves.
[2]Let him who has ears hear.

The parable of the Leaven is found in Matthew, Luke, and *Thomas*. In Matthew and Luke the parable is virtually identical, indicating it probably derives from the Q source. Of course, Matthew uses "kingdom of the heavens" because Jewish usage avoided the name of God and the stock substitute was "heavens." The version in *Thomas* introduces a contrast between a "little" leaven and "large" loaves. The little/large contrast is found in several parables in the *Gospel of Thomas,* but is not usual in Jesus material.

The parable, however, often has been preached as a little-to-large promise. A little leaven = the church, and a big loaf = the world; someday the whole world will be leavened by Christian missionary activity. The interpretation is prompted by Matthew and Luke, both of whom couple the Mustard Seed parable and the Leaven and suppose, mistakenly perhaps, that both are stories of triumph. But, though exhilarating, such an interpretation is a mistake. Robert Funk notes that leaven in the Bible, without exception, is used as a symbol of corruption by unclean or sinful things (Funk 1975, 51–71). Does not Matthew himself quote Jesus as saying, "Beware of the leaven of the Pharisees and Sadducees" (Matt.16:6)?

Contrary to most modern translations, leaven is not yeast. Leaven is a chunk of leavened bread that has been stored in a dank place until it molds; in effect, the bread is rotten. Often the dough it leavens will have a sour taste and smell. As a result, leaven became a familiar metaphor for corruption. Israelites were forbidden to eat leavened bread during the Passover festival. Indeed they could not have even a crumb of leaven in their houses. Here is the tradition for the Feast of Unleavened Bread:

> Seven days you shall eat unleavened bread; on the first day you shall remove leaven from your houses, for whoever eats leavened bread from the first day until the seventh day shall be cut off from Israel. . . . In the first month, from the evening of the fourteenth day until the evening of the twenty-first day, you shall eat unleavened bread. For seven days no leaven shall be found in your houses; for whoever eats what is leavened shall be cut off from the congregation of Israel, whether an alien or a native of the land. You shall eat nothing leavened; in all your settlements you shall eat unleavened bread.   [Ex. 12:15–20; see also Ex. 13:3–7 and Deut. 16:1–8]

What's more, leavened bread could not be used as a fire offering because, according to Leviticus 2:11, its smoke would not be a pleasing odor to the holy God. Throughout the Hebrew scriptures, leaven is a symbol of the unholy, indeed, of the ungodly!

The symbol does not change in the Christian documents. The major text is in 1 Corinthians 5:6–8 where Paul, scandalized by a church member who is cohabiting with his father's wife, asks for his expulsion:

> Don't you know that "a little leaven leavens the whole batch" of dough? Get rid of the old leaven so you can be new unleavened dough. For our passover, Christ, was sacrificed. So let us keep the feast, not with old leaven, nor with the leaven of malice and of evil, but with the unleavened [bread] of sincerity and truth.

Again, in Galatians Paul reaches for the same metaphor. Some Galatians are insisting that members of their community must be circumcised under the law of

God. Paul is livid: "You who want to be justified by the law have cut yourselves off from Christ; you have fallen away from grace." (Gal. 5:4) He is appalled:

> You were running well; who blocked you from being persuaded by truth. The one who called you [i.e. Christ] did not so persuade you. "A little leaven leavens the whole batch." (Gal. 5:7–9)

Evidently, "A little leaven leavens the whole batch" is a quoted folksaying warning of corruption because Paul uses the phrase in both contexts. Without exception leaven is a biblical symbol associated with sinfulness.

To make matters worse, Jesus tells about a woman "hiding" leaven in bread. The odd word "hiding" (*krypto*) conveys something surreptitious. Of course, mention of a woman does not enhance the situation, for women were associated with menstrual impurity. If they were not impure, women were definitely considered second-class citizens. Most men were delighted that they were not "born a woman or a slave." So here we have a conjunction of rather negative associations: woman, leaven, and a surreptitious "hiding."

The parable gets worse, for the woman is hiding leaven in "three measures of flour." The phrase "three measures of flour" will mean little to a modern congregation, but in the Bible three measures of flour, an "ephah," is associated with the sacred (Scott 1989, 327). When Abraham welcomes the three divine messengers, one of them being the Lord, he has Sarah bake up cakes from three measures of fine flour to celebrate (Gen. 18:1–6). When an angel of the Lord shows up before Gideon, Gideon prepares a feast with an ephah of unleavened flour (Judg. 6:19). Later, when Hannah dedicates her son, Samuel, she offers an ephah of flour in the temple (1 Sam. 1:24). An ephah, three measures, is around fifty or sixty pounds of flour (Jeremias 1963, 147), enough nowadays to fill a big bakery truck with bread. According to the parable, the sacred ephah of flour was all leavened, that is, corrupted. Notice the absurdity of a woman baking bread with fifty pounds of flour in a small clay oven.

Why is the kingdom of God like a bakery-truck load of corrupted bread a woman has produced by sneaking in a hunk of leaven? Though Matthew and Luke have paralleled the parable of the Leaven with the Mustard Seed, from a little to a lot, the more obvious parallel might be Jesus' words to the chief priests and the elders in Matthew 21:31: "Truly I tell you, the tax collectors and the prostitutes are going into the kingdom of God ahead of you." At the time of Christ there was a huge concern for purity. How could God's kingdom be comprised of anything other than the morally and ritually pure? As a result, there was a denigrating of people considered socially impure. But here Jesus opens up the kingdom of God to the impure. Good heavens, he not only opens a door to admit the impure, he announces that "*all* was leavened."

The use of bread as a symbol may be fortunate. Remember, Jesus hosted dinner parties for the riffraff, those excluded by right of impurity. Many scholars suppose that in so doing Jesus was enacting a parable, he was hosting small-scale messianic banquets, kingdom feasts, ahead of time. Whenever we break eucharistic bread, we can recall the parable. We are sinners at table, yet sinners anticipating God's new order where we will be welcomed to a table as large as the cosmos with room for all humanity.

How do preachers preach a parable that requires so much background information? Congregations must know what leaven means symbolically. They must realize that we are dealing with an ephah, around fifty pounds of flour, enough for a huge banquet. They must understand the exclusion of the impure from God's anticipated kingdom in first-century religious thought. They must admit that a parable featuring a woman as a central character was suspect. How can we preach without a church school class for the whole congregation?

Maybe we can design an introduction that will orient our congregation. We can ask what to do with a parable that pictures a woman baking bread in a tiny clay oven but using fifty pounds of flour! A crazy parable, perhaps, but watch out, it may be full of meaning. Such a start will alert a congregation to expect the unusual.

Obviously we will have to identify leaven as a symbol of corruption. To do so we might describe cruddy leaven, covered with mold, before explaining that, naturally, it was a symbol of corruption. Jews must sweep their houses to get rid of the unholy leaven. And Paul, dealing with a reported sex scandal, tells the congregation in Corinth to expel the sinner for, after all, "a little leaven corrupts the whole."

The symbol of leaven ought to trouble us. We also tend to picture the kingdom of God in terms of purity; righteous people, saints, fill up the kingdom, we say. If the kingdom is not packed with the righteous, at least it is populated with true believers, those who have been justified by grace through faith. But if leaven is a symbol of sin, of evil, of rank unbelievers, well, what's going on?

A preacher, then, may bring in the good news of God, a God who loves sinners, *us* sinners. To grasp the nature of such a God we will see Jesus Christ hoisting a few with sinners—even dying on a cross, condemned for sinners. Rejoice, the kingdom will welcome us broken, scuffed-up children of God.

WEATHER REPORT
(Matthew 16:1–4; Luke 12:54–56)

MATTHEW 16:1–4

[1]Coming up to test him, the Pharisees and Sadducees asked him to show them a sign from heaven. [2]But, answering, he said to them, "At sundown you say, 'Fine weather! The sky is red.' [3]At dawn you say, 'Today, stormy weather! The sky is red and threatening.' Hypocrites! You know how to interpret the look of the sky, but why can't you interpret the signs of the times? [4]A wicked and adulterous generation seeks a sign, and no sign will be given, except the sign of Jonah the prophet." Leaving, he went away from them.

LUKE 12:54–56

[54]He said to the crowds, "When you see a cloud rising in the West, immediately you say, 'Rain is coming.' And it does. [55]When a south wind blows, you say, 'It's going to get hot,' and it does. [56]You hypocrites! You know how to interpret the appearance of earth and sky, but why don't you know how to interpret the present time?

While the two versions of the parable are slightly different, the essential idea is the same—you know how to interpret the weather, why can't you read the signs of the times? The contexts where the parable appears in Matthew and Luke, however, are very different.

Matthew brackets the parable with material he has used before in 12:38–39, where the scribes and Pharisees ask for a sign and Jesus replies using the same words we find here: "A wicked and adulterous generation seeks a sign, but no sign will be given except the sign of Jonah the prophet." But Matthew has located the image of the weather report immediately after the story of the feeding of the four thousand, a miracle which should be sign enough. Right after the parable the disciples show up in a dither because they have no bread. Jesus tells them to "beware of the leaven of the Pharisees and Sadducees" who, after a miraculous display, were still asking for a spectacular sign. In response to their refusal to believe, Jesus asks "Do you not remember . . . seven loaves for four thousand?"

In Luke the pericope is located after a somewhat labored second-coming comparison between a responsible slave who cares for other slaves and thus merits a reward and an irresponsible slave who is beaten up for failing to do his returning owner's work. Suddenly Jesus announces, "I came to bring fire to earth." He will not bring peace, but division: "father against son and son against father, mother against daughter and daughter against mother," an allusion to Micah 7:6. Then he tells the parable of the Weather Report and follows it with still another imagistic warning: "When you go with your accuser before a magistrate, on the way make an effort to settle the case." In Luke the context is judgment in view of a delayed, but certain, second coming. The material is probably drawn from Q^2 but has been patched together somewhat clumsily by Luke.

Still, the images of the parable apply. They describe us and our more modern world. Nowadays we are into forecasting. Old-timers (along with Matthew) chant, "Red sky at night, sailor's delight; red sky in the morning, sailor take warning." But we are much more sophisticated these days. If you are a computer buff, you can call up a radar picture and predict weather on the way. You can even screen multiphased pictures, temperatures, cloud movement, and sophisticated in-motion depictions of probable weather patterns a day or two in advance. We watch the weather, particularly these days with the dismaying prospects of global warming.

But it's not merely weather. We try to predict the future with some precision in other ways. We have developed a list of economic indicators in order to read financial prospects. We read political polls, population growth statistics, all sorts of social trends, from tastes in music to dietary preferences. And there are people who try to read significance in the motion of the stars. Most newspapers carry a daily horoscope—What will your day be like if you're a Taurus or a Gemini or a Scorpio? When it comes to medical matters, after a batch of tests, doctors can offer us a probable prognosis. Nowadays we try to read the future by discerning "signs of the times."

Nevertheless, Jesus would snarl his verdict: "Hypocrites!"

The passage shows up in both Matthew and Luke. Was it originally an apocalyptic warning? The end is near, the day of the Lord is at hand; can you not read the signs of the times? In the Greek, the word is *kairon,* not merely times (*chronos*), but *crisis* times.

Certainly our age seems to be in crisis. "The times they are a-changin'," Bob Dylan sang prophetically back in the sixties.[13] Our modern world seems to be falling apart, and something new, perhaps a new world epoch, seems to be forming in the midst of the cultural debris. We talk of "postmodern" but no one seems to know exactly what *post*-postmodern will be. All we know is that the brave new world that began with the Renaissance/Reformation, an "enlightened" world that Paul Tillich once labeled "The Protestant Era," is clearly over. Will nations fade and be replaced by economic blocs? Will religious "free enterprise," namely, denominationalism, wane as world religions begin to contend on Main Street, U.S.A.? A few years ago there was a cartoon that showed two men sporting beards, long robes, and sandals, each carrying a sign: "The end is near!" and "Prepare to meet your God!" One man is saying to the other, "Have you noticed? They're not laughing anymore." The world appears to be in crisis. But who can discern the signs of the times?

Why can't we read the signs of the times? Perhaps because we do not read the world as a world related to God. When we predict the future we merely project our own human accomplishments. So Detroit can design a model car of the future, basing it on in-the-works technology. And computer buffs can guess there will be rapid-fire modems in the future and many different kinds of internets to explore. We can dream a spaceship world with technological miracles everywhere, but, of course, we are only projecting tangents of current science and industry. Always we are forced to add a grim footnote: "But we may be dead." The only way to go beyond either an inflated human pride or a dour acknowledgement of mortality is to read God's purposes, purposes that are alive in all things. How can a secular world grasp the purposes of God? Answer: We can't! No wonder Jesus labels us hypocrites!

Is there a clue to the future? People still buy those awful "newspapers" in the supermarket checkout lanes that rehash the prophecies of Nostradamus, supposing that the future has been preprogrammed by divine decree. But fatalism is a far cry from faith. In love God works with our free choices, elaborating from our errors wondrous things, ever seeking to save us from our will to self-destruction. If God does give us large freedoms then the future is not "set" in advance, but will be worked out improvisationally—freedom and *grace*—as God's sovereign purposes and human desires interact. Yet we must affirm that God's purposes are ultimate.

To read the shape of the future we must admit to basic human reality: We are astonishing, imaginative, creative beings made in the image of God, but we die, and, to be truthful, we can be demonic. Because of our complex nature, the future is always both remarkable and deadly. Short-term human achievement is bleak.

The promises of God, however, are sure. Someday God and humanity will "tent" together in some great "shalom." The Spirit will have transformed all human enterprise so that, by the Spirit of God, the true humanity we name, Christ will be all in all. What will be the shape of God's future? The shape of "The Great Commandment," a wide humanity in love with one another and with God.

Years ago in a Pennsylvania Presbyterian church we saw a child's crayoned picture taped up on the wall of a classroom. The picture showed stick-figure people all over the page, in pairs or threesomes, bowing to one another, their arms reaching out to serve. In big letters underneath the child had written a caption: "Kingdom of God." If God's world is moving toward a "kingdom of God," we should be able to read the signs. Moreover, we should be able to change our ways accordingly. If the world will end in the glad exchanges of mutual service, then the Pentagon budget must be sliced and our Peace Corps enhanced. If the world under God's influence is moving toward familial love, then racism is an inexcusable social blunder. We can learn, taught by the visions of scripture and some modicum of theological reasoning, to read the signs of the times. All our times are in God, who, in spite of our chronic defections, loves us.

Every age is in *kairos,* crisis. And in every age, the crisis is a crisis of faith. To read the signs of the times we must remember that, hidden modestly behind the sometimes fearful red sky, is nothing but grace, God's amazing grace.

LOST SHEEP
(Matthew 18:10–14; Luke 15:4–7; Thomas 107)

MATTHEW 18:10–14

10Look out that you do not despise one of these little ones, for I tell
you their angels in heaven gaze on the face of my Father in heaven.
12What do you think? If a man has a hundred sheep and one of them
strays, won't he leave the ninety-nine on the mountains and go to seek
the strayer? 13And if he should find it, I tell you he'll rejoice over finding
it, more than the ninety-nine who didn't wander.
14So it is not the will of your Father in heaven that any one of these
little ones be lost.

LUKE 15:1–7

1Now there were tax collectors and sinners gathering around to hear him. ²And both the Pharisees and the scribes grumbled loudly, saying, "This man welcomes sinners and eats with them!" ³So he told them this parable:

⁴Suppose one of you has a hundred sheep, and, loses one of them, won't he leave the ninety-nine in the wilderness and go after the lost one until he finds it? ⁵And finding it, he'll carry it on his shoulders rejoicing. ⁶Coming home, he'll call his friends and neighbors together, saying to them, "Party with me, for I have found my sheep which was lost."

⁷I tell you, there will be more joy in heaven over one repenting sinner than over ninety-nine righteous people with no need of repentance.

The parable of the Lost Sheep has inspired much Christian piety, hymnody, and art. In Luke the parable is told in response to criticism: "This man welcomes sinners and eats with them." Luke sees Jesus on a missionary expedition to rescue "the lost." Thus he lines out three parables—the Lost Sheep, the Lost Coin, and the Prodigal (lost) Son—all in a row to demonstrate the faithful divine love that Jesus embodies. With Matthew the context is somewhat different; it is "parish oriented." Matthew is concerned with the recovery of lapsed members.

The parable comes from the Q source and clearly draws on imagery from the prophet Ezekiel:

> For thus says the Lord GOD: I myself will search for my sheep, and will seek them out. As shepherds seek out their flocks when they are among their scattered sheep, so I will seek out my sheep. I will rescue them from all the places to which they have been scattered on a day of clouds and thick darkness. I will bring them out from the peoples and gather them from the countries, and will bring them into their own land; and I will feed them on the mountains of Israel, by the watercourses, and in all the inhabited parts of the land. I will feed them with good pasture, and the mountain heights of Israel shall be their pasture; there they shall lie down in good grazing land, and they shall feed on rich pasture on the mountains of Israel. I myself will be the shepherd of my sheep, and I will make them lie down, says the Lord GOD. I will seek the lost, and I will bring back the strayed, and I will bind up the injured, and I will strengthen the weak, but the fat and the strong I will destroy. I will feed them with justice. (Ezek. 34:11–16)

The tradition of God as "the shepherd of Israel" repeats in the Hebrew scriptures, particularly in Jeremiah 23:1–4 (which no doubt prompted Ezekiel's imagery) and in Zechariah 11:4–17, as well as Psalms 23, 77:20, 80:1. Although the Hebrew Bible passages seem to link scattered sheep with the exiles, Matthew and Luke take the image and relate it to sinners, lapsed and lost.

The parable is designed artfully in both Matthew and Luke. Some scholars read Matthew's version rhetorically as a chiasmas (Scott 1989, 410), and others arrange Luke's version in a somewhat similar manner (Bailey 1976, 144–45):

Matt. 10a	"one of these little ones"
10b	"my father in the heavens"
12b	"has gone astray"
12c	"the ninety-nine"
12c	"the one"
13b	"the ninety-nine"
13b	"went astray"
14	"your father in the heavens"
14	"one of these little ones"

In Matthew, "little ones" are apparently lapsed members of the community, for, following the parable, there is a procedure to govern affairs: "If another member of the church sins against you . . ." (Matt. 18:15–20). Then Matthew adds another parable, the parable of the Unforgiving Servant (Matt. 18:21–35). Matthew's entire chapter is a carefully designed argument for seeking and forgiving lapsed members of the community.

The lead-in to the parable of the Lost Sheep is rather strange with its odd reference to "their angels in heaven gaze on the face of my Father in heaven." Apparently Matthew is referring to the Jewish notion that God, out of love, has appointed a guardian angel for each person. As you can imagine, the odd reference has been chomped over by scholars. Preachers would be wise to concentrate on the parable itself; there is quite enough pop angel stuff these days without adding to the confusion.

In some ways the parable is disturbing. Shepherds in first-century Palestine were regarded with some dismay. They would come down from the hills like bikers roaring into a startled village to do some rowdy partying. Though the parable draws on traditional biblical imagery, the social position of shepherds may have skewed the parable a bit. Also, as it stands, the parable is simply absurd. If a man has a hundred sheep and one wanders, won't he leave the ninety-nine on the hills and go for the one? Answer: No. What responsible shepherd would think of abandoning a flock! Some scholars have argued that the parable must be referring to a two-shepherd operation, with one to seek and one to guard (Jeremias 1963, 133; Bailey 1976, 149–50), but there is no mention of another shepherd in the parable.

The problem of leaving the sheep may have led to the peculiar version found in the *Gospel of Thomas:*

> Jesus said: "The kingdom is like a shepherd who had a hundred sheep. One of them, the largest, went astray. He left the ninety-nine and looked for that one until he found it. When he had gone to such trouble, he said to the sheep, 'I care for you more than the ninety-nine.' (*Thomas* 107)

By inserting "the largest," *Thomas* tries to justify the neglect of ninety-nine. But the rationalization scarcely can be aligned with a gospel of God's love for all humanity.

Are we then left with an absurdity? Quite likely. But we have seen how again and again Jesus' parables surprise an audience and then disclose. Although no human shepherd would risk the flock for the sake of one, God's particular love is for each and every "little one," even the lapsed sinner—perhaps especially the lapsed sinner.

Does Matthew's version of the parable challenge church management these days? Perhaps. Parish ministers are much more management oriented than once they were; they do not chase after dropouts with evangelical fervor. Neither do their parishes, particularly if there is any scent of obvious sinfulness. Thus God's passionate concern for the wandering sheep is a huge corrective to our parish life. Sheep are not the smartest animals around; they just graze their way into lost-ness. Most lapsed members are smarter than sheep, but in a secular age not much more insightful. Churches must be under Matthew's instruction and, more than Matthew, Jesus' own parable.

In Luke the setting is quite different. As with Matthew, a whole chapter is carefully designed. At the outset, Luke pictures "tax collectors and sinners" coming near to hear Jesus. Whereupon Pharisees and scribes remark, "This man welcomes sinners and eats with them." So Jesus tells them the Lost Sheep parable, then another, the Lost Coin, and still another, the Prodigal Son. The Lost Sheep and the Lost Coin are stylistically joined. In each case something is lost, there is seeking and finally finding, whereupon the finder calls in "friends and neighbors," saying, "Rejoice with me for I have found [something] which I lost." Finally, after each parable, Luke adds a phrase such as, "So, I tell you there will be more joy in heaven over one repenting sinner than over ninety-nine righteous persons with no need of repentance." After the Lost Coin, Luke also mentions "angels of God," which may indicate that there was some reference to angels in the Q source.

In Luke the parable of the Lost Sheep is virtually identical to Matthew's version except for the substitution of "wilderness" for "mountain" and the picture of the shepherd with the sheep on his shoulder. What joins all three parables is the partying to celebrate finding the lost. The partying is, of course, an image of heavenly joy over "one sinner who repents." Luke is a very evangelical evangelist!

There are some problems for preachers. First, we must be very careful with the word "lost." In some sermons, "lost" means consigned to perdition, that is "eternal damnation." But the parables use "lost" for wandering off from God's love. Inasmuch as the parables imply God's love for those who have wandered, we must preach with such constant love in mind. We must never risk evangelism by threat. Worse, we never must succumb to getting homiletical kicks out of "damnation." The notion of a damning wrath is essentially a contradiction of the gospel. The word "repent" should not conjure images of a "sawdust trail" with hot tears and quivering remorse. In the Bible, repentance is a return to the will of God; it is ethical change.

Second, we may be tempted to portray Jesus as a saccharine lamb-cuddler. The status of shepherds may help to dispel such nonsense — remember the "biker" analogy. Shepherds were rough, tough men doing difficult but responsible work. Cuddling was not quite the way it was done. A remarkable painting by Alfred Soord of "The Lost Sheep" pictures a shepherd, muscles straining, leaning precariously out over a rocky precipice to reach for a stray, while overhead, predatory birds already are circling in a stormy sky. Such an image is more like it!

But for Luke the real picture is partying. Preachers may wish to link rejoicing with Eucharist, which may have been in Luke's own mind. As a Gospel writer, Luke is most interested in the Lord's Supper. Does he see Jesus' partying with sinners as a symbol of eucharistic acceptance? Probably. Does he read Eucharist into celebrations over the lost who are found? Almost certainly. For Luke, as it should be for us, the end of evangelism is not names on a church roll, but places at table in the midst of eucharistic joy.

FEAST
(Matthew 22:2–14; Luke 14:12–24; Thomas 64:1–2)
Italicized words represent editorial additions by Matthew and Luke to the parable they received from Q.

MATTHEW 22:2–13

2The kingdom of the heavens is like a man, *a king,* who gave a *wedding* banquet *for his son.* 3He sent his slaves to call those who had been invited to the *wedding* banquet, but they didn't want to come. 4Again he sent other slaves, saying, "Tell those who have been invited: Look here, I have fixed my dinner, my oxen and my fat calves have been slaughtered, everything is ready; come to the *wedding* feast." 5But they paid no attention and went off, one to his farm, another to his business, 6*while the rest seized his slaves, humiliated and killed them.* 7*So the king was enraged. He sent his army to destroy those murderers and burn their city.* 8Then he said to his slaves, "The *wedding* feast is ready but those invited didn't deserve to come. 9So go out into the avenues and invite everyone you find to the *wedding* banquet." 10Going out into the streets those slaves collected everyone they found, both good and bad alike; so the banquet hall was filled with guests.

11*When the king came in to visit his guests, he noticed a man who wasn't dressed for a wedding.* 12*He said to him, "Friend, how did you get in here without being dressed up for the banquet?" The man was speechless.* 13*Then the king said to his waiters, "Tie him up hand and foot and throw him into the dark outside." There will be weeping and grinding of teeth.* 14*For many are called but few are chosen.*

LUKE 14:12–24

[12][Jesus] said to the person who had invited him: "When you give a luncheon or a supper, do not call up your friends, your brothers or sisters, your relatives, or your rich neighbors. Probably they will return the favor and you will be repaid. [13]But when you throw a ·party, invite the poor, the crippled, the lame, and the blind. [14]Then you will be blessed, because they cannot repay you. You will be repaid in the resurrection of the just."

[15]Hearing him speak, one of the dinner guests said to him, "Blessed are those who eat bread in the kingdom of God!" [Jesus] said to him:

[16]"A man prepared a huge dinner and invited many guests. When it was dinnertime, [17]he sent slaves to those invited, saying, 'Come now because everything's ready.' [18]But one by one they began to make excuses. The first said, 'I just bought a farm and must go and look it over. Please excuse me.' [19]Another said: 'I bought five teams of oxen and I'm going off to try them out. Please excuse me.' [20]And another said, 'I married a wife and so I can't come.' [21]Coming back, the slave reported everything to his master. The master of the house was furious; he told his slave, 'Quick, go out into the streets and alleys of the city and bring back *the poor and the crippled, the lame and the blind.* [22]The slave reported, 'Sir [kyrios, Lord]· I have followed orders and there is still room for more.' Said the master [kyrios] to the slave, [23]'Then go out to the back roads and country lanes and force people to come in so that my house will be filled. [24]I'm telling you, not one of those originally invited will taste my dinner.'"

THOMAS 64:1–2

[1]Jesus said, "A man had received visitors. And when he had prepared dinner, he sent his servant to invite the guests. He went to the first one and said to him, 'My master invites you.' *He said, 'I have claims against some merchants. They are coming to me this evening. I must go and give them my orders. I ask to be excused from the dinner.'* He went to another and said to him, 'My master has invited you.' He said to him, 'I have just bought a house and am required for the day. I shall not have any spare time.' He went to another and said to him, 'My master invites you.' He said to him, 'My friend is going to get married, and I am to prepare the banquet. I shall not be able to come.' He went to another and said to him, 'My master invites you.' He said to him, 'I have just bought a farm, and I am on my way to collect the rent. I shall not be able to come. I ask to be excused.' The servant returned and said to his master, 'Those whom you invited to dinner have asked to be excused.' The master said to his servant, 'Go outside to the streets and bring back those whom you happen to meet, so they may dine.' [2]*Businessmen and merchants will not enter the Places of My Father.*

We have three versions of the parable of the Feast. Probably Luke is closer to the original, but all versions display editorial revision. Italicized text in the three versions shows where scholars guess some additions have been made. Matthew turns the feast into a wedding banquet for a king's son, adds the very hostile verse 7, and, of course, tags on the addendum about a wedding garment. Luke, who has a special concern for the oppressed, refers to "the poor and the crippled, the lame and the blind." Luke also adds a second, wider recruitment of guests, perhaps because of his interest in the missionary spread of the church. The version in *Thomas* appears to have been rewritten to add the extra invitation to a merchant. The merchant and businessman have more elaborate excuses so as to set up the peculiar moral to the story: "Businessmen and merchants will not enter the Places of My Father." Though the versions have been heavily edited, a basic scenario is quite clear (Funk 1966, 165–66).

Behind the parable of the Feast is an image of the great messianic banquet, a symbol of worldwide salvation. Here is a vision of the banquet that appears in Isaiah 25:6–10:

> On this mountain the LORD of hosts will make for all peoples
> > a feast of rich food, a feast of well-aged wines,
> > of rich food filled with marrow, of well-aged wines strained clear.
> And he will destroy on this mountain
> > the shroud that is cast over all peoples,
> > the sheet that is spread over all nations;
> > > he will swallow up death forever.
> Then the Lord GOD will wipe away the tears from all faces,
> > and the disgrace of his people he will take away from all the earth,
> > for the LORD has spoken.
> It will be said on that day
> > Lo, this is our God; we have waited for him, so that he might save us.
> This is the LORD for whom we have waited;
> > let us be glad and rejoice in his salvation.
> For the hand of the LORD will rest on this mountain.

Think of it! Our world will not end with a bang or a whimper, but in a cosmic-sized party with God and humanity feasting together!

During the intertestamental period, the festive vision was narrowed in two ways, both of which Jesus sharply opposed: (1) In *1 Enoch* 62 we are told that the elect will relax and eat at table with the Son of Man forever. These same elect ones will laugh as Gentile leaders—"kings, governors, officials, and landlords" are ousted and punished. (2) In the Qumran community there is also expectation of a messianic banquet, but only for the pure and the righteous. Gentiles and the impure will be excluded along with self-evident sinners, such as the lame, the halt, and the blind.

Obviously, national pride and ritual purity had begun to control the guest list. No wonder Jesus enacted a different image; he partied with riffraff, with known sinners and with those considered impure. He restored an inclusive vision.

Although both Matthew and Luke tell the parable differently, the basic scenario probably goes back to Jesus.

Matthew tells the story of the Feast immediately after the parable of the Tenants and before a series of controversies—questions on taxes to Caesar, on levirate marriage and resurrection, on the Great Commandment—which climax in a torrid series of "woes" against the scribes and Pharisees. Matthew interprets both parables, the Tenants and the Feast, as allegories of salvation in which Israel rejects God's son (see italicized text) and is replaced by Matthew's Jesus-believing community. Israel will be punished for faithlessness. Matthew, stirred no doubt by synagogue persecution, adds to the parable of the Feast that they "seized his slaves, humiliated and killed them," phrases he also used in the parable of the Tenants. And in verse 7 Matthew adds punishment: "So the king was enraged. He sent his army to destroy those murderers and burn their city." Then, Matthew draws the parable into his developing theme of moral judgment by adding the story of the wedding garment. Thereafter the generous grace of the parable has been edited into a familiar conclusion: "There will be weeping and grinding of teeth."

Most scholars suppose Luke's version is closer to original Jesus material. But Luke has provided a clever setting for the parable. Jesus is attending a dinner party at "the house of a leader of the Pharisees." He notices that the guests are crowding the head table to grab "places of honor." He advises guests to choose instead the lowest places so they may be invited up, for "those who humble themselves will be exalted." There are a number of rabbinic parallels to the instruction (Young 1989, 246–49), which may have been prompted by Proverbs 25:6–7.

Then Jesus discusses dinner invitations. Don't invite the rich, he advises, for they can repay you with a return invitation. Instead Jesus adds, "invite the poor, the crippled, the lame, and the blind." They can't afford a return party, so you will be "repaid in the resurrection of the just." Notice that those Jesus recommends match those recruited in the parable after original guests refused to attend.

The tag line, "resurrection of the just," prompts one enthusiastic guest to rise and intone piously, "Blessed are those who eat bread in the kingdom of God!" an obvious allusion to the great messianic banquet. In reply Jesus tells his parable.

Luke's version of the parable contains some amusing excuses. "I just bought a farm," says one man, "and must go and look it over." The excuse is an obvious sham, for no one would buy farm property without first looking it over. According to Kenneth Bailey (1980, 95–96), contracts for the sale of land had to describe all features of the property (trees, wells, etc.). Moreover, a dinner party would begin in the late afternoon; why hadn't the man checked out his real estate during the day? The excuse is patently an excuse and nothing more.

"I bought five teams of oxen," a second man says, "and I'm going off to try them out." Here is another phony excuse. Bailey supplies an amusing parallel:

> I cannot make it home tonight for dinner because I have just signed a check for five used cars, which I bought over the phone, and I am on my way down to the used car lot to find out their age and model, and see if they will start. (Bailey 1980, 98)

The second guest's excuse is not only hopelessly absurd, but insulting as well. He suggests that time with his animals is more important than dining with his host. A barefaced snub at best!

"I married a wife and so I can't come," says a third invited guest. Again, the excuse is not merely an excuse, but a crude excuse as well. Presumably the man had accepted the invitation, so why must he suddenly stay at home to service his wife? He could not have been married during the day of the party. Marriages were planned well in advance, and he would not have accepted the dinner invitation on a wedding day. Moreover, Semitic people do not discuss marital intimacies in public. To do so would be considered appallingly crude. So, again, the excuse is not only transparently false, but insulting (Bailey 1980, 98–99).

Many ministers are tempted to allegorize the excuses—land, possessions, family affairs—that keep people from God ("from church" in most sermons). Though both Luke and *Thomas* may be playing with allegorization, the issue here is not occupations or busyness. The issue is that all the excuses are outright fibs and an insult to the host. If the host is God, then these people are not too busy for God because their priorities are askew. No, they are deliberately rejecting God. The great Arab mystic al-Ghazzali says it plainly:

> Listen my friend, if you do not want to be with God, it is not because you are too busy; but because you do not like him, do not want him and you had better face the fact.[14]

There is another feature to the Lukan version. There is a double recruitment to fill the banquet table. First, servants are told to bring in "the poor and the crippled, the lame and the blind." The phrase was used in the parable's introduction and repeats. From Jesus' initial preaching in Nazareth (Luke 4:18), Luke believes the gospel message calls us to a special concern for the poor rather than the rich, and for the handicapped rather than the strong. But what about the recruiting of people from "the back roads and country lanes"? Luke seems to have symbolized his missionary concern for the spread of the gospel to other lands and peoples.

All in all, Luke's version of the parable is a pleasure to preach. But here is a warning: Watch out for Luke's final phrase—"I'm telling you, not one of those originally invited will taste my dinner." If we find ourselves feasting at Christ's table, we must not castigate those who have refused the invitation, particularly nowadays when we feast in a strangely secular land. We are not better than the secularists. No, for we may have been dragged in during the second recruitment. The secular world is nevertheless a world God loves. Inasmuch as the party has been going on for nearly twenty centuries and is still going on, God may ask us to recruit still others. After all, the messianic banquet is as big as the whole wide world.

Turn back now and ask a blunt question: What can we do with Matthew's cruel allegory? Obviously we will not hesitate to delete, "So the king . . . sent his army to destroy those murderers and burn their city." We need not turn

Matthew's outrageous hostility into "word of God." Unless we are fundamentalists, we need not canonize the sub-Christian! So, cheerfully, we will preach an expurgated version of the parable. When religious people will not come to God's party (probably because they wouldn't want to mingle with the company), God will gather in the very people we would exclude. In fact, God always gathers those we might exclude—people of other races, political rivals, those we consider evil such as sexual offenders and drug addicts. We can declare the good news from an amended version of Matthew's parable.

Here is another question: What on earth do we do with the added story of the man inappropriately dressed for a wedding? Matthew may have borrowed the story from Jewish tradition (Young 1989, 103):

> R. Johanan b. Zakai said: "This may be compared to a king who summoned his servants to a banquet without appointing a time. The wise ones adorned themselves and sat at the door of the palace, said they, 'is anything lacking in a royal palace?' The fools went about their work, saying, 'can there be a banquet without preparations?' Suddenly the king desired [the presence of] servants: the wise entered adorned, while the fools entered soiled. The king rejoiced at the wise but was angry with the fools. 'Those who adorned themselves for the banquet,' ordered he, 'let them sit, eat and drink. But those who did not adorn themselves for the banquet, let them stand and watch.' "15

In preaching Matthew's added section, two options present themselves: (1) We can simply drop the extra section on the wedding garment from the parable and preach no more than the first ten verses. After all, most parable scholars believe Matthew added the extra story. Or (2) we can design a system that works from the illogic of the odd postscript parable. You can give a congregation the puzzling addition—When you invite tramps to a party, how can you throw them out for not wearing tuxedos? They will want a solution. Obviously, Matthew's moral sense has been strained. He wants us to realize that, if we answer the call of God, we will have to spruce up our conduct.

Sermon

Here is a sermon on Matthew's version of the Feast preached in Chicago over thirty years ago and revised a decade later for a Baptist church in the South.

Introduction. Not all the parables of Jesus were original with him. Some of them were familiar stories that Jesus borrowed and retold in his own way. Probably the parable of the Great Feast was one of these, for there was an old Jewish story about a tax collector who tried to buy his way into society by throwing a party for the important people in his town. When they snubbed him by refusing his invitation, he sent servants to haul in beggars to fill his banquet table. Can you imagine his horrified neighbors watching bug-eyed as a ragtag procession of tramps paraded by their windows? Well, Jesus borrowed the story, changed it a bit, and told it as a parable. Said Jesus: "The kingdom of heaven is like a king who prepared a feast."

1   "There was a king who prepared a feast." Jesus' parable should surprise us, for if there's one thing we wouldn't think of as a picture of the Christian life, it would be a party, a great feast. We describe the Christian life as duty, as discipline, as a dread struggle with dark evil, as a somber walking with the Lord—but as a party? Never. The image is too frivolous, too glad for us. After all, living for God is serious business, isn't it? And yet Jesus told the parable and it stands in our Bibles. The kingdom of God is like a banquet. No black-suited saints with blacker Bibles, no prim souls, grim and repressed, but of all things, a party. Remember the old hymn we sing sometimes in church?

> They stand those halls of Zion
> All jubilant with song;
> The song of them that triumph,
> The shout of them that feast.[16]

There it is: Joy! The kingdom of God is joy to enter. Like a feast, said Jesus, and a wedding feast at that.

2   Well, perhaps that's why it fooled the invited guests in the parable. And perhaps that's why it fools us too. When you come right down to it, there are more important things in life than parties. There is money to make, business to conduct, and family affairs no one should neglect. If we must give up precious time, at least let it be for something more important than a party—or than a mythical kingdom of God for that matter. Be honest now, absolutely honest. If I tell you that here and now God invites you to enter the kingdom, you will listen, you will hear the words, but scarcely take them seriously. Talk of an unseen kingdom strikes us as pleasant enough, but not really real or urgent. Besides, in the back of our minds we remember that tomorrow we must get up and go to work in the world, the real world, with letters to dictate, laundry to sort, or pupils to teach. So God's invitation gathers dust in our lives. The R.S.V.P. goes unnoticed. A king invited guests to a feast but "they made light of it and went off, one to his farm, another to his business." Who's got time for a party anyway?

3   Listen: "They made light of it!" Is the parable pointing to a deeper motive? To something that lives in each of us? Wasn't it an Arab mystic who probed the diagnosis: "Listen my friend, if you do not want to be with God, it is not because you are too busy; but because you do not like [God], do not want [God] and you had better face the fact." Perhaps we'd better. The fact is, we do not want God running our lives. We prefer to make our own plans, to seek our own goals, to live free of God's interference. "Sorry God, I can't answer your call—got a previous commitment." That's exactly the term, "a previous commitment," to what? To ourselves. The excuses slide from our lips— casual, polite, but saying "No." Just as religious leaders long ago heard Jesus and turned away. Like the invited guests in the parable, "they made light of it" and refused God's invitation.

4 So, the king was furious. He said to his servants, "The feast is ready . . . Go out to the main thoroughfares and invite everyone you can find." The thoroughfares were broad highways where beggars gathered and visitors gawked, a place for the poor and for strangers passing. Perhaps the first followers of Jesus saw themselves in the parable, for they weren't what you'd call the best people in town—day laborers, slaves, outcasts, crooks; but at least they had answered Christ's call, while the religious people, the social in-group, failed to follow. Listen, and listen well! God extends the invitation now. If we will not answer, why God will find others ready to come, perhaps among the beatnik bunch or from the shout-and-holler crowd in some South Side pentecostal church. And if American Protestant people fail to hear God's claim, will not God find eager folk in India or Africa or behind the "iron curtain?" In the parable, the king sent out servants to snare beggars and lepers and outsiders for his banquet, and they came.

5 But please note: They came "both good and bad alike," says the parable, and we are shocked. Did the king in the parable have no moral values? Didn't he care what kind of people he welcomed? And can this be an image of the God we worship? Yes it can! God doesn't check references. God doesn't demand a placement test. Our neat, too neat notions of morality God sweeps aside. It doesn't matter what you've been or what you've done or how much of a mess you've made of your life. We are none of us good in the sight of God, but all of us are loved and invited to God's table. Did you read about the little girl who was found weeping because she couldn't attend a party for handicapped children? "I can't get in," she cried. "There's nothing the matter with me." On that basis, we are all eligible, for there is something the matter with all of us. Call it evil, call it sin, call it what you will, but none of us, no none, is good enough to deserve God's invitation. Yet it comes to each of us personally, and it comes now.

6 "Go out to the main thoroughfares and invite everyone," said the king; "so the hall was packed with guests." All God requires is a willingness to come. Hungry folk come quickly. Beggars hop up without question. Outcasts warm to the welcome. "Come," says God, and waits for our response. It isn't a matter of being nice or neat, pious or terribly pure; God wants your immediate response to the call. There's a family in New York City with a wonderful custom. Every Thanksgiving Day, they set tables with as many places as they can cram in their house. Then they go out into the streets and invite folk to join them—the hungry, the lonely, the homeless. Strange to say they always get a number of refusals; pride and mistrust get in the way. But others stare for a moment, wide-eyed with surprise, and they get up and follow along. Always the table is filled. Pride and suspicion still get in the way: our pride, our fear, our suspicion. But God's kingdom will be filled. In the parable the banquet hall was packed with guests.

7 The hall was packed with guests, says the parable. Then, suddenly, there's a change in the story. A strange last chapter is written for us to read. As the king walks among his guests, he spots one of them wearing a smudged, grubby robe. He points a finger at the man: "Bind him hand and foot and turn him out," he shouts to his servants. Suddenly, what seemed like a comedy turns into harsh tragedy. We don't understand. We wish the parable had ended with the filled-up banquet hall — "the song of them that triumph, the shout of them that feast" — but it didn't, and it doesn't. A strange postscript is added to the parable to trouble us. And trouble us it should, for it points to something we'd rather forget. If you enter the kingdom of God, your life must change. God calls you, yes, and the invitation is free, but if you answer, if you say, "Lord, I will follow along with you," then your whole way of life will have to change. Did you read about the TV prize contestant who won a week at the Waldorf with all expenses paid? Well, she burst into tears because, said she, "I've got to get everything new." She wanted to dress for the occasion. What else does the parable demand? God hands out an invitation we know we don't deserve, so, yes, we should want to dress our lives up in the best.

8 What does it mean for you and for me? Nothing but new life. If you come into the kingdom of God, do you think you can wear the same old prejudice you wear now? The kind of prejudice that says, "Nigger," or comments idly, "Just like a Jew." And do you really think you can get away with occasional charity? No, dress up. You will want to match God's own unlimited generosity with an extravagant love for others, particularly others in need. Anything less would be out of place in the kingdom. Anything else will seem so old and shabby. Put on the new — new attitudes, new compassion, new loves. Your old life doesn't belong at God's great party. "To use an old expression," says writer Ignazio Silone, "it's a matter of conversion. It's a matter of becoming a new [person]."[17]

Conclusion   What about the parable? Will you pass off God's call as just another parable, a quaint story from the Bible? Or will you hear the invitation now? God addresses you now. God says, "Come into the kingdom." You mustn't put it off; there's an R.S.V.P. on all God's invitations. Time to change your lives.

Discussion

The sermon's pattern is almost a verse by verse reading of the parable. Any homiletic excitement must happen in the interpretation and the language.

Introduction   The introduction works from the idea of a borrowed parable and basically retells the story. My research seems to indicate that congregations do not listen to written prose selections very well, even the biblical prose of scripture readings. Therefore, usually, we will need to put the bare plot of a parable in their minds. The last line gives listeners the sense of a story about to begin.

1   We began with the idea of a party, which is seldom the way church people think of the kingdom of God. The move is a simple system. We are surprised by the image because we define the Christian life in a somber, quite disciplined way. But the party image is glad. The quote from the hymn, "Jerusalem the Golden," evokes a little partying—shouts, songs, jubilation.

2   What I decided not to do was to slide into allegory by dealing directly with the excuses. Luke plays with the excuses, Matthew does not. In Matthew's version the guests simply did not want to come. So I trivialized the party image: "If we must give up precious time, at least let it be for something more important than a party." Then I addressed the congregation quite directly, "If I tell you that here and now . . . ," with the idea of the kingdom. Members of the congregation can discover their own tendency to dismiss the notion of a kingdom of God in favor of "real world" obligations, much as the invited guests skipped the party.

3   Here I try to penetrate the excuses with a quote from the mystic al-Ghazzali. I follow up by playing with the phrase "a previous commitment." The move may not be long enough or strong enough to register. We end the move by returning to the plot of the parable. In preaching parables we use plot movement to move the sermon along, but with this sermon I rely too much on quotes from the text.

4   Whereas the first three moves of the sermon dealt with the party invitation and our response, in move 4 we turn to the host. The shift in character creates a substantial shift in focus. Though the sermon was preached in the early sixties, it was somewhat prescient. Because mainline American Protestantism has cold-shouldered God, African and Asian Christian churches are welcoming crowds while our congregations dwindle.

5   "Both good and bad alike"—the start of the move is a bit too abrupt. As a rule, I do not think that quotes from scripture are a useful way to introduce moves. Quotes tend to split the focus of a congregation just as they are entering a new idea, for they must remember scripture and, at the same time, orient toward something new. Nevertheless, the move works out pretty well, and the illustration is on target. Of course, the move is hurt by too many sentences with the word "it."

6   The final move of the basic parable features fulfillment. The illustration of the Thanksgiving dinner should have been developed a bit, perhaps, with a little dialogue connected with pride and suspicion: "What's the catch?" or "I ain't good enough for you folks." The illustration does well but then may seem to go flat. The move ends where the first part of the parable ends: The banquet hall is filled with guests.

7   The move does not begin abruptly enough. Foolishly, I echo the last line of the previous move, and then work into the additional Wedding Garment parable, losing any abrupt surprise. Then I deliberately try to involve the congregation with the puzzling addition. I needed to use more imagery such as, "When you invite bums to dinner, can you expect a tuxedo?" The illustration of the woman crying when she wins a prize is a good one.

8 The final move is badly developed. What's more, the move ends in a quote, which is never wise. (Preachers should speak directly toward the end of a sermon and not import quoted voices.) If the examples of prejudice are blunt (and they are), then images of new life must be brighter and more compelling (and they are not). The preacher must have been getting tired! The move should be redeveloped and, above all, vividly imaged.

Conclusion   The conclusion is dreadfully weak. As a result, I suspect I "rewrote" the conclusion as the sermon was preached. But I have no rewritten text available. Often preachers will sense a weakness in conclusion and ad lib a new ending. I can only hope I did so.

The parable of the Feast must never be historicized—those Jews refused God's invitation, but we Christians can feast with God. Anti-Semitism is simply disallowed in Christian pulpits. No, the parable speaks of God and God's call which is for all humanity. The sermon should feature an evangelical articulation of God's call, and our response.

CLOSED DOOR
(Matthew 25:1–13; Luke 13:25)

MATTHEW 25:1–13

¹The kingdom of the heavens then will be like ten girls who took their lamps and went out to meet the bridegroom. ²Five were wise and five were foolish. ³When the foolish took their lamps, they did not take any oil along; ⁴but the wise took containers of oil along with their lamps. ⁵Because the bridegroom was delayed, they became drowsy and they all fell asleep. ⁶But at midnight, there was a shout, "Look, here comes the bridegroom, come out to meet him." ⁷Then all the girls got up and trimmed their lamps. ⁸The foolish said to the wise, "Give us some of your oil for our lamps are going out." ⁹But the wise ones answered saying, "No, we don't have enough for us and you, go to dealers and buy some for yourselves." ¹⁰But while they went off to buy the bridegroom came, and those who were ready went with him to the wedding feast. The door was shut. ¹¹Afterward the other girls came, saying, "Lord, Lord, open up for us." ¹²But he answered and said, "I'm telling you, truly, I don't know you." ¹³So watch, for you don't know the day or hour.

LUKE 13:25

Once the homeowner has got up and shut the door and you're standing outside knocking at the door, saying, "Lord, open up for us"; answering, he will say to you, "I don't know where you're from."

Most contemporary parable scholars suspect that the Closed Door is not original Jesus material. Matthew is quite certain that Christ will return to judge the wicked and vindicate the righteous, so he has assembled a series of four harsh parables all in a row (Matt. 24:45–25:46)—the Unfaithful Servant, the Closed Door, the Talents, and the Last Judgment. But did Jesus tell the Closed Door?

The Closed Door is probably a non-Jesus scenario for five reasons: (1) Many modern scholars do not suppose that Jesus told parables about the return of a "Son of Man," particularly if the mysterious cloud-borne Son of Man is Jesus himself. (2) The parable is a moralistic message without much depth. A full-scale parable from Jesus that adds up to little more than the Boy Scout motto, "Be Prepared," is unlikely. (3) Most Jesus parables seem to have a kind of trickiness, a sudden reversal or, sometimes, a kind of funny wit. The Closed Door is too obvious. (4) The parable delivers an appeal-based threat. Jesus does not normally voice such appeals. (5) Finally, for good reason, recent scholarship considers second-coming material secondary, a product of eager early Christianity.

Whether Jesus told the parable or not, it is still in our Christian writings and is often included in lectionaries for preaching. Preachers probably will have to deal with the Closed Door, or with some of the parallel material in Luke 13:22–30. What do we do?

The problem is intensified by the cosmic background. We can preach "Be Prepared," urging people to be alert, watch for opportunities to serve neighbors in need, or recognize crises in which Christians must testify to their faith. But the parable seems to presume a second-coming "Day of the Lord" in which the world will conclude and a new aeon commence. Bluntly, contemporary churchgoers, though as gullible as any, do find it difficult to suppose a triumphant return of the Lord Jesus. Such passages cannot be reduced to personal crisis sermons. Somehow the cosmic dimension must emerge. The question is, How?

Another feature of the parable might be noted. When the door is closed, the girls cry, "Lord, Lord, open up for us!" The double "Lord, Lord," has been used by Matthew before. Remember the conclusion to Matthew's Sermon on the Mount:

> Not everyone who says to me, "Lord, Lord," will enter the kingdom of heaven, but only the one who does the will of my Father in heaven. On that day many will say to me, "Lord, Lord, did we not prophesy in your name, and cast out demons in your name, and do many deeds of power in your name?" Then I will declare to them, "I never knew you; go away from me, you evildoers."
>
> "Everyone then who hears these words of mine and acts on them will be like a wise man who built his house on rock. The rain fell, the floods came, and the winds blew and beat on that house, but it did not fall, because it had been founded on rock. And everyone who hears these words of mine and does not act on them will be like a foolish man who built his house on sand. The rain fell, and the floods came, and the winds blew and beat against that house, and it fell—and great was its fall!" (Matt. 7:21–27)

In the passage, Matthew not only uses the phrase, "Lord, Lord," but he also sets up a contrast between the wise and the foolish, a pattern we can see in the Closed Door. Matthew has set up a concluding warning at the end of the Sermon on the Mount and then, later, he brings back the same contrast ("wise" and "foolish") and the same confessional cry ("Lord, Lord") in the parable of the Closed Door.

There was a rabbinic debate in first-century Judaism over which was the most virtuous, the study of Torah or the obedient doing of Torah. The same debate is reflected in the parable of the Two Children, where there is a debate over intent, "I will," and action, "I do" (Young 1989, 252–54). Matthew wants action.

The parable does require some biblical background about first-century wedding practices. Jeremias offers research to support the notion that weddings might commence with a bridegroom showing up at night, greeted by bridesmaids with their lamps lit. Then the bridal party would parade to the house of the bridegroom's father for a ceremony and banqueting celebration (Jeremias 1963, 171–75). But wise preachers will always avoid long descriptions of biblical practice in their sermons. Sermons are not Bible study sessions; they preach a gospel *now*.

Sermon

Here is a sample sermon from 1965, subsequently published in an abbreviated form in *Presbyterian Life:*

Introduction   Weddings in Palestine were seldom on schedule. Instead the bridal party would gather and wait. They waited because they never knew when the groom would arrive and the festivities begin. Sometime during the day or the night a messenger would run the streets to announce the bridegroom's coming. Come he would! If the bridesmaids were not ready, they could be left behind and miss the celebration. If you were a bridesmaid, you had to be ready, prepared to follow at a moment's notice.

1   "Be prepared" is what the parable says, the parable of the Ten Bridesmaids, be prepared, be alert, be on your toes. We wonder why Jesus told such a story. Did he sense that a crisis in his own life was near? Did he dimly see the shadow of the cross, the thorny crown, the climb to Calvary? Perhaps he knew his death would be terror and doubt for his disciples. How could they stay loyal while a crowd cried against him? How would they fare when he was gone? The moment of trial was near, so Jesus told the parable of the bridesmaids to say, Be prepared.

2   "Be prepared" is what the parable says today. You never know the hour when you will be asked to stand loyal to Christ. Any day, perhaps every day, is crisis. Surely we who have lived through the traumas of this mid-century world should understand the parable. Did not the push for civil rights catch churches unprepared? And the belated welcome mat we tossed out to a people who were justly impatient was a sign of our unreadiness. Now the crisis of military escalation quickens fantasies of atomic fury. Are we prepared to speak out for the Lord of Peace? How hard it is to shake awake and obey the Lord. You never know the day or hour unless you're alert, unless you're prepared.

3 Is there anything worse than to miss the moment? The parable says there isn't. Nothing is more painful than to sense that the time is passed and it's too late; you didn't speak, you didn't act. You shrug your shoulders, shake your head, but you can't fade the memory of failure. "Too late" is a pathetic epitaph. The foolish five in the parable missed their moment. Said the bridegroom: "I declare I do not know you."

4 The parable says more. It says that the crisis in which we live involves the whole world—all nations and races. Early Christians believed that they were living in the last act of a cosmic drama. Christ had come saying, "The kingdom of God is at hand." His disciples were sure that it was only a matter of time before God would ring down the curtain on this world, destroy evil, and establish the promised kingdom. The world would not whirl on forever but would come to a grand conclusion in God's purpose.

5 Of course, it hasn't happened, has it? The world goes on now as always, no worse, no better. We wonder if talk of a Last Day is not a pious pipe dream, an ancient superstition the Bible once believed which we have outgrown. So we hang a sign on our lives saying, "business as usual," and laugh away all thought of final crisis. No hurry over social righteousness. No need to accelerate the march for civil rights. No push for peace in our generation. "Business as usual," we say; the end is not in sight.

> Starch the bedroom curtains,
> Shine the silver tray,
> Put on a little make-up—
> Here comes the Judgment Day.[18]

The chorus to that tune ends in silly laughter!

6 The early Christians shared the same doubts. Their world didn't end as expected. Christ did not come conquering, and evil seemed inconsiderately stubborn. But then they remembered the parable and told it to each other, for the parable reminded them that the earth is not timed by orbits, by turn of the moon or flame of the sun, but by God's will. God has written the script, beginning and end. We cannot ask the day or the hour, nor can we know. But we can be alert to God's word every day, and prepare to serve God come what may. Says the parable: Be prepared.

Conclusion   But for what? For what do we make ready? For joy. That's what the parable holds before us, joy. Does not Jesus picture a wedding celebration, festive and glad? We do not live our lives cringing before the threat of singeing hell, or cowering before the rap of a judge's gavel. No, we make ready for a joyful hullabaloo we wouldn't want to miss. The Lord is coming, says the parable—be alert, be faithful, prepare for the day. Something worth waiting for, isn't it? And living for.

Discussion

The sermon is designed to begin in our day-to-day lives, talking about prepared-ness. But notice that with move 4, the sermon shifts to a worldwide, human-history dimension.

Introduction   I designed an introduction to deliver a little biblical back-ground. Thus a congregation received information about Semitic weddings as well as a thematic, "Be Prepared." What's more, I have accomplished all in seven sentences, which is about right for an introduction.

1   I look back at this sermon written in 1965 and am distressed. Obviously I accepted a more conservative reading of the parable. I assumed Jesus told the parable of the Closed Door and, therefore, tried to explain how and when he might have done so. Now I would talk of the parable as a product of early Chris-tian understandings and never attribute it to Jesus, not even in a sermon. Why don't people know about biblical scholarship? Maybe because we preachers hide facts regarding scholarship in our sermons. But this sermon, written more than twenty years ago, explains how Jesus must have told the parable.

2   The start of the move switches time to the present day. Then a "you" sen-tence seems to set a personal tone—"you will be asked to stand loyal to Christ." But quickly (and deliberately) we shift to a social example. Virtually all ethical commands in the Christian scriptures are addressed to a corporate body, the church. The Christian sense of corporate identity precluded much discussion of one-to-one ethics. In the sixties the church (belatedly) was coping with civil rights issues, and was beginning to speak out on issues of war and peace.

3   Here a move has been abbreviated to reduce the sermon for publication, but the character of the move is obvious. Here I have personalized the experience of "Too late!" The move ends with a hard line from the parable: "I do not know you."

4   Now I attempt to broaden the parable reference to a cosmic drama. I use dramatic imagery—"last act," "ring down the curtain," "grand conclusion"—to portray early Christian conviction.

5   Then I turn to a contemporary reaction: The kingdom hasn't come; there-fore, we can ignore Christ's ethical demands and pursue business as usual. I pick up the social issues posed earlier in the sermon, civil rights and peace. Then I add an edgy satiric poem by Edith Lovejoy Pierce.

6   The sermon now turns back to the early Christians who were skeptical when the world didn't end and the kingdom had not arrived. But then I affirm that the world is not mindless motion, orbiting in space. No, creation is still ulti-mately under God's governance. We are responsible to God's purposes.

Conclusion   All of a sudden, I pick up the theme of a wedding celebration. Though Matthew may use second-coming passages as a moral threat, we must not forget that the idea of the second coming includes a great messianic banquet. In God's purposes, the world ends neither with a bang nor a whimper, but a "glad hullabaloo." We look forward to a party.

The conclusion suggests a strategy for preachers who must interpret somewhat intense second-coming passages. Ultimately such passages must be transformed by the gladness found in both Jewish and Christian eschatology. What do we wait for? A party, of all things, a party!

ENTRUSTED MONEY
(Matthew 25:14–30; Luke 19:11–27)
Italicized words represent editorial additions by Matthew
and Luke to the parable they received from Q.

MATTHEW 25:14–30

[14]When a man was leaving home, he called in his slaves and turned his business affairs over to them. [15]To one he gave ten thousand dollars, to another four thousand, and to another two thousand; to each according to ability. Then he went away. [16]The one getting ten thousand immediately went out and by trading earned another ten. [17]In the same way, the one with four thousand earned another four. [18]But the one who got two thousand dollars dug a hole in the ground and buried his boss's money. [19]Then, *after a long time*, the boss came back to settle his accounts with the slaves. [20]Coming up, the one getting ten thousand brought another ten, saying, "Boss [*kyrie* = Lord], you gave me ten thousand dollars; look, I've earned another ten." [21]The boss said to him, " Well done, good and faithful slave; you were faithful over a few things, I will put you over many; *come on, celebrate with your boss* [literally, "enter into the joy of your Lord"]." [22]Coming up also, the one getting four thousand dollars said, "Boss, you gave me four thousand; look, I've earned another four." [23]The boss said to him, "Well done, good and faithful slave; you were faithful over a few things, I will put you over many; *come on, celebrate with your boss.*" [24]And coming up also the one getting two thousand said, "Boss, I knew you to be a hard man, harvesting where you haven't sown, and gathering where you haven't scattered, [25]so, afraid, I went off and hid your money in the ground; look, here you are." [26]Answering him, the boss said, "You no-good, lazy slave! You knew I harvest where I haven't sown, and gather where I haven't scattered, [27]you should have turned my money over to brokers so that I could have received it back with interest. [28]Therefore, take the two thousand dollars from him and give it to the man with ten thousand. [29]*For everyone who has shall have more, but from those with little even what they have will be taken away.* [30]*Throw the useless slave out into the dark—there will be wailing and grinding of teeth!*

LUKE 19:11–27

[11b]Jesus told a parable because as he was nearing Jerusalem, [the disciples] thought the kingdom of God would suddenly appear. [12]So he said, *A certain nobleman went off to a distant country to secure a kingdom for himself and then return.* [13]Calling in ten of his slaves, he gave them each a thousand dollars, and said to them, "Trade while I'm away." [14]*But his citizens hated him and sent a delegation after him with a petition, saying, "We don't want this man to rule us."* [15]*It so happened, after he returned from securing a kingdom,* he called in the slaves to whom he had given money, wanting to see if anyone had made a profit trading. [16]The first one came saying, "Boss, your thousand made ten thousand more." [17]He said to him, "Well done, good slave; because you were faithful over a small matter, you will be in charge of ten cities."[18]The second came saying, "Boss, your thousand dollars made five thousand more." [19]He said to him also, "You will be in charge of five cities." [20]Another came saying, "Boss, look, *I wrapped up your thousand and put it safely away,* [21]for I was afraid of you. You are a hard man; you take out what you haven't deposited, and you reap what you haven't sown." [22]He answered him, "By your own words, I will judge you, you no-good slave. Since you knew I was a hard man, taking what I haven't deposited, and reaping what I haven't sown, [23]why didn't you put my money in the hands of a banker [literally, "on the table," meaning a money changer's table] so when I returned there would be earned interest? [24]Then he said to those standing by, "Take the thousand dollars from him and give to the one with ten. [25]*They said to him, "Sir, he already has ten thousand."* [26]*"I tell you to everyone who has, more will be given, and to those who don't even what they have will be taken away.* [27]*Now, about those enemies of mine who didn't want me to rule them, bring them here and kill them in my sight."*

There are two versions of the parable of the Entrusted Money, one in Matthew and another in Luke. Both versions have been heavily edited so that the vocabulary is quite different, yet the underlying structure probably goes back to an original Jesus scenario. In Matthew the parable appears following the "little apocalypse," which ends with contrasting images of faithful and unfaithful servants (24:45–51). Then Matthew has three parables in a row: the Closed Door, the Entrusted Money, and the climactic vision of the Last Judgment. Obviously Matthew has interpreted the parable of the Entrusted Money as referring to the second coming of Christ. Matthew's editing shows up with "after a long time" in verse 19, as well as the phrase "enter into the joy of your Lord" that occurs twice and would have been understood as a reference to the great eschatological banquet. Finally, Matthew has added verses 29–30 with his familiar picture of those who do not pass muster before the Lord: "Throw the useless slave out into the dark—there will be wailing and grinding of teeth!"

Even with his editing, Matthew's version appears to be closer to the original scenario than Luke's rather labored parable of the *mnas,* "minas." Luke makes the "boss" into a nobleman who goes off to make a deal securing a territory for himself. Unfortunately, the people in the territory protest, "We don't want this man to rule us." The subplot concludes with an added verse 27: "Now, about those enemies of mine who didn't want me to rule them, bring them here and kill them in my sight." But the added material, an overdrawn theological allegory, does not fit the structure of the parable terribly well. By spotting the editorial additions, we can reduce the parable to a basic shape for discussion.

The amounts of money involved are quite different. A talent today would be worth around three hundred thousand dollars, so that the five-talent servant would be investing more than a million dollars. Yet Matthew has the boss praise him for being faithful over a little. By contrast, Luke's mina would be worth no more than five thousand dollars. But the amounts are not terribly important in the way the parable works—in translating, I have used much lower figures. The issue is not how much money, but what the servants do with their cash.

Though there are three servants involved (storytellers tend to employ triads), actually they may be scaled down to type A and type B. Type A invests money, earns a return, is praised, and is given more responsibility. In contrast, type B plays safe; he buries the money and when his boss returns he hands back the cash without loss. After all, putting money in the ground is normal protection in an age without banks. (Luke has his play-it-safe servant wrap the money and stow it away.) Nonetheless, the type B servant is condemned, "You no-good, lazy slave!" his boss declares. The parable reads like a TV Western—the good guys versus the bad guy, all cut and dried. But watch out, the parable may be trickier than it seems.

Check out the dialogue. The type B servant explains himself. He safely buried the cash because, "I knew you to be a hard man, reaping where you haven't sown, and gathering where you haven't scattered so, afraid, I went off and hid your money in the ground." Often sermons castigate the servant for his fears; surely he has misunderstood his generous boss and, confused by his own fears, mismanaged the money. But no, the boss agrees with the servant's appraisal. He says in effect, Yes, indeed, I am unscrupulous: "I reap where I haven't sown and gather where I haven't scattered." Therefore the boss is blunt: "You should have turned my money over to brokers so that I could have received it back with interest." We get the picture! If we deal with a ruthless, greedy boss, we have to invest and produce a return or we need not expect a reward.

But what happens to the parable if we reverse the figure of the boss (as we would with the crooked judge) and say, "Look, our God is not a ruthless, exploitive God"? If we reverse the boss's moral status, then we end up out of the parable, trying to figure out how to conduct our lives in response to a free-grace God. We don't play it safe, because God is patient and ever merciful. But we don't *have* to invest, produce, and hand over a profit either to get along with God. No, if God is a free giver, we can step out of the parable and be free givers as well.

Has our espousal of capitalism prevented us from hearing the parable? Perhaps. Or maybe clergy using the parable in connection with church fund-raising have blinded our sight. Without really hearing the parable, we tend to assign hero status to the investors. Of course, Matthew has done the same thing — morally investing yourself will earn approval when God hands out rewards and punishments in the judgment.

How do we preach the parable? Initially, let's admit that the parable has nothing to do with innate abilities, with what we sometimes call "talents." The word "talent" comes from the parable, but should not be used to interpret the story. The parable may have been spoken to Sadducees and Pharisees. The Sadducees lived within the law, playing it safe, guarding their religious purity. The Pharisees, on the other hand, were pietists; they intended to extend God's law into all areas of their lives, investing their energies in virtue so as to glean a reward in the resurrection of the just. Although Jesus guards God's law — "not one iota, not one stroke of a letter, will pass from the law until all is accomplished" (Matt. 5:18) — and indeed urges radical virtues, obviously his love commandment poses a broader way.

The parable of the Entrusted Money may be the trickiest parable we have. Although it is fun to preach, the reversals in the parable are difficult to manage. Obviously Matthew, and also Luke, has turned the scenario into a reward/punishment story, but a careful reading of the dialogue — "Boss, I knew you to be a hard man" and "You knew I harvest where I haven't sown, and gather where I haven't scattered" — will display the boss's admission. (In Luke, the admission is even more obvious: "Since you knew I was a hard man . . .") The boss is indeed a "hard man" who openly admits his ruthlessness! The parable must be reversed: Our God is not ruthless.

Sermon

This "sermonette" from 1982 was originally designed to fit into a brief theological seminary chapel service, but was recently revised:

Introduction A few years ago there was an off-Broadway show. The show was a satire on TV Westerns. At the beginning of the play, you knew who the characters were because some wore white hats and some black, heroes and villains. But halfway through the show the actors started trading hats, and by the final curtain there were no hats at all. Some of the parables of Jesus are as tricky. Servants who take a risk are rewarded; they're heroes, while the servant who buries his cash is clearly a villain. But by the end of the parable, you're not so sure. What began as melodrama has turned into theater of the absurd. Well, here we are — curtain going up on a parable.

1 Do you have any doubt about the villain in the parable? He's the man who played it safe. "No-good, lazy servant," says the boss, and we agree. Is there anything worse than a play-it-safe, no risk, hold-on-for-dear-life human

being? Or a play-it-safe church for that matter? The fact is our mainline
Protestant churches have been playing it safe ever since the frightening nineteen sixties. That old missionary chant, "The World for Christ in Our Generation," has given way to a more cautious slogan; something like, "Cut your
losses." Even the Southern Baptists have succumbed. The old evangelistic
bravado, "A Million More in '74," has been scaled down: "Lord, let's be
sedate in '98." As for ministers, we are equally cautious. We talk of the virtues
of pluralism, take courses in conflict management, and above all, hand out
positive self-images from the pulpit. Remember the famous French bishop
who was asked what he did during the Revolution? "I survived," he said
sweetly. Motto for churches in the nineteen nineties: "Survive!" But is there
anything worse than play-it-safe Christianity? "You lazy, no-good servant,"
cried the boss. At least the villain is easy to spot.

2 But now, who are the heroes? Heroes in the parable are as obvious: some of
the workers took a risk. They invested themselves and earned a return. "You
should invest," the boss says, and they did. They risked everything they had
and came up winners. "Good and faithful servants," says the boss. You almost
can see him handing out the gold watches, or perhaps the vice-presidencies.
Oh, we know ministers should not be workaholics, that every minister should
take time off for personal pleasure, else risk burnout. Nevertheless, down
deep, most of us respect the minister who gives and gives and never stops giving. If the phone rings in the middle of the night, it's off to the hospital at once.
If there's a nasty marital mess in the parish, the minister's not afraid to wade
in. As for the pulpit, we do admire the minister who takes a brave stand whatever the risks. Last summer a tiny Michigan town honored a part-time pastor
who'd served there—Would you believe it?—for thirty years. They handed
him a plaque: "Good and faithful servant," it said across the top. And underneath there was a wonderful one-liner: "You gave yourself away." A hero, our
kind of hero. "Since I am ruthless," the boss announced, "Since I am ruthless,
you should invest!" Some workers did invest themselves. So you know who
the heroes are, don't you?

3 Wait a minute, hold on, what was it the boss said? "Since I am ruthless . . ."
Look, our God is a God of love. You spell God's name, L-O-V-E. God is not
ruthless, demanding you produce in order to earn a reward. No, we affirm
God's love. What else do you see at Calvary but love? "Love so amazing, so
divine," it takes your breath away. See a balky, self-interest world rung round
the cross—clanking soldiers, power politics, cautious priests, and a carnival
crowd whooping it up for capital punishment. And what do you hear? "Forgive them. Forgive them, they know not what they do." Well, you can't label
those words ruthless. They are the substance of love. Heard about a Catholic
church up in Indiana. After Vatican II, they tore down their crucifix—life-
sized, with a spear in Jesus' side and blood painted on his brow beneath
a crown of thorns. Instead, they strung up a chain of letters across the chan-
cel—L-O-V-E. But, after a while the wall seemed a little saccharine until

somebody got the bright idea of hanging the old crucifix over the words. You look at the cross and the only way to make sense of it is to talk of love. "Since I am ruthless," the boss said, "Since I am ruthless, you should invest." But, guess what, our God isn't ruthless.

Conclusion   Question: How do we do a common ministry—you and your minister together? Answer: On the far side of the parable! The parable offers too few options: either we play it safe or we invest for a reward. The options are too few. Instead, guess what? You're going to have to figure ministry out for yourselves. How do we minister in a free-grace world, where hidden, huge, behind all that comes our way, is love, nothing but LOVE spelled out in great God-sized letters? The only way to be a Christian church and a Christian minister is to walk clear out of the parable and, once and for all, shut the door behind you. You can live in the strange, eerie, insecure world of grace. And, in such a world do your ministry.

Originally the sermon was limited to fit into a brief chapel framework, limiting moves and forcing a final move-conclusion combination. But a number of the seminary's students, thrown a bit by the sermon's open-endedness, hung around to talk about what they had heard.

Discussion

Introduction   The introduction is a little trickier than it seems. We set up an image of the Western satire—white hats and black hats—and then subvert the image. Then we liken the image to Jesus' parable. Why? We want our congregation to anticipate a switch of some sort, so, though they will recognize heroes and villain, they will be a little unsure, ready for a surprise.

1   In the first move, we deal with the servant who buries his money, but we line up the image with cautious mainline Protestant denominations. The gag line about the Southern Baptists was deliberate; there were Southern Baptist seminarians also on hand. Notice that the critique begins with denominations being cautious before turning to ministers. Congregations will accept personal criticism more easily in such a stepped-down structure, from the social to personal. The move is framed by dialogue from the parable, "You lazy, no-good servant!"

2   The second move recognizes the "heroes" who are rewarded. Notice that I deliberately leave off the Matthean "enter into the joy of your Lord." In the second move, I reverse the pattern and deal with personal ministerial patterns of behavior. I am eager to have my audience affirm ministers who will risk themselves. The second move also is framed in dialogue from the parable, "You should invest," and then as the move concludes, "Since I am ruthless, you ought to invest."

3   The next move counters the dialogue: Our God is *not* ruthless. If I had had more time, I could have developed the legalisms of "you should invest"—basically a form of "works" theology. Instead I stressed the alternative: Our God is love. I introduced the image of the cross. The illustration puts the cross and love together.

Conclusion   The conclusion is half a conclusion and half a new move, a dangerous practice. But we had to establish that ministry, authentic free-grace ministry, has to step out of the parable, beyond either playing it safe or investing for a reward.

The parable of the Entrusted Money in Matthew and Luke is used frequently to encourage pledges for the church, presumably suggesting that there may be a reward in the offing. Disastrous! Can you put together going for a payoff with the bulk of Jesus' teaching? No, not at all. Matthew is clearly urging moral investment in order to secure a place at table in the messianic banquet. But we can step beyond Matthew and recover the power of an original parable. When we read the parable of the Unjust Judge who finally gives in to the widow, we must reverse the image, saying our God is not an unjust judge. Likewise, in the parable of the Entrusted Money, we must reverse the one-liner, "Since I am ruthless . . ." When we do so, the impulse for investment or playing it safe both dissolve. We are left to live our ministry outside the terms of the parable.

8

Parables in Luke

Luke draws on Mark for four parables and on Q for nine. But eleven of Luke's parables are from some unknown source that scholars label "L." Most of the major parables are told on Jesus' way to Jerusalem in Luke's famous "travel narrative" (Luke 9:51–19:44).

Luke's special parables are quite different from those in Mark and Matthew. John Drury (1985, 112–14) argues that the parables match Luke's theology of history. Luke regards Christ Jesus as the midpoint in the human story; he is the crux of history. Parables in Luke also seem to display crucial turning points.

Luke's Gospel begins with a two-chapter "Christmas Oratorio" featuring solo voices and angel choirs. Chapter one begins the story with, "In the days of King Herod of Judea . . ." Chapter two switches: "In those days a decree went out from Emperor Augustus . . ." Luke has constructed a perfect prologue to his two-volume work of Gospel and Acts.

Volume one, the Gospel, is a story of Jesus in Israel. After his baptism by John, his temptation, and the rejection in Nazareth, Jesus calls disciples and begins his ministry in Galilee. Almost at once he tangles with Jewish leaders. In his Gospel, Luke pictures Jesus moving with determination on the way to Jerusalem, where conflict with Jewish leadership will harden into organized opposition. The Gospel ends in Jerusalem with Jesus' climactic death, his resurrection, and his astonishing Elijah-like ascension.

Volume two, Acts, is about the Jesus movement. In Acts, Luke tells the second half of his story, a story that begins in Jerusalem but widens out into the empire. Apostles, instructed by the word of Christ and animated by his lively Spirit, preach good news to every land. The church spreads out all over the world. For Luke, Jesus' death and resurrection in Jerusalem is the turning point of human history.

Drury argues that most of Luke's major parables seem to feature a turning point, a crisis midway in the story. The prodigal son is in crisis, starving in the far country. The dishonest steward is in crisis when he is suddenly fired from his position. The rich farmer faces the crisis of an enormous harvest he must manage. The rich man and Lazarus are in crisis when suddenly they die. Not every parable fits Drury's schemes, but many do.

Often crisis is signaled by an internal dialogue. There are such "soliloquies" in the Rich Farmer, the Prodigal Son, the Dishonest Steward, the Unjust Judge, the Tenants, and the Pharisee and the Publican. The inner dialogues sum up the plight of a central character and prompt new resolve. For example, the prodigal says to himself, "How many of my father's hired hands have plenty of bread, while I am dying of drought. I will get up and go to my father, and I will say . . ." Thus, in crisis, he decides to head for home.

Everyone has noticed that Luke's characters seem to be flesh and blood human beings; they are not stock representational figures.[1] They have motivations, they display passion, they err, they reach for redemption. Of all things, Luke features a number of crooks as central characters: a resentful older brother, a ruthless profiteering boss, a clever but dishonest manager, a corrupt judge, a nouveau riche "rich man," a pompous Pharisee, a sleazy publican. What an astonishing collection!

Many of Luke's characters have trouble with money. The prodigal wastes it, a servant fails to invest, a widow presses a case involving money, the rich man will not share with a beggar, and so forth. Luke supposes that money, if not the root of all evil, is definitely a problem.[2] He seems to approve of the dishonest steward who marked down bills owed his boss in order to make some friends, for, though prompted by self-interest, at least he stepped out of the profit motive and into charity.

Throughout Luke's parables is special concern for the poor, the handicapped, and social outcasts. Early in the Gospel, Jesus announces his role as an evangelical liberator: "to bring good news to the poor . . . to proclaim release to the captives and recovery of sight to the blind, to let the oppressed go free." No wonder Lazarus, a scaly beggar, is elevated and a rich man dropped into hot Hades. And Luke describes substitute guests in the parable of the Feast as "the poor and the crippled, the lame and the blind." He also champions the widow who pleads for justice.

Many of Luke's parables feature food. The Closed Door and the Feast mention banqueting. In the Friend at Midnight, though growling, a neighbor provides bread. The Lost Sheep and the Lost Coin end up in joyful parties. The Rich Man and Lazarus features banqueting. And the rich farmer looks forward to eating and drinking. There should be fruit to eat on the Barren Tree. The dishonest steward hopes to be welcomed at table in the homes of those whose bills he reduced. Some scholars wonder if Luke's fondness for feasting derives from his eucharistic interest that shows up often in both the Gospel and Acts.

Luke seems to smooth the edges of Matthew's more spiky parables of judgment. There is more humor in Luke's parables and sometimes a delight in surreal exaggeration. Luke is less intense and seems to have a broader tolerance for human error and moral failure.

Chapter fifteen is a crucial chapter. In it Jesus is accused by scribes and Pharisees who say, "This man welcomes sinners and eats with them." In reply Jesus heaps up parables: the Lost Sheep, the Lost Coin, the (Lost) Prodigal Son. In each case there is joy in finding a lost sinner who repents. The chapter is not only the heart of Luke's Gospel but the theme of many parables (Donahue 1988, 146–62). In Jesus Christ, God visits humanity with mercy—wide, wide mercy.

PARABLES IN LUKE

Good Samaritan	Luke 10:30–35	
Friend at Midnight	Luke 11:5–8	
Rich Farmer	Luke 12:16–20 *Thomas* 63:1–2	Sermon
Barren Tree	Luke 13:6–9	
Lost Coin	Luke 15:8–9	
Prodigal Son	Luke 15:11–32	Sermon
Dishonest Steward	Luke 16:1–8a	Sermon
Rich Man and Lazarus	Luke 16:19–26	
Undeserving Servants	Luke 17:7–10	
Unjust Judge	Luke 18:2–5	
Pharisee and Publican	Luke 18:10–14a	

GOOD SAMARITAN

LUKE 10:25–37

25See, this lawyer stood up and tried to trap him, saying, "Teacher, what must I do to inherit eternal life?" 26[Jesus] said to him: "What is written in the law? How do you interpret it?" 27And, answering, he said, "You shall love the Lord your God with all your heart, with all your soul, with all your energy, and with all your mind; and your neighbor as yourself." 28And he said to him: "You've got it right. Do so and you will live." 29But wanting to justify himself, he said to Jesus, "And who is my neighbor?" 30Replying, Jesus said:

"A man was going down from Jerusalem to Jericho and fell into the hands of robbers. They stripped him, beat him up, and went away, leaving him half dead. 31It so happened that a priest was going that way but, seeing the man, he circled around him. 32Likewise, a Levite, coming to the spot, took one look and circled around. 33But a traveling Samaritan came on him and was all choked up. 34Going to him, he bandaged his wounds, pouring on olive oil and wine. Putting the man on his own animal, he got him to an inn and took care of him. 35In the morning, he took out eighty dollars and, giving it to the manager, he said, 'Take care of him and, if you spend more, I'll settle up when I come through again.'

36In your opinion, which of the three was neighbor to the man who fell into the hands of robbers? 37He answered, 'The one who showed compassion to him.' Jesus said: 'Go and do the same.'"

Is the story of the Good Samaritan the most familiar of all parables? Perhaps. The phrase "good samaritan" has entered our language. We give "Good Samaritan" awards for persons who offer unusual, lifesaving helpfulness. We establish "Samaritan" counseling centers and "Samaritan" hospitals. The parable is usually preached as Luke presents it: the Samaritan is good, the perfect model of neighborly love, and we should all go and do likewise. But lately scholars have questioned if Luke's interpretation could have been what Jesus had in mind.

Luke has written a prologue and an epilogue to the parable. The prologue, involving questions from a lawyer, is peculiar because it seems to echo the story of the Rich Young Ruler (Luke 18:18–25): "Teacher, what must I do to inherit eternal life?" Does Luke want readers to associate the two episodes? In any event, the lawyer recites the Great Commandment, which combines the Shema (Deut. 6:4–5) with Leviticus 19:18 on neighbor love—the combination had become a kind of credo within early Christian communities. Jesus responds: "Go and do so!" Whereupon the lawyer has a follow up question: "Who," he asks, "is my neighbor?"

The question is a good one, now as then. Does proximity make a neighbor? Does our common humanity? Are neighbors the like-minded? In an "us" and "them" world, are there exclusions, enemies we would not include in a list of neighbors? Do national or racial boundaries define a "hood" and therefore neighbors? The questions are still live issues. In answer to a good question, Luke follows with the parable of the Good Samaritan.

After the parable, Luke adds an epilogue. Jesus asks the question, "Which one of the characters in the story was neighbor to the man in the ditch? Answer: "The one who showed compassion." Then Jesus repeats his urging, "Go and do." But notice there is a kind of disjunction between prologue and epilogue. In the prologue the question is, Who is neighbor? Now in the epilogue the question seems to have turned into, What is neighborliness? The prologue/epilogue framework seems somewhat contrived. But remember, Luke is recasting a very Jewish parable for a quite different Gentile audience.

The parable itself is unusual because, of all the parables, it features actual place names, Jerusalem and Jericho. Parables, like fairy tales, are usually in a fictional "somewhere," and do not include place names. A boss goes off somewhere and then returns. A farmer sows seed somewhere. A woman loses a coin somewhere. A gardener digs manure around a barren tree somewhere. There is seldom mention of any particular "where." Here, a particular road, the road from Jerusalem to Jericho, actually is identified. The story of the Good Samaritan is a Jewish story with Jewish place names and decidedly Jewish characters, a priest and a Levite.

Now let us ask an odd question. In Palestine at the time of Jesus, with whom would an audience identify? Rather obviously, a first-century Jewish audience would identify with the victim, the man in the ditch (Funk 1966, 212; but see Scott 1989, 194). Why? Because Israel always seemed to be beaten up by brigand nations all around. The list was long—Babylonians, Assyrians, Persians, Greeks, and Romans. Roman squadrons clanked through the streets of Jerusalem. A Roman governor had turned the Jewish king into a puppet ruler. There were skirmishes because people dreamed of freedom from Roman oppression, but such protests were always put down by cruel force. Of course the Jewish audience would identify with the victim; poor little Israel, a chronic victim, always beaten up in a ditch.

Who will deliver the victim? Protestant people are apt to accept a failure on the part of Jewish religious leadership; perhaps anticlericalism has always lurked within the Protestant soul. But you cannot discover any such disrespect in Israel. Priests and Levites kept the temple going and, in turn, the temple was a symbol of Israel's identity, particularly in contrast to Roman power. God was with Israel, and temple worship was absolutely crucial to Israel's identity. So priests who offered daily sacrifice and Levites who assisted in ritual were absolutely necessary. Many of them lived in Jericho and commuted back and forth to the temple (Scott 1989, 195). Jesus' audience might be dismayed by their religious leaders circling around the battered man, but there was a justifiable reason.

The priesthood had to guard purity before God. Leviticus 21:11 is explicit with regard to a high priest: "He shall not go where there is a dead body; he shall not defile himself even for his father or mother." The Levite, who functioned in the temple assisting the priests, was to keep pure also if only by association. If the victim were dead, they had better keep their distance. If they could not be certain; they had to play it safe. In Samuel Beckett's *Waiting for Godot,* the two tramps simply cannot pick up a fallen neighbor because, as they say, "We are waiting for Godot."[3] In the parable, the religious leadership was clearly waiting on God.

There is much scholarly debate over the injunction in Leviticus 21. Were there any exceptions to the rule? Provisions in the Mishnah and the Talmud do seem to permit exceptions, particularly with regard to a neglected corpse (Scott 1989, 195–97). But, strictly speaking, the commands in Leviticus 21 would be binding (Derrett 1970, 212–14).

Scott (1989, 198) and others have marshalled evidence of hierarchical patterns in Jewish culture. For example, in the Mishnah:

> A priest takes precedence over a Levite, a Levite over an Israelite, an Israelite over a *mamzer* [bastard], a *mamzer* over a *Netin* [temple slave], a *Netin* over a proselyte, a proselyte over a freed slave.[4]

The Good Samaritan story shows such a potential pattern: a priest, a Levite, and then, quite naturally, an Israelite; the audience would expect a pious Jewish layman to come along and be the hero. A symbolic Jewish hero should save a Jewish victim. Indeed there are scholars who suppose the original Jesus scenario featured a Jewish layman and that Luke himself substituted "Samaritan." But the argument is unconvincing (Scott 1989, 199, n. 50).

What happens instead? Why a traveling Samaritan comes down the road and the Jewish victim must accept deliverance from the hand of an enemy! One of "us" must be saved by one of "them." Can you imagine how the parable might have disturbed Jesus' audience? Not only is deliverance provided by the enemy, but it is generously provided. The wounds are treated and bound, the man is carried on the Samaritan's own beast, and taken to an inn. The Samaritan pays for the man's stay and promises additional funding as necessary. A *good* Samaritan reverses normal Jewish expectations.

Luke has inherited the story but must present it to a Gentile audience. Luke's audience will have no sense of oppression; after all, they are Roman citizens. So Luke, already eager to blame crucifixion on Jewish leadership, is quite willing to portray the priest and Levite as insensitive, indeed as unneighborly. Likewise he is delighted to elevate a non-Jewish hero, the Samaritan. (In Luke's Gospel, "Samaritan" almost seems to be a code word for Gentile.) Thus Luke writes a new framework around the parable and turns the story into an object lesson: Please go and be neighborly to those who need your helpfulness.

In a way, we have two parables to preach, a good-deed object lesson and a rather shocking story in which salvation comes to us via our enemies, from one of "them." Inasmuch as most white, mainline Christian congregations are not exactly oppressed, preachers usually follow Luke. But once in a while the story can go in a different direction. Some years ago an excellent Catholic student preached the parable to a Chicano congregation in Arizona. He told his people of a Chicano in the ditch, beaten up, a victim, and his audience nodded; they understood—Chicano people have been oppressed. He then described a plump monsignor driving by in an Oldsmobile 88, followed by a permanent deacon in a Chevy on his way to Mass. "Who will save us?" the preacher asked with passion. "Who will come down the road to deliver us? Look, there he is, Tico Taco!" "Tico Taco" is an insulting term, equivalent to saying "Uncle Tom" in an African American congregation. The parable was so troubling that the student's congregation stayed after services to discuss, trying to come to terms with the force of the story.

Parables still have power. The scenarios performed again can profoundly disturb any audience. The Samaritan is "good," but unexpectedly so. The problem for most preachers is how to preach the parable to settled, often oblivious American congregations. Like Luke's congregation of Roman citizens, we are proud of our status and usually unaware that we are regarded as oppressors by many impoverished peoples. The only shock left is that the hero is not "one of us." We must be compassionate like the Samaritan, such is the moral of the story, though the hero is an odd figure. We reduce the shock of the parable by focusing on the compassion and helpfulness. The big problem is that we are no longer in the ditch. Preachers can emphasize the need of those who are in ditches, and issue a call to compassion.

How to preach the parable? White Americans in mainline churches do not view themselves as victims. Though the bite may no longer be in the parable, it is still a story worth telling, as Luke discovered. A call to compassion is a call worth issuing.

FRIEND AT MIDNIGHT

LUKE 11:5–13

[5]He said to them, "Suppose one of you has a friend, and you go to him at midnight and say to him, 'Friend, lend me three loaves of bread, [6]because a friend of mine has come in from a trip and I have nothing to serve him.' [7]From inside there's an answer, saying: 'Don't bother me, my door's shut and the children are in bed with me. I can't get up and give you anything.' [8]I tell you, even if he won't get up out of friendship to give him anything, because of his persistence he will get up and give him as much as he needs.

[9]"I tell you, ask and it will be given you; seek and you will find; knock and it will be opened to you. [10]Everyone asking receives, and whoever seeks will find, and to the person who knocks it will be opened.

> [11]"What father among you, when your son asks for a fish will hand him a snake instead? [12]Or if he asks for an egg will hand him a scorpion?

> [13]"If you who are evil know how to give good gifts to your children, how much more will the Father in heaven give the Holy Spirit to those who ask."

Luke is interested in prayer. He is the Gospel writer who tells about Jesus' prayer life. He is also the evangelist who, in Acts, pictures apostles at prayer as well. Luke urges us to a life of prayer.

Here he tells a rather amusing parable on prayer. The only trouble with the parable is that it seems to imply that we must pray stridently and repeatedly so as to command God's attention. He hands out much the same advice in connection with the parable of the Unjust Judge: "He told them a parable that they should pray all the time and not lose heart" (Luke 18:1). There have been Christians who have tried to pray all the time, murmuring "Jesus" under their breath while going about their daily doings. But the notion that, repeatedly, we must bang on the doors of heaven if we are to catch God's attention is hardly an appropriate theology of prayer.

The parable is a bit trickier than it appears. In biblical times hospitality was a nondebatable obligation. And hospitality was not merely an obligation for the host alone, but could involve an entire village. In the parable, a guest, traveling at night to avoid the heat of the day, has arrived late. The host has nothing to offer and must scurry around to neighbors. How could you honor a guest by serving leftovers? Besides, bread is more than food; bread is also an implement with which to dip and eat food (Bailey 1980, 123–24). The plot is not as bizarre as it may seem to us.

The sleepy neighbor's protest sounds reasonable. But, no, he is as bound as the host to provide hospitality for an unexpected guest. His grumbling reply borders on insult. He forces the embarrassed host to keep on banging on the door for bread.

There is scholarly debate over the word we have translated "persistence" (*anaideian*). The debate centers on two problems: First, the word can mean "persistence," but normally it would mean "shamelessness," or perhaps a kind of impudent "brazenness." Second, whose "shamelessness" would we be talking about? Does the word "his" refer to the desperate host or to the sleepy neighbor? Some scholars suppose that the grouchy sleeper gets up out of shame; in other words, he knows that hospitality is flat-out required and is ashamed to have stalled (Bailey 1976, 124–33). The problem with this suggestion is that while it may resolve some philological problems, it could lead us toward a theological morass. Is God a reluctant grouch who answers prayer out of divine shame?

Of course, the problem with the parable—as with the parable of the Unjust Judge—is that Luke seems to suggest we will have to keep at our praying in order to get God's attention. In the case of the Unjust Judge, we can reverse the parable by observing that God is not a corrupt judge; ergo, God wants to give to our needs. Perhaps we must spin this parable the same way—our God is not a gruff neighbor. Nevertheless, Luke's push for persistence is theologically peculiar.

Verses 9–10 seem to counter the idea that we need to bang on the door of heaven to receive an answer to prayer; after all, "ask and it will be given you . . . knock and it will be opened," sounds less strenuous. And verses 11–13 toss in two additional images in order to argue that, "If you who are evil know how to give good gifts to your children, how much more will the Father in heaven give the Holy Spirit to those who ask." God wants you to ask so that, in turn, God can give you good gifts.

If we preach the parable, we must correct the impression that we must pray all the time urgently or God will not respond. God is not a sleepy friend who does not want to get up in the night. No, God stirs up our prayers. We should know that our inadequate prayers are, nonetheless, the result of God's prior initiatives. Paul understands, for he tells us that though "we don't know how to pray," the Spirit among us stirs our prayers (Rom. 8:26–27). When we preach on prayer we should not suppose that the model "we pray/God answers," is valid; such a model will lead inevitably to those turgid discussions on why God does or does not answer prayers. No, reverse the model, and you come close to a biblical theology: "God initiates prayer/we respond by praying." In other words, we pray because God has stirred our prayers. There is no question of God answering or not answering; God is already attentive prior to our praying.

We can improve the model further by realizing that our praying is both learned and urged by our life in a liturgical community of faith. The lone saint climbing mystic ladders to God is not a biblical model. In experience we learn language within linguistic communities; we learn prayer the same way. In scripture, community is always prior to individual.

The "ask, seek, knock" material following the parable is from the Q source, as is the section on giving gifts to a son. Matthew has "bread" and "fish"; Luke "fish" and an "egg." Matthew has God giving "good gifts" and Luke has God conferring "Holy Spirit." Matthew's version is probably truer to the source because bread and fish were staples of the Middle Eastern diet as well as symbolic foods in biblical narrative.

These added sections do correct the parable somewhat. God knows how to give us good gifts and all we have to do is ask. God knows our needs before we speak, but God wishes to draw us into relationship through prayer. Luke may not embrace the idea that God knows needs in advance, for, above all, Luke wants us to pray and pray and pray.

When you preach the parable you can play around with the amusing aspects of the story. But you must avoid the conclusion that persistence will pay off in prayer. In other words, be sure to add verses 9–13 to the parable. If we try to pray all the time, it is not because we must, but because we can enjoy God's gracious presence.

RICH FARMER
(Luke 12:13–21; Thomas *63:1–2)*

LUKE 12:13–21

[13]Someone in the crowd said to him, "Teacher, tell my brother to divide the inheritance with me." [14]But he answered him, "Man, who appointed me your judge or arbiter?" [15]And he said to them, "Look out! Keep yourselves from all forms of greed; for life is not measured by the stuff [we] possess."

[16]And he told them a parable, saying, "The land of a rich man produced a huge harvest. [17]Debating within himself, he said, 'What'll I do, I don't have anywhere to store my produce?' [18]Then he said, 'I know what I'll do, I'll tear down my barns and build bigger barns, and I will store all my grain and my goods, [19]and I will say to myself, "Self, you've got goods laid up for years to come, take it easy—eat, drink, and be happy."' [20]But God said to him, 'Fool, tonight your self will be demanded from you! And who will get the stuff you've piled up?'

[21]That's the way it goes with [those] who treasure up for [themselves] and are not rich toward God.

THOMAS *63:1–2*

[1]There was a rich man who had much money. He said, "I shall put my money to use so that I may sow, reap, plant, and fill my storehouse with produce, with the result that I shall lack nothing." Such were his intentions, but that same night he died. [2]Let him who has ears hear.

The parable of the Rich Farmer is often preached as a warning: "You can't take it with you!" After all, such a pattern is in the parable. A man builds big barns to secure his future, only to die before his future begins; the parable seems obvious. And the version of the parable in the *Gospel of Thomas* has been reduced to just such a stark message.

Parables are often developed out of biblical passages. They function as illustrations of ideas or teachings (Stern 1991, 48–49). Did both versions, Luke and *Thomas*, derive from Sirach 11:18–19?

> One becomes rich through diligence and self-denial,
>   and the reward allotted to him is this:
> when he says, "I have found rest,
>   and now I shall feast on my goods!"
> he does not know how long it will be
>   until he leaves them to others and dies.

But Luke's parable is not merely a dour "you-can't-take-it-with-you" warning. The parable is not as simple as it seems. Bernard Brandon Scott (1989,

127–40) has written an interpretation of the parable entitled, "How to Misman-
age a Miracle." The title is apt. The farmer in the parable is not merely an all-
American entrepreneur; no, he has failed to understand that his good fortune is a
miraculous gift of God.

The key to unpacking the parable is in a biblical tradition. The scourge of the
ancient world was drought; therefore, bumper crops were viewed as gifts of God,
providing for the future when lean years would arrive. Above all, bumper crops
were designed for wide, generous distribution. Put succinctly, in God's economy, big harvests are for the poor.

Remember the story of Joseph who told pharaoh to store up huge harvests in
preparation for seven years of famine that would befall the land of Egypt (Gen.
41:25–36)? The same foresight shows up in the stories of how Israel, wandering
in the wilderness, gathered twice as much manna before the sabbath day of rest
(Ex. 16:22–27). Sabbatical year customs are of the same tradition:

> When you enter the land that I am giving you, the land shall observe
> a sabbath for the LORD. Six years you shall sow your field, and six
> years you shall prune your vineyard, and gather in their yield; but in the
> seventh year there shall be a sabbath of complete rest for the land, a
> sabbath for the LORD: you shall not sow your field or prune your vine-
> yard. . . . Should you ask, What shall we eat in the seventh year, if
> we may not sow or gather in our crop? I will order my blessing for you
> in the sixth year, so that it will yield a crop for three years. (Lev.
> 25:2b–4, 20–21)

The rich farmer should have received the enormous harvest as a miraculous provision for famine years to come. Initially he appears to act appropriately, for he
plans to build bigger barns to store his crops. Like Joseph in Egypt, we suppose
he will prepare to feed his neighbors, especially the poor. God's command is
blunt: "The land is mine; with me you are but aliens and tenants" (Lev. 25:23).
Thus farming must be socially responsible.

The rich farmer has other plans; he is looking out for "numero uno." Listen to
him figure out his future: "Self [*psyche*], you've got goods laid up for years
to come, take it easy—eat, drink, and be happy." His words echo an Epicurean
slogan: "Eat, drink, and play with love; all else is nothingness."[5] Variations of
the slogan were well-known in the first century world. The phrase shows up and
is ridiculed in scripture (Isa. 22:14; Tobit 7:9; 1 Cor. 15:32) as well as in the parable (Scott 1989, 136). In the Bible, wealth is given for sharing, but the rich farmer
is stacking up goods to guarantee his own pleasant future. He is reveling in profit
while forgetting the poor.

Charles Hedrick believes the rich farmer made a tactical error; instead of harvesting and storing what he can in his facilities, he determines to build bigger
barns: "He dies, his fields overflowing with abundance and his storage facilities
yet unmodified" (Hedrick 1994, 160–61). But Hedrick's argument is not entirely
convincing.

Only in this parable does God play a speaking part: "Fool, tonight your self will be demanded from you! And who will get the stuff you've piled up?" The man is a practical atheist, ignoring both God's law and his neighbors' need; no wonder he is called a "fool"—"The fool says in his heart, 'There is no God'" (Ps. 14:1, RSV). And the man is assuredly foolish, for he dies even as he is gleefully rubbing his hands in anticipation of a soft life. Incidentally, God is not carrying out a punishment; the man is not killed by God. The text reads literally, "This night the self they will take back from you," perhaps a reference to the pop-religious idea of angels of death. In any event, he simply dies and can't take it with him.

The last line is the real question: Whose will it be? "Who will get the stuff you've piled up?" A Jewish audience hearing the parable would know the answer. Ultimately the goods will be distributed to the hungry according to God's purposes.

As usual, Luke has contrived a framework. A man shows up asking Jesus the rabbi to offer a judicial ruling: "Teacher, tell my brother to divide the inheritance with me." Two sons would inherit land together. If one son requested division, usually the other son would normally comply. But Jesus rejects a judicial role: "Man, who appointed me a judge or divider over you?" Instead Jesus warns against "all kinds of greed," and then tells the parable.

For Luke a wealthy Christian is a contradiction in terms. The theme of wealth and poverty shows up not only in his Gospel but in Acts where, for example, we come across the story of Ananias and his wife Sapphira (Acts 5:1–11), zapped by the Spirit because they held private property when there was common need. Luke takes seriously the injunction: "Blessed are the poor," adding an appropriate, "Woe to you rich." And he agrees with Jesus' amusing hyperbole that it is harder for a rich man to enter the kingdom of God than for a camel to sway through the eye of a needle. Again and again, Luke turns to glower at the rich and at those who want to be rich. He believes Christians are to share goods in common, family style. Therefore "rich Christian" should be an oxymoron.

Middle-class, mainline Protestant churches generally soften Luke's harsh words about money. Perhaps we are afraid to counter capitalist ideology. Or perhaps we do not wish to trouble wealthy church contributors—Who was it that quipped, "The church has always been willing to trade 'treasure in heaven' for cash down"? But the call to Christian poverty echoes through the Bible. Luke concludes his parable by citing Jesus' teaching, "I'm telling you, don't worry about yourself, what you're going to eat, or about your body, what you're going to wear." The word translated "worry," *merimna,* is an action word; it might be translated, "Why are you all *driving* yourselves to get food or clothing?" To do so would be "pagan." No, Christians are to trust God's good providence, share in common, and give freely to those in need.

> Don't be afraid, little flock, for your Father is delighted to give you the
> kingdom. Sell your possessions and give to charity; have yourselves

purses that never wear out, a sure treasure in the heavens, where no thief will come near and no moth destroy. Where your treasure is, your heart also will be.   (Luke 12:32–34, DGB)

"Treasure in heaven" is a familiar Jewish euphemism for charity; it is not a term for some sort of world-renouncing spirituality. In God's economy, what we give away is "treasure in heaven."

Sermon

Here is a very short sermon on the parable. It was preached in 1996 at a morning prayer service in Washington's National Cathedral presided over by the Reverend Canon Erica Wood. The congregation was mostly clergy attending a study conference at the College of Preachers. How do you manage to read lections, preach, and have Eucharist in less than forty minutes? Answer: You design a brief "sermonette":

Introduction   There was an old story about a man who thought he had the future licked. By some magic he had gotten hold of a copy of the *New York Times* dated a year in advance. What a bonanza! He knew what stocks to buy and sell, what properties to purchase. He rubbed his hands together with glee, until he turned a page and read his own obituary. The story's a shocker, but no more shocking than the parable Jesus told. A rich man has a bumper crop. So, he built bigger barns, and thought he had the future licked—he could eat, drink, and make merry. Then God spoke: "Fool! Tonight your life will be required of you." Listen to the parable of the rich fool.

1 Question: What do you do with a bumper crop, the kind of crop that happens every twenty years or so? What do you do with prosperity? Answer: You become a capitalist, which is what the farmer in the parable did. We Americans tend to admire the man; he was an entrepreneur, tearing down in order to build bigger barns for bigger crops for bigger profits. And what's the motive? You don't have to have an MBA to figure out the motive: self-interest. He was providing for his own security. A few weeks ago while wandering the library of a management school, we came across a sign on the wall of a student carrel reading, "Self-interest Makes the World Go Round." Would you believe it was written in Gothic type? Listen, in an age of downsizing, a future free from money worries sounds pretty good—eat, drink, and enjoy! Could anyone describe the American dream any sweeter? Food enough, wine on the table, and time—time for ourselves. What do you do with a bumper crop? Easy, you become a capitalist.

2 But what does God say? God speaks and speaks bluntly: "Fool! You fool!" Notice the word, a special biblical word reserved for people who no longer believe in God: fool! The man in the parable was a practical atheist, for he had drawn a tight circle of self-interest around himself leaving out neighbors and, if neighbors, then also God. "You fool!" God hands out a verdict, a verdict, incidentally, written all over our American free enterprise. We have neighbors who are hungry — eighty percent of the earth to be exact. We even have such neighbors here in America — a third of all American school children are undernourished, most of them black or Spanish-speaking. Instead of sharing our wealth these days we are building bigger barns so the rich can be richer, and designing welfare plans to penalize the poor for being poor. You wonder whether the churches here in Washington, D.C. have spoken out about the irony of rich senators trying to legislate morality for the poor! All the man in the parable wanted was a little security, an IRA, and ease in old age. "Fool," said God, "today your life will be required of you." So God speaks to our American dream.

3   Now listen, for Luke the moralist adds a tag line. "Be rich toward God," he advises us. So how are we rich toward God? Luke is not talking about spirituality. Spirituality without charity isn't spiritual, it is simply a nasty little form of religious perversion. No, "being rich toward God" was a fine ancient-world metaphor for almsgiving. What do you do with a bumper crop? Why, you give it away, with a fine, free, and gleeful carelessness. You make sure the hungry are fed, the poor have funding, the aged are cared for, and the sick are healed. You give your gain away. John Calvin will never be accused of being a stand-up comic. But hear his advice on divvying up a church budget: You give one fourth to the poor, one fourth for the training and maintenance of the ministry, one fourth for the work of the church, and one fourth to the poor![6] Add it up, and you can almost see the twitch of a smile dimpling Calvin's cheek. The farmer was a fool; he tried to secure his own life. But he could have been rich toward God, serving God's special friends, the poor.

Conclusion   Look, we clerical types preach the parable, but we figure we're poor and therefore exempt. But mainline clergy these days are scarcely poor. So the parable speaks to us. We can love the Lord with an easy grace and give ourselves away! For heaven's sake, we need not be religious fools!

Discussion

The sermon is compressed, probably too much. We have had to neglect the theological rationale behind bumper crops and God's concern for the poor. The problem with a compressed twelve-minute sermon is that the preacher can only say two or three things. Sermons then tend toward moralism or brief inspiration; they lack theological depth. The old adage, "No souls are saved after ten minutes," is neither true nor helpful. A bishop coined the phrase and, after reading his sermons, I tend to agree; in his case no souls were saved after thirty seconds! But brevity means a tight design and little room for homiletical error. Brevity also can lead to banality. Nonetheless the sermon was designed for brevity.

Introduction   The introduction is right on the cusp of being too long. But it does reinstate the story in everyone's mind, plus add a bit of a shock. I would never assume that people hear scripture readings, so a rehearsal of the parable's plot will be useful.

1 While I could not explore biblical background because of time constraints, I raise the question, "What do you do with a bumper crop?" Notice that instead of the "you" leading to a personal sermon on personal wealth, immediately I set the sermon in a corporate context: "You become a capitalist." The approach leads into the cultural assumptions behind personal wealth. Unless we can dent cultural assumptions we will not change personal behavior which, of course, is never "personal." The other reason for using the word "capitalist" is that we Americans seem to suppose that our economic system is divinely mandated, along with democracy. But Calvin, who argued that a limited capitalism was probably necessary given the hard fact of human sinfulness, was closer to the truth. Maybe it is time for the pulpit to open critical dialogue on the subject of our all-American belief in ungoverned capitalism. Move one is somewhat compressed for it combines action and motivation.

2 The start of the second move is choppy. I introduce God's voice, but then I focus on the word "fool," chase the biblical meaning of "fool," and depict the farmer, before returning again to God, the speaker. Not good! The start is a series of nervous point-of-view shifts. Nevertheless, I do need to emphasize the initial shift to God's speech firmly. Note the aside, namely, a remark about the irony of rich senators trying to legislate morality for the poor. Instead of laboring prophetic comment, a brief aside, a barb, is often more useful.

3 The move is too brief, but otherwise is on target. Notice that it contains a contrapuntal beginning, "Luke is not talking about . . ." The phrase "rich toward God" is often preached as being concerned with spiritual things. But as a Jewish metaphor for charity it does not focus on religious things, but urges a cash-down love of neighbors. The Calvin citation is amusing, but needs more follow-up than two brief sentences.

Conclusion The conclusion addresses the audience—clergy. Whenever clergy speak on the subject of wealth and poverty, they categorize themselves as either in-between or poor. Actually, American mainline clergy (and particularly theological faculty members) are doing rather well. Compared to world income, we are rich indeed. The last two sentences should be reversed in sequence.

The parable is blunt, edgy, and fun to preach.

BARREN TREE

LUKE 13:1-9

[1]At the same time, there were some present who told him about the Galileans whose blood Pilate mixed with their sacrifices. [2]Answering, he said to them: "Do you think that because those Galileans suffered they were worse sinners than all other Galileans? [3]No, but I tell you, unless you repent you all will perish

the same way! [4]Or the eighteen who were killed when the tower
of Siloam fell and killed them; do you think they were worse sinners than all the others living in Jerusalem? [5]No, but I tell you,
unless you repent, you all will perish in the same way."

[6]And he told this parable: A man had a fig tree planted in his vineyard, and
he came looking for fruit and found none. [7]He said to the vinedresser,
"Look, for three years now I have come for fruit from this fig tree, and I
found none. Dig it out, it's taking up space." [8]But answering, he said to
him, "Leave it for another year, sir, until I dig around it and throw on
[manure]. [9]If eventually it produces fruit . . . , otherwise you can dig it out."

Fig trees often show up in the Bible. In Joel 2:22, a fig tree in leaf is a sign of
harvest blessings. We need not fear, for "the tree bears its fruit/the fig tree and
vine give their full yield." Likewise in the Gospel of Mark (13:28), the sudden
blossoming of the fig tree is a symbol of a coming salvation (Jeremias 1963,
119–20). Mark also tells the story of Jesus cursing a fig tree, full of leaves, but
without any figs (11:12–14). To Mark the unfruitful tree seems to be a symbol
for the temple cult that is no longer bearing ethical fruit. Biblically, fig trees function in positive and negative ways.

You do not have to be an expert on fig trees to catch on to Luke's parable. If
you have ever seen an orchard, you understand. When you are starting an orchard
from scratch, with infant trees planted in rows, you know that for a few years
the orchard must mature before you will begin to see any fruit to pick. No
owner would look for fruit until after the first three years. But there is an odd text
in Leviticus 19:23 that seems to suggest a longer delay before the fruit can be
harvested:

> When you come into the land and plant all kinds of trees for food, then
> you shall regard their fruit as forbidden [i.e., uncircumcised]; three years
> it shall be forbidden to you, it must not be eaten. In the fourth year all
> their fruit shall be set apart for rejoicing in the LORD. But in the fifth year
> you may eat of their fruit, that their yield may be increased for you: I am
> the LORD your God.

Does the text begin after the initial three-year maturation, plus one, thus in the
eighth year, or skip the initial three years for a young tree to grow? Even the rabbis were unsure:

> Until [what stage of growth are trees] called "saplings"? R. Eleasar b.
> Azariah says, "Until they become permitted for common use [until they
> are five years old, for Lev. 19:23–25 forbids the consumption of fruit in
> the first four years of a trees growth]." R. Joshua says, "[They are] seven
> years old."[7]

Why the disagreement? When do we start counting—after or including three
years of maturation, three years plus one, or six years plus one? If the owner has

been looking for fruit for three years, he would not have begun looking until the fifth year; so the parable must be referring to an eighth year. But whatever the calculation, the fig tree is completely dead!

"Dig it out!" the owner says sensibly. An audience would agree with the owner at once, realizing a nonproductive tree is useless. Why should the bad tree take up valuable space in an orchard?

Peculiarly, the vinedresser appeals for a little more time: "Leave it for another year, sir, until I dig around it and throw on [manure]." There is a more earthy word in the Greek, though most translations are decorous and use the word "manure." The King James Version has a blunt "dung." But a more earthy word is likely because the Greek, *kopria,* is root for a number of slang terms applied to people, people who are "stinkards, dirty fellows, low buffoons," says Liddell and Scott's *Greek-English Lexicon,* sedately.

The vinedresser is more optimistic than Jesus' listeners would have been; barren trees simply do not produce. And the vinedresser himself does not seem entirely sure that the tree will ever be productive: "If eventually it produces fruit . . . , otherwise you can cut it down." Many modern translations fill in the elliptical gap, "If eventually it produces fruit, *well and good,* otherwise you can cut it down," but some versions of the text do not. They end with a chancey ellipsis.

Luke's chapter 12 has begun with a hard promise of judgment. He warns the crowds to interpret the present time:

> When you see a cloud rising in the west, you immediately say, "It's going to rain"; and so it happens. And when you see the south wind blowing, you say, "There will be scorching heat"; and it happens. You hypocrites! You know how to interpret the appearance of earth and sky, but why do you not know how to interpret the present time? (Luke 12:54–56)

Then Jesus drops in another image, with advice on going to court, warning the crowd to straighten out their lives in view of the coming judgment: "Settle the case, or you may be dragged before the judge, and the judge hand you over to the officer, and the officer throw you into prison" (Luke 12:57–59).

Finally, there is a peculiar section dealing with two recent tragedies (13:1–5). Jesus tells of Galileans "whose blood Pilate mixed with their sacrifices." Did the crowd suppose that the Galileans were worse sinners than others in Galilee? In other words, was their slaughter a punishment designed by God? "No," says Jesus, "but unless you repent you all will be destroyed like them." Then Jesus cites the case of eighteen workers crushed when a tower fell on them. Did the crowd imagine that they were "worse offenders than all the others living in Jerusalem?" He answers, "No, I tell you; but unless you repent you all will perish just as they did." Then Jesus tells the parable of the Barren Tree.

What is the meaning of "the present time?" It is time to repent in view of the all but absurd mercy of God, a God whose patience has stretched quite beyond reasonable expectation. We all live in a huge, grace-filled ellipsis!

A sermon on the parable might reach back to the beginning of chapter 13. We can begin with an objective study of the problem of theodicy. Why do terrible things happen to people? Towers still tumble and devout persons can be cruelly gunned down; we live in a violent time. But victims do not deserve the tragedy according to Jesus; they were not worse sinners than neighbors who are not suffering.

Then, unexpectedly, Jesus interrupts the objective discussion, calling for us to repent. We are all sinners in the sight of God, blithely living in the mercy without changing our lives. Repentance is not a matter of salt tears and sawdust trails; in the Bible repentance is change, a deliberate, smart redesigning of lifestyles.

The parable is an encouragement. We live in the midst of God's absurd mercy, unbelievably patient and generous. Let us then respond to grace, grace stretched wide, and repent! God is waiting, waiting. . . . Quick, take advantage of the divine ellipsis.

LOST COIN

LUKE 15:1–10

1Now there were tax collectors and sinners gathering around to hear him. 2And both the Pharisees and the scribes grumbled loudly, saying, "This man welcomes sinners and eats with them!" 3So he told them this parable:

4Suppose one of you has a hundred sheep, and, loses one of them, won't he leave the ninety-nine in the wilderness and go after the lost one until he finds it? 5And finding it, he'll carry it on his shoulders rejoicing. 6Coming home, he'll call his friends and neighbors together, saying to them, "Party with me, for I have found my sheep which was lost."

7I tell you, there will be more joy in heaven over one repenting sinner than over ninety-nine righteous people with no need of repentance.

8Suppose a woman with ten drachmas loses one, will she not light a lamp and sweep the house and search carefully until she finds it? 9Finding it, she will call together friends and neighbors, saying, "Party with me, because I found the drachma that was lost."

10I tell you, there is joy before the angels of God over one repenting sinner.

Luke has designed the two parables so they parallel one another in both plot and style. And he has added a somewhat similar conclusion to each about the joy in heaven over one sinner repenting. Luke then proceeds to tell the story of the Prodigal Son, a story he ties into the previous parables by referring to the prodigal, who "was lost and is found."

At the beginning of the chapter, Luke has told a story of Jesus eating with sinners:

> Now there were tax collectors and sinners gathering around to hear him. And both the Pharisees and the scribes grumbled loudly, saying, "This man welcomes sinners and eats with them!" (15:1–2)

So Luke has set up a situation for Jesus to address: Why does Jesus party with sinners? Luke's answer: Jesus is trying to save lost sinners. After all, Jesus represents a God who loves sinners. Thus Luke arranges three parables and, by rewriting, manages to turn them all into lost and found stories, with the climactic story being the parable of the Prodigal Son. The three parables now comprise a thematic chapter on repentance. Previously we have discussed the Lost Sheep (see pages 152–56). In the next section we will discuss the Prodigal Son. Here we will look at the story of the Lost Coin.

Luke tips his theological hand in advance. He has reported the critical reaction of scribes and Pharisees to Jesus, who is evidently enjoying the company of sinners: "This man welcomes sinners and eats with them!" Then he lines out the two parables, each ending with a somewhat similar announcement: There is joy in heaven over a sinner who repents. Luke portrays Jesus as God's living missionary expedition. The message is clear, but the parables are strange indeed.

Once more Jesus tells a parable featuring a woman, incidentally, a woman who will represent God! There are several such parables: the Leaven, the Closed Door, the Lost Coin, the Unjust Judge. In a patriarchal society where pious men could pray, "Blessed be God that he [*sic!*] has not made me a woman," Jesus' stories with central female characters would be startling, if not offensive. Moreover, for a woman to be in any way a representation of God's rule would be even worse and doubly shocking. The unabashed use of women heroes in Jesus' parables is quite remarkable.

Of course, the whole idea of the parable of the Lost Coin is a bit odd. The woman has ten drachmas, each worth a little less than a field hand's daily minimum wage. Nowadays migrant workers may clear forty dollars a day if they are lucky, but in first-century Palestine, a poor country, the buying power of a day's farm work would be minimal. So the woman has lost a coin, she cannot seem to find. She lights a candle to search in the dark corners of the house; she gets a broom and sweeps the floor to find the coin. Finally, after considerable effort, she locates the coin. Then what does she do? She throws an expensive party for friends and neighbors to celebrate the recovery. Does the parable seem just a bit odd? Perhaps even absurd?

In order to explain away the absurdity, Joachim Jeremias (1963, 133) speculates that the coin was probably a dowry coin, perhaps strung together with other coins and worn as a kind of headdress. As dowry, the coin might be of sentimental value. But as other scholars have pointed out, the parable says nothing about a dowry. The absurdity remains; the party had to be more expensive than a misplaced coin. The woman's extravagance is almost as absurd as leaving ninety-nine sheep unprotected to chase down a stray!

Some scholars have attempted to set up a parallel between the Lost Sheep and the Lost Coin. Because the search for a lost sheep could be dangerous, they have argued that the woman's house held dangers as well. Maybe the house had flooring, and the coin could have slipped through a crack between the boards. Because of snakes and spiders, a search under floorboards would be both strenuous and risky. The argument is unconvincing. In general, only wealthier homes would have had cypress flooring. The woman in the parable appears to be modestly poor—she is desperate to find a coin—so her floor was more likely made of clay or flat stones. Besides, there is no mention of searching under floorboards. If the coin is not a dowry coin and there is no flooring in the house, we are stuck with a parable that is pleasantly nutty.

The odd reference to "angels of God" matches a reference to angels in the "preface" to Matthew's version of the Lost Sheep (Matt. 18:10), and therefore may indicate some sort of angel reference in the Q source. But Matthew seems to have dropped the Lost Coin story, perhaps because it did not fit his context.

The Lost Coin parable is so brief (and silly) that it may be difficult to preach. But congregations are made of human beings, and who has not lost something inconsequential around the house and gone crazy trying to find it? More significantly, we tend to misplace people. If lapsed members of the congregation, or those usually regarded as "sinners," have gradually disappeared, the loss may be a matter of "out of sight, out of mind." After all, they were never really "one of us."

In the parable the woman searches. She lights a candle (because houses were dark) and looks in every crevice, every shadowy corner. The persistent seeking is part of Luke's message. Though we may forget to search, God keeps looking.

The party for her friends and neighbors is a surprise. Anyone who does much entertaining knows that parties do not come cheap, particularly evening parties. Luke is underlining heavenly joy which, down our way, may seem impractical or even absurd. But God loves sinners and is eager to have them turn in a "godward" direction. Each of the two "lost" parables strains credulity—a foolish shepherd who risks his flock to find a stray; a peculiar woman who throws an expensive party when she finds a misplaced coin. An audience would be surprised by both parables. Surprise doubles when a preacher adds, "Just like God!"

There is a danger in Luke's chapter. He tells these stunning parables to respond to a criticism launched by the scribes and Pharisees: "This man welcomes sinners and eats with them." There are two problems: First, if we overstress Christ's missionary motivations, we may obscure the fact that he may have enjoyed partying as well as the company he was keeping. Preachers should not portray Jesus as uncomfortable with sinners, as if he truly would not want to eat with them but, sacrificing himself, does so to save them. No. Remember that Jesus was accused of being a glutton and a drunk (Luke 7:34). Presumably he had fun at parties. How else can we love sinners?

Second, if we preach Christ with sinners, they must be real sinners and not secretly "nice" sinners. Some years ago, a critic complained that preachers were turning all the sinners in Christian scripture into nice if wayward people; he labeled the tendency, "the whore with the heart of gold syndrome." If Jesus liked the sinners, preachers suppose, they had to be good at heart. But such logic misses the point. Jesus loved the not nice—the venial prostitute and the slick, racketeer-type tax collector—and, apparently, partied with them. We probably would not encourage them to attend our church family-night suppers.

We must also be very careful that the word "lost" does not tumble into damnation, eternal punishment for unrepentant sinners. Notice the real surprise in the passage: Though Luke mentions joy over repenting sinners, there is no feature in the Lost Coin or the Lost Sheep that represents repenting; the lost sheep does not apologize, the lost coin does not shed tears of remorse. No, the joy is in finding the misplaced coin or restoring a sheep that has wandered.

The parable is full of joy because God loves sinners. The parable tells news of a God who will not lose us, each one of us, no matter what. God seeks and finds us. And, yes, there's a great hullabaloo over the finding. Maybe when love finds, it turns into joy—gleeful, giggling, celebrative joy.

PRODIGAL SON

LUKE 15: 1–2, 11–32

¹Now the tax collectors and sinners were all crowding around to hear him. ²The Pharisees and scribes muttered, "This man welcomes sinners and eats with them."

¹¹Then Jesus said, "A certain man had two sons. ¹²The younger of them said to the father, 'Give me the share of the property coming to me.' So he divided the estate among them. ¹³Not many days later, getting everything together, the younger son went off to a distant country and squandered his estate in high living. ¹⁴Having spent everything he had, a severe drought swept through the land, and he began to be in need. ¹⁵He went and hired out to one of the citizens of the land who sent him out into the fields to feed pigs. ¹⁶He longed to fill his belly on the husks which the pigs ate, but nobody gave him any. ¹⁷When he was off by himself, he said, 'How many of my father's hired hands have plenty of bread, while I am dying of drought? ¹⁸I will get up and go to my father, and I will say to him, "Father, I have sinned against heaven and in your sight. ¹⁹I am no longer worthy to be called your son. Make me one of your hired hands."' ²⁰So, getting up, he went to his father."

"While he was still far away, his father saw him and was moved with pity; running, he embraced and kissed him warmly. ²¹The son said to him, 'Father, I have sinned against heaven and in your sight. I am no longer worthy to be called your son. . . .' ²²But the father said to his workers, 'Quick! Bring the best robe and dress him; put a ring on his hand and sandals on his feet. ²³Get the fatted calf, kill it, and let's party, ²⁴because this son of mine was dead and lives again, was lost and is found!' They began to celebrate."

25"But his older son was in a field. As he came in and neared the house, he heard music and dancing. 26He called over one of the boys and asked what was going on. 27[The boy] said, 'Your brother has arrived, and your father has killed the fatted calf because he got him back in good health.' 28He was angry and did not want to go in; so his father came out and pleaded with him. 29Answering, he said to his father, 'Look, I've worked for you for years and never disobeyed one of your orders, and you never gave me so much as a goat so I could party with my friends. 30But when this son of yours, having used up your inheritance with whores, shows up, for him you kill the fatted calf!' 31The father said to him, 'Dear child, you are always with me. Everything I have is yours. 32But it is right for us to celebrate and be glad, for this brother of yours was dead and lives again, was lost and is found.'"

The parable of the Prodigal Son is beloved. For centuries the parable has brought news of God's welcoming mercy to all of us sinners. As a result, the parable is conventionally preached as a call to repentance and as an assurance of pardon. The younger son is our exemplar and the older son is generally castigated by contemporary interpreters. With the conventional understanding firmly fixed, what can preachers preach that is new? Not much. But a rehearsal of recent parable research may help us to understand the parable of the Prodigal Son at a deeper level.

The prodigal is not merely a wayward child. Usually he is pictured as a young person, free from family constraints, who goes astray. A familiar story. Is he wicked? Let's call him a typical young man flexing his freedoms, for "wicked" does sound a bit excessive. We have tamed him. But in Jesus' day, the prodigal son was a fairly offensive person:

First, he insults his father by asking for his inheritance in advance. Does he not imply that he wishes his father were dead? Sons simply did not ask for an inheritance ahead of time. To do so would have been a terrible slap at a parent and a social scandal. Kenneth Bailey admits that a parent could set up a will, dividing property between sons, and do so ahead of time. Then he remarks:

> But the startling fact is that, to my knowledge, in all of Middle Eastern literature (aside from this parable) from ancient times to the present, there is no case of any son, older or younger, asking for his inheritance from a father who is still in good health.   (Bailey 1976, 164)

The prodigal is treating his father as if he were already dead.

Second, he severs any relationship with his brother. David Daube cites the Hebrew term *yashabh yahadh* ("to dwell together") as a biblical ideal: "How very good and pleasant it is when kindred live together in unity!" (Ps. 133:1). Land is family property and confers status on a family in the community. Thus two brothers living together on the land after a father's death is the preferred resolution because it retains the package of land as a whole in the name of the family.[8] When the prodigal wants his share of the property so as to sell the land and pocket the cash, he forces a division of the land. The division of land in turn will lessen family status in the wider community. Maybe the brothers are already alienated, but division of the estate is a radical step.

The third reason the younger son is offensive is that his action suddenly exposes the family to community criticism. The boy himself would be treated as a pariah, a social outcast, for evidently he does not respect his father and has no regard for his brother. But, more, his action will have brought ridicule on his father. What kind of father lets a son ride roughshod over him, reduce his economic status, and offend his brother? Sirach warns against such a situation:

> To son or wife, to brother or friend,
>   do not give power over yourself, as long as you live;
> and do not give your property to another,
>   lest you change your mind and must ask for it.
> While you are still alive and have breath in you,
>   do not let any one take your place.
> For it is better that your children should ask from you
>   than that you should look to the hand of your sons.
>   (Sirach 33:19–21, RSV)

The father now is ridiculed for his impotent foolishness, the family status in the community is reduced, and the young son has alienated his own brother.

All in all, the young son is a bum. Because the parable is preached as a conversion story, preachers portray the young man as good at heart; all he has to do is "to come to himself," confess his sin, and return home to his father. Besides, in telling the parable, Jesus—with a little help from Luke—obviously is pleased with the young fellow. Can we not suppose he is good-hearted? Misguided, yes, but ultimately good-hearted.

No, when preachers portray sinners, let them be honest. The boy may be young and misguided, but he is still a self-centered scoundrel.

Also, let us not romanticize his trip to a far country. Having converted property into cash, the young son promptly lives it up. Some preachers blame the older brother for being snide when he observes, "this son of yours, having used up your inheritance with whores," but to be truthful, the older brother was probably on target. The Greek uses two terms to describe the young son's lifestyle, *dieskortisen* = "wasted," and *zoa asotos* = "self-destructive living"; both terms are often associated with sexual excess. The young son engages in high living, expensive high living. When drought strikes the land, he is broke and, think of it, as a Jewish man, he must go and tend pigs! Scott (1989, 114) quotes a Talmudic aphorism: "Cursed be the man who would breed swine, and cursed be the man who would teach his son Grecian Wisdom." The prodigal ends up feeding pigs while working for a Gentile.

Now an oddity: The first-century Jewish audience would expect the boy to come through and be a hero; scapegrace younger sons in Jewish stories usually come through. Although stories seldom take younger sons to the dramatic level of degradation as in this parable, younger sons are stock characters in a familiar plot—they will come through and be heroes. An audience will not be surprised that the young son turns around and heads home; no, the audience is sure he will come out all right. Bernard Brandon Scott argues that there is a long biblical tradition in which younger sons, often rogues, are heroes and older brothers are villains.

> One need only call to mind the stories of Cain and Abel, Ishmael and Isaac, Esau and Jacob, Jacob's favorite son Joseph, and, after his supposed death at the hands of his brothers, Benjamin. Many of the stories of these younger brothers follow a stereotype. Younger sons frequently leave the house of their father to find their wealth; there is something slightly scandalous or off-color in their stories, and they are the favorites.   (Scott 1989, 112)

When the son turns back home, the audience is not surprised. People expected him to be a winner all along. So, in spite of variations, we are dealing with a stock ploy. We cheer a younger son, and we usually boo an older brother.

What about conversion? Obviously the older brother is still recalcitrant at the end of the story. We do not know if he will ever return his father's affection, or be reconciled with his brother, or even drop in on the party. Though we do not know, a happy ending does not seem likely. As far as we know, the older brother is unconverted. But what of the younger brother? Luke certainly has conversion in mind, conversion and joy. But to be honest, you have to wonder. See the sequence of the young son's thoughts:

> How many of my father's hired hands have plenty of bread, while I am dying of drought. I will get up and go to my father, and I will say to him, "Father, I have sinned against heaven and in your sight. I am no longer worthy to be called your son. Make me one of your hired hands."

The statement, "I have sinned against heaven and in your sight," may sound properly pious. But what prompts his piety is blatantly obvious: "How many of my father's hired hands have plenty of bread, while I am dying of drought." Yet doesn't the parable say plainly, "When he came to himself . . . "? Jeremias (1963, 130) claims that the phrase, *eis heauton de elthon* = "he came to himself," is an Aramaic expression for repentance, but other scholars are a bit skeptical. After all, the phrase might simply mean, "off by himself, he said . . . ," even though Luke usually introduces interior monologues with, "he said to himself." Although the boy seems to have voiced repentance, his supposed conversion may be mostly a "soup kitchen conversion"—he's hungry! His formal recital, "I have sinned against heaven and in your sight," certainly sounds like a liturgical formula, but is said following his vision of farmhands eating well at home. Remember, the audience expects the young scoundrel to come home, so his turn toward home is not surprising.

What is surprising? The father's behavior. Scott (1989, 117) says it has "the quality of burlesque." The audience would expect some dignity, passion perhaps, but also righteousness. The father is, after all, a patriarchal figure. He might well go out to meet his son and, as a sign of forgiveness, kiss the boy. Such a public display would announce to the crowd around that the boy would be received back into the family on some kind of reduced basis. After all, the property that was to be his is gone, and the family status is clearly less than it was.

If burlesque humor is extravagant, a humor of surreal exaggeration, then the father's actions qualify as burlesque! He goes overboard. First, he hikes up his robes and runs at top speed out to greet his son—there goes dignity. He kisses the boy passionately. Then he interrupts the son's solemn speech with excited commands. He hands out "the best robe," perhaps his own ceremonial robe. He puts a ring on the boy's finger, probably a signet ring conveying position and authority. He tells slaves to put sandals on his son's feet, thus indicating that the boy will not be a hired hand but will be served by servants. Patriarchs do not receive backsliders as equals, but this father, in a frenzy of joy, fully reinstates his son.

The fatted calf being killed is a further symbol. Bailey observes that such a large animal will feed a whole community. Although the community has nothing but disapprobation for the boy, now they are invited to a massive barbecue.

> A calf is slaughtered for the marriage of the eldest son, or the visit of a governor of the province, or some such occasion. The calf means at least a joy so great that it must be celebrated with the grandest banquet imaginable. (Bailey 1976, 187)

So the father in the parable is playing a role no proper Semitic patriarch would enact. He has left his honor behind, his position, his community standing. In a way, he is behaving like a mother—kissing, dressing, feeding. Perhaps Bernard Brandon Scott is correct in arguing that Jesus' image of God has broken with patriarchal authority, with absolute sovereignty, and been feminized:

> When the son returns home, the father runs immediately to him and kisses him. Many have objected to this behavior because running offends the dignity of an Oriental man. Even more, he demands no proof of repentance from the son. The son is in no way punished or tested. Most scandalously, the father kisses the young son. The Greek word, *katephilesen,* has overtones of an affectionate kiss of the type exchanged by husbands and wives. Many try to avoid this connotation, but the father here behaves like a mother. This father abandons male honor for female shame. (Scott 1994, 64)

The scene is climactic, if quite bizarre—a manic daddy racing around with symbol after symbol of extravagant restoration, not to mention party plans all at once.

The symbol of the father stands in contradiction to legal and sovereign definitions of God.

But the story is not over: There is the elder brother. The elder brother who was
silent and uninvolved at the start of the parable now returns from a field and nears
the house. (Is distance here symbolic?) A slave announces, "Your brother has
arrived, and your father has killed the fatted calf because he got him back in good
health." The parable establishes relationships all over again—"father" and
"brother." But the elder brother is angry. He will not join the party; He will not
be his brother's brother. So the father comes out to him, as he did when the prodigal returned.

All of a sudden the elder brother's bitterness, formed over many angry years,
spills over:

> Look, I've worked for you for years and never disobeyed one of your
> orders, and you never gave me so much as a goat so I could party with
> my friends. But when this son of yours, having used up your inheritance
> with whores, shows up, for him you kill the fatted calf!

Of course, the elder son is quite right. He has slaved for his father and, what's
more, will have to support his father until the old man dies. He has been faithful,
if grudging, whereas the younger son has not only damaged the family finan-
cially, brought disgrace to the family name, and, by consorting with whores,
besmirched the family line. No wonder he is appalled.

> I've worked for you for years, and never disobeyed one of your orders,
> and you never gave me so much as a goat so I could party with my friends.

Do you see? The elder brother has defined his own position in terms of slave
labor, obedience, and reward.

Then once more the father behaves untypically. "Dearest child," he says. The
phrase is movingly tender. Then the father reaffirms the elder son's position:
"Everything I have is yours." The statement is a formal declaration. Under inheritance custom, the eldest son receives two-thirds of an estate. Here the father
announces that the son will receive everything. Once more, the father's behavior defies every expectation. He does not rebuke a resentful, outspoken, uppity
older son. No, he hands over everything. The father will be destitute, for he has
given himself away!

Sermon

How do you preach the Prodigal Son when everyone has heard it before? Here
is a quirky sermon, written with brevity in 1989 for an Anglican theological
school's morning chapel service with Eucharist.

Introduction   There's a book about American folklore. You find it in most
   libraries. In the book, there's a section entitled, "Rogues, Scalawags, and

Wastrels." Have you noticed, we Americans seem to love scamps? We cheer a movie like *The Sting,* all about con artists. We buy a book like *Catch-22* with that irrepressible rascal Yossarian. Rogues, scalawags, and wastrels! No wonder we like the story of the Prodigal Son; the prodigal son is a first-class rogue, a wastrel through and through. But he's our hero, for though he may sow wild oats, he still winds up at a party. Listen again to the parable from Jesus.

1 Let's be honest: The younger son, the prodigal son, is a stock character. The younger son is scarcely original. There are thousands of stories about scapegrace younger sons. We see him on the television soaps. Perhaps we see him in ourselves. He is a rogue, a thoroughgoing rascal. Doesn't he con his father out of a bundle of cash? Too bad you've lived so long, Dad; how about an advance on the old inheritance? Then, with a bulging wallet, he's off and running. See him run, with a Benny Hill smirk on his face, off to where the action is. Talk about wine, women, and song. He quaffs wine like water, sings every ribald song, and, as for women, well, they may be expensive, but every growing boy should have a hobby. How was it Saint Augustine described his own wild oats? "The sizzling . . . of unholy loves," he wrote.[9] Well, the young son in the story sizzles—he sizzles, that is, until the cash runs out. Then there he is, broke, hungry, and homeless. "Prodigal" is too nice a word for him; to be truthful, the boy is a bum.

2 But, mark this, the prodigal son is not stupid. Like most rogues, he has a shrewd, canny, calculating mind. Here he is hungry while, in his thoughts, he could picture his father's farmhands feeding on three square meals a day. Aha! he says to himself, I know what I'll do. I'll go to Daddy and sound religious: "I've sinned against heaven and in your sight. . . . Please pass the mashed potatoes!" Look, we want the story to be about conversion; we want a religious motive and a religious reward; after all, the story is in the Bible. But, to be honest, is the prodigal son all that religious? There was a wonderful novel some years ago about a Salvation Army soup kitchen where bums could line up for a handout lunch. One old bum in line advised a young tramp standing behind him, "Always eat good," he says. "Take a dive for Jesus every day!"[10] Leave your religion behind when you hear the story of the Prodigal Son and you'll have to agree; if he's converted, it's not much more than a soup-kitchen conversion. I'm hungry, father's farmhands are eating well. . . . I know what I'll do! Listen, the prodigal son may be a rogue, but he isn't dumb.

3 Hold on now, suddenly the story turns surreal. Enter the father, stage right. Enter the father, rushing out to welcome his wastrel son! Before the boy can unreel his canned, carefully memorized speech, the father interrupts and starts bellowing orders. "Get him a three-piece suit," he shouts, "tasseled loafers, and a dozen new shirts. Put a ring on his finger, my own signet ring. Sell the stock portfolio," he roars, "let's party tonight!" In one of Frederick Buechner's novels there's an old evangelist who throws a party for every prodigal soul he can find, which is to say, all the bums in town. There are tables of food,

table after table, and wine punch, tray after tray; and people singing, everything from "Roll Out the Barrel," to "Praise God from Whom All Blessings Flow."[11] What a party! A small-scale Mardi Gras! A party for prodigals. Notice please, there are no recriminations—"I told you so"; no lectures on moral theology, no probationary period. No. There is nothing but joy—like a rock band beating out joy in the middle of a church service instead of a prayer of confession. So the father rushes out to welcome his wastrel son.

4 But then, as in most stories, unfortunately there's a complicating factor. There's always an elder brother! The father must turn around and deal with an elder brother, a self-righteous, tedious elder brother. What's a father to do? The older boy won't join the party, not on your life. He won't acknowledge his own brother: "This son of yours," he snarls at his father. He can't even contain his own simmering resentments: "You never gave me so much as a pot roast so I could party with my friends." What's a father to do with such an insufferable son? Answer: Why, forgive him, for that is what the father does. "Dearest child," he says, "Dearest child." Then with a sweep of his hand he announces, "Everything I have is yours." So guess what? The elder brother walks off a winner; he gets two-thirds of the inheritance to begin with and everything else as well. Talk about theater of the absurd! The story is shocking because the villain we've booed and hissed all along turns out to be a winner. "Dearest child," the father says, and hands his son the world.

5 Now take a second look. Nobody has repented. Nobody has repented, but everyone has been forgiven. Repeat: Nobody has repented, but the father has forgiven both sons. And if the father is a stand-in symbol for the God we worship, then we are stuck with a strange, unsettling theology. We sing, "There's a Wideness in God's Mercy," but this is ridiculous, for here there is no limit to mercy at all. Obviously the father forgot to read Bonhoeffer's scathing remarks on the subject of cheap grace. No, he gives and gives and gives and gives until he is reduced to nothing, nothing more than a naked laughable God—a God almost as ridiculous as naked Jesus nailed to a cross! In south Philadelphia there used to be the ugliest church you ever saw. Flat-roofed, it was made of cinder block with cloudy windows that looked like they had been provided by the Department of Sanitation, all but one window that was stained glass, filched from some church being torn down. It was ugly too, all yellow and green, with words, "Come to the mercy seat." The window was lit from the outside so that for people in church the words would glow like neon. But there was a light on the inside too, so that outside in the dark, people could read the same message—"Come to the mercy seat." Think of it, the same message for those inside the church and those on the outside; the same message for those who confess, and those who don't; the same message for those who believe and for those who may never believe. Think of a God who doesn't have mercy, but *is* mercy. Think of a God who is willing to give up everything, yes, even give up being God—there's the laughable man on the lone cross on a hill outside Jerusalem—yes, give up being God to forgive us all.

Conclusion   Look, the story of the Prodigal Son is more radical than we know. We can't file the story away under "C" for conversion. What are we going to do? If God's mercy is unconditional, our churches may be undercut, our revivals superfluous. What are we going to do? We can do what we should do. Dear friends, let us repent and join the party, a party that's been going on for twenty centuries! The table is filled with the mercies of God. The wine is blood red. Come, let us hoist the cup with joy.

Discussion

The problem for preachers can be restated simply: Everyone has heard the parable before. So what else is new? People already understand the story is about conversion, that God is like the father, and that tight-sphinctered religious types are like the elder brother. The problem is how to introduce any other interpretation.

Frequently a preacher can solve such a problem by reordering plot sequence. For example, we could enter the story at the point of the prodigal's welcome home, review the elder brother's resentments, and then switch over to a more personal point of view and see what the welcome must have meant to the prodigal. We tend to think of stories as beginning at the beginning and moving along, episode after episode, but human consciousness is no longer so slavish; in plotting stories, we can enter a sequence of events and, by flashbacks, recall previous happenings, and so forth.

But the problem with the Prodigal Son is that the plot itself is overestablished. Therefore the only solution I could find was to retain the traditional story line, but then change the imagery and illustration to undercut traditional interpretation. Let's review the sermon move by move.

Introduction   The introduction is designed to establish the prodigal as a rogue, a scalawag who is, nonetheless, our hero. Today, examples would have to change—both *The Sting* and *Catch-22* are now dated; but when preached they were still viable examples. Note that the prodigal is "our hero" because "he may sow wild oats, but he still winds up at a party."

1   Here we want to establish that the prodigal is a rather nasty rogue and not merely a wild-oats youngster. Instead of discussing biblical scholarship, we have established (1) his attitude toward his father—"Too bad you've lived so long, Dad; how about an advance on the old inheritance?" and (2) his destructive, indeed salacious behavior—"See him run with a Benny Hill [also dated] smirk on his face, off to where the action is." The phrase "where the action is" is common parlance in any urban area. The cynicism with regard to women, "they may be expensive, but every growing boy should have a hobby," is deliberately sleazy. Why Saint Augustine? I still keep the story of the prodigal in church (at least temporarily) while labeling his activity, "The sizzling of unholy loves." But, all in all, we are trying to convey that "the boy is a bum."

2   The next move is crucial. I have to shake the usual conversion reading of the parable—no easy task. The real key is in the phrase, "I know what I'll do. I'll go to Daddy and sound religious." Note the coupling of the religious confession with the crassness of "please pass the mashed potatoes." The illustration adds to the assault on conventional interpretation. Can anything be more calculating than, "Always eat good. Take a dive for Jesus every day"? We end the move with a second rehearsal of logic: "I'm hungry, Father's farmhands are eating well. . . . I know what I'll do."

3   Now I shift focus sharply and establish a different mood. I pick up a dramatic metaphor, "Enter the father stage right." Actually I began to draw on the dramatic metaphor early in the introduction with the mention of performance works, *The Sting* and *Catch 22*. I mentioned further that the young son was a stock character you could see on TV soaps. We have set the retelling of the parable in dramatic scenes. Move three begins in a kind of frenzy, as the father, interrupting, starts bellowing orders. Deliberately I skipped the significant biblical images — robe, ring, sandals — in favor of contemporary equivalents. Interrupting sermons with Bible study stuff is not always helpful. Instead we have a three-piece suit, tasseled loafers, a signet ring, and a stock portfolio. I add a scene from a Frederick Buechner novel that vividly captures the mood and, with "everything from 'Roll Out the Barrel' to 'Praise God from Whom All Blessings Flow,'" couples secular partying with religious meaning. Then I do more biblical background in disguise with "no recriminations . . . no lectures on moral theology." In the move I have tried to catch a touch of burlesque.

4   Problem: I jam two things in one move, normally a disaster. I try to deal with the elder brother's attitude and the father's response all together. (Theological school chapel services, particularly those with Eucharist, are timed carefully.) The move first establishes the elder brother's attitude, but within the framework of "the father must deal with . . . " This device allows me to turn to the father's reply without completely splitting the move. Finally, I interpret the exchange as theater of the absurd, because the villain ends up with everything after all.

5   The final move is crucial. It shatters expectations with "Nobody has repented, but everyone has been forgiven." Conventional interpretations have been dumped. I then depict God's radical grace, "We sing 'There's a Wideness in God's Mercy,' but this is ridiculous." The quip, "Obviously the father forgot to read Bonhoeffer's scathing remarks on the subject of cheap grace," was designed for the theological students attending. Do you notice the strategy of two asides — "a God almost as ridiculous as naked Jesus nailed to a cross," and subsequently, "there's the laughable man on a lone cross on a hill outside Jerusalem"? In each case I have alluded to Christ crucified in relation to statements about God. But, deliberately, I have slipped them into the sermon as if to create a subliminal association. They flank the rather lengthy illustration about the cinder-block church in south Philadelphia. The move portrays extravagant mercy from a God who "gives and gives and gives and gives" (rhetorically, a fourfold repetition conveys unlimited excess) and who will even "give up being God to forgive us all"!

Conclusion The conclusion picks up an earlier phrase, "We can't file the story away under "C" for conversion." Then follows the rather desperate phrase, "What are we going to do?" repeated as a bracket around our fears—"our churches may be undercut." Finally, without any identification with the elder brother, I suggest "repent and join the party." The last lines move us toward the Eucharist: "The table is filled with the mercies of God. The wine is blood red."

Is this interpretation correct? Who knows? It is not Luke's understanding of the parable. Luke has a conversion/repentance story. But my treatment is not illegitimate and, for preaching to a bunch of pleasant seminarians, rather fun to design.

DISHONEST STEWARD

LUKE 16:1–12

1There was a certain rich man whose manager was accused of squandering his property. 2Calling him in, he said, "What's this I hear about you? Hand in an audit of your dealings, because you're not going to be manager anymore." 3The manager said to himself, "What am I going to do when the boss fires me? I can't dig ditches and I'm ashamed to beg. 4I know what I'll do to open up some doors* after I'm fired." 5So he called in every one of his boss's [*kyriou* = lord] debtors. He said to the first, "How much do you owe my boss? 6And he answered, "Five hundred gallons of olive oil." So he said to him, "Take the bill, sit down and, quick, write two hundred fifty." 7Then he said to another, "How much do you owe?" He answered, "A thousand bushels of wheat." He told him, "Take your bill and write eight hundred." 8And the boss praised the crooked manager for his shrewdness

—for the children of this world are shrewder in dealing with their generation than are the children of light.

9I tell you, make friends for yourselves with your crooked cash so that when you go broke, you may be welcomed into eternal housing.**

10The person faithful in little matters will be faithful in much, and the person unrighteous in little matters will be unrighteous in much. 11If you have not been faithful with unrighteous cash, who will trust you with true riches? 12And if you have not been faithful with someone else's things, who will give you anything for your own?

* Literally, "receive me into their houses." *The Complete Gospels* suggests "so doors will open."
** Literally, "eternal tents" or, perhaps, an "eternal campground."

The parable has embarrassed Christians for centuries. Clearly the parable embarrassed Luke, for he keeps adding verses—8b, 9, 10–12—trying to find an acceptable moral for the story. How could Jesus tell the story of a crook and, what's more, seem to approve of the crook's behavior? Yes, Jesus told some stories in which a lead character is unsavory: a crooked judge, a ruthless boss who reaped where he did not sow, a king who sentences an agent to torture. But how could a boss applaud the manager for marking down bills, particularly bills owed the boss? And, if the *kyrios* in 8a is translated "Lord," referring to Jesus, how could Jesus endorse a crook?

The prior question is, Where does the parable end? If it ends with verse seven then it sounds unfinished, as if some sort of "punch line" has been lost. If it concludes with 8a, then we must figure out if Jesus ("Lord") is speaking, or the "boss." Scholars are split. Most contemporary parable scholars dismiss verses 9–11 as later attempts to find a redeeming message in the story. Although Jeremias argued that all of verse 8 is Jesus material (Jeremias 1963, 45–47), most recent scholars have differed. Fitzmyer notes that the structure of the story, a story that begins with a boss, almost demands some response from the boss in conclusion.[12] Many recent interpreters agree and include 8a as part of the story; the boss, not Jesus, commends his crooked steward.

If the boss commends the crooked manager, the question is, Why?

There have been several solutions to the problem. One answer has been put forward by J. Duncan Derrett (1970, 56–59), an expert in biblical law and custom. He notes that an agent would collect a boss's debts, but add a "commission" for himself—often a substantial sum. The practice was usual. Threatened with an audit, the agent takes off his added commission, thus winning the debtors' friendship.[13] Moreover, because Levitical law was explicit—Jews must not charge fellow Jews interest (Lev. 25:36–37; Ex. 22:25; Deut. 23:19–20)—he is inadvertently virtuous. In view of the law, there was nothing his boss could do but praise his behavior.

We do know that, in order to sidestep the demands of the law, lenders could write up a loan in terms of produce—so many bushels of wheat, so many measures of oil. In the parable, the loans were obviously usurious, and the agent, though a rascal, either removed his own commission or his boss's usurious interest. The interpretation has a certain appeal: The crook gets off free, and the boss is trapped into giving him a pious commendation. Such bemused trickiness is very much within Jesus' storytelling style. The beauty of Derrett's scheme is it explains everything—the crook's shrewdness and the boss's prompted approval. Nevertheless, there is something labored about the explanation.

John Donahue, S.J. (1988, 161–69) has another observation. He notes that the parable follows after the story of the Prodigal Son and he spots stylistic repetitions that seem to link the two stories. Both begin with "a certain man" (*anthropos tis*), both begin and end with speeches from the initial character, both involve characters who "squander" (*dieskorpisen*), both have characters who are in life-threatening situations—the prodigal is starving and the manager is unemployed—both parables feature inward "I know what I'll do" dialogue, and in both cases there is a surprising acceptance, by the father and by the boss. Therefore Donohue argues that the parable is actually about the accepting boss. Maybe.

Bernard Brandon Scott (1989, 260–65) has offered an interesting recent interpretation. In part he accepts a classification tendered by two other scholars (Crossan 1973, 192–221 and Via 1967, 159–62): The parable is a familiar "trickster-dupe" narrative in which a clever rogue tricks the dupe into going along with his chicanery. Then Scott looks at how the story functions in a listener's mind. He argues that the parable traps listeners into a kind of admiration for the crooked manager's slick deals until, suddenly, the boss voices approval. Then listeners are forced to reexamine their own support of a crook, admitting their own laxity—"the audience's moral holiday" (Scott 1989, 263–64). Scott's reading is quite perceptive, but also may be problematic. Is meaning altogether reducible to patterns of internal audience response?

Maybe we must ask about why Luke tells the story. Luke is usually something of a moralist, even a pious moralist. He tells the story of a crooked judge and turns it into a lesson about persistence in prayer. He contrasts a tax collector and a Pharisee, and explains God's favor toward the racketeer as a response to the man's repentance. Here Luke spars with the parable in 8b–11, trying to find a moral lesson. He comes up with three morals tacked onto the story: (1) children of light should be as shrewd as the worldly (v. 8b), (2) we must use crooked cash faithfully to ensure "eternal housing" (v. 9); (3) we must be faithful with cash in order to be trusted with more cash (vv.10–12). Though he seems to be ruining a good story by tacking on morals, Luke may actually be on the right track. What does the crooked manager do? He quits trying to make money and instead makes friends. He puts relationships above cash which, of course, is what we all should be doing. His motives may be lousy, but at least he has stepped beyond profit to relate to his neighbors.

Still, we are left asking, Why does the boss praise his crooked manager? The problem with Scott's interpretation is that the boss's praise is designed to throw an audience for a loop. As a device the approval has meaning but, within the plot of the story, it does not. At the beginning of the story we have an arbitrary boss who, even before an audit, has condemned his manager. The manager in turn supposes he will be fired (an admission of guilt?). So he marks down all the bills to the delight of the creditors. Then in an inexplicable reversal, his boss approves. We must either buy some version of the Derrett-Fitzmyer scheme or we must argue that the boss cannot afford to alienate his borrowers and, therefore, has to approve his manager's generosity. We cannot stay within the plot of the story and argue that the boss's approval forces us to examine our "moral holidays." Could verse 8a have been a rewrite of an earlier, but now missing, punch line? We could drift toward some version of the Donahue proposal, in which case we end up with the justification of a sinner—*Simul Iustus et Peccator*.

Scholars and homileticans both leave the text with a bundle of unanswered questions. But, questions or not, the parable can be preached. And in our society, a nation that lives by the dollar and that frequently admires profiteering as "good business," the parable may have peculiar power. In a world where soon economic blocs may replace nations, the parable may speak even more loudly than in early times. We prosecute embezzlers, business cheats, and the like; financial deviation is a scandal to us. But we do not punish those who dehumanize in the name of "good business," who exploit neighbors with high interest credit cards, who treat customers as losers from the start. The manager in the parable, though a crook operating out of self-interest, at least is relating to neighbors with friendship and generosity. Would that the children of light were as dedicated.

Sermon

This sermon on the parable was preached in 1998 at a Presbyterian church:

Introduction   We Christians are easily shocked. So the parable of the crooked manager has troubled us for centuries. The parable tells the story of an out-and-out crook whose boss seems to approve of his being crooked! Even the Gospel writer, Luke, is embarrassed by the parable. He keeps adding morals to the story trying to make it respectable. We tell the parable of the Good Samaritan to our children. In church, we cheer the prodigal son when he seems to repent, but what can you do with a crooked manager? How could his boss praise him? Worse, how could Jesus tell the story as if it were some sort of religious truth? What can we do with the parable of the crooked manager?

1   Begin by admitting that the whole Bible is as embarrassing. Again and again God seems to favor crooks. The favoring begins early in the Bible. Remember: God rescues a murderer, Cain, who's killed off his own brother, and protects Cain from punishment. And what about Jacob—a mama's boy who cheated his older brother out of a fortune? He's one of God's favorites. Then there's King David, the Bill Clinton of Israel. His sexual episodes involving a swell-looking Jewish girl named Bathsheba would have driven a Kenneth Starr bonkers. Yet the Bible says God loved King David especially. Wasn't it Mark Twain who snorted his contempt for the Bible? As far as he could see, the Bible was a spectacular collection of the immoral—liars, cheats, adulterers, murderers, con artists, megalomaniacs, all of whom appeared to be loved by God! Well, to tell the truth, Twain was right, the God of Israel does seem to lean overboard in support of a host of sleazy types who live fast and loose on the edge of the Ten Commandments. So let's admit the truth: The Bible, the whole Bible, can be downright embarrassing.

2   Of course, here's a thought: Maybe the Bible is only embarrassing to those who think they are righteous. Ever since Scott Peck decided the world could be split up into good people and bad people, most of us tend to list ourselves under the heading "good." Bad, are people like Saddam Hussein, hiding chemical weapons in Iraq, or Osama bin Laden, the terrorist. Of course, we do make distinctions: some people are pretty bad, others not-so-bad, and there's kinda' bad, but always the "bads" are separate from the good list where our own names appear. But look here, we are Presbyterians and ever since Mr. Calvin preached in Geneva we have believed that every one of us is both good and evil; we are morally ambiguous creatures. Mixed motives undercut all our virtues—good heavens, even our prayers can be packed with self-interest. Robert Penn Warren has a corrupt politician, Willie Stark by name, sum up truth: "Just plain simple goodness," he says, "You can't inherit that from anybody. You got to make it out of badness. Badness." "You know why?" he asks. "Because," says he, "there isn't anything else."[14] A very Presbyterian conviction—perhaps a biblical conviction. No wonder the Bible is so embarrassing.

3 Well, the crook in the parable is certainly B-A-D, bad. And yet, please note, we sort of admire the man. He's clever, isn't he? Look, he knows he's about to get canned—an audit will show him up. "What am I going to do?" he exclaims. He looks down at his smooth Presbyterian hands: "I can't dig ditches," he says. He looks to his own smooth Presbyterian pride: "I'm certainly not going to beg." So what's he going to do? Well, talk about "slick." The manager calls in all the people who owe his boss money one after another. "What do you owe?" he asks. "Five hundred gallons of oil? Here's the bill, quick, sit down and write two-hundred fifty gallons." "And you, a thousand bushels of wheat? Here, mark your bill eight hundred." One after another he slices all the bills. He figures he had better make friends, for when he's fired, he's going to need friends. The manager is quick, he's slick, and he's saved his own neck. To tell the truth, we kind of admire him, don't we? Lawrence Block has written a series of books about a professional thief, Bennie Rodenbarr. Bennie is slick and smart and witty. One reviewer said it nicely, "Bennie is such an outrageous character . . . you wish he were real."[15] The manager in the parable is outrageous, and he's as crooked as crooked can be, but in a way, well, we nudge each other and wink and cheer him on.

4 Of course, we can offer an excuse for his behavior. Let's face it, the whole economic situation in the parable is not what you'd call moral. Read your Bible: Exodus, Leviticus, Deuteronomy—they all announce God's law, you don't charge interest on loans, particularly of fellow Jews; to do so was considered wicked usury. But there's always a way around God's law, isn't there? If you wanted to loan a thousand dollars, you merely wrote out an invoice for bushels of corn, one thousand five hundred dollars worth of corn. And then you added more so the manager got a cut—make it eighteen hundred dollars worth of corn. The whole system was devious. But then think of our own credit cards: "4.9 percent interest" the ads proclaim, but then there's those three little letters, APR—"above the prime rate"—and suddenly people can be paying fifteen percent which by anyone's calculations borders on the

usurious. Yes, the man may have been a slick operator, but look, everyone's involved, the whole system was corrupt. Maybe all we can ever do is shrug, and borrow Kurt Vonnegut's favorite phrase, "So it goes, so it goes."[16] So it does go in anyone's human world.

5 But look out! All of a sudden the parable ends in a strange way. The boss approves of the crooked manager; he praises him for his shrewdness. Notice two words are in the Bible side by side: He's *shrewd* (we figured that out) and he's a *crook*. Somehow we had begun to forget the fact. We had begun to suspend judgment, to drift off on a kind of moral holiday. But now, suddenly, we're shaken. The boss admits the man is a crook, and yet praises him. Deeper still, why does Jesus himself endorse the little crook by telling us his story? Is the moral of the story a crass "go out in the world and be shrewd?" If so, Jesus disappoints us; Jesus who died in self-giving love. Something's wrong here. There is an astonishing story by Friedrich Duerrenmatt about a group of retired jurists—a judge, a prosecuting attorney, a defense attorney, an executioner—who schedule what they call "entertainments." They invite an unsuspecting traveler, a Mr. Traps, to join them for a mock trial. By a series of questions they expose the criminal actions hidden in Traps's life. But then, while delivering a guilty verdict, at the same time they celebrate their guest, embracing him affectionately, toasting him at a banquet in his honor.[17] So in the parable—the manager is a crook and at the same time he is celebrated. *Simul Iustus et Peccator*—that's a Latin phrase going all the way back to the Reformation—"at the same time justified and a sinner." Maybe, suddenly, the boss has become a stand-in for the mercy of God.

6 Wait a minute! There is a good reason to praise the crook. Did you see what the man did? For the first time in his life he suspended the profit motive and put his neighbors ahead of cash. In desperation he turned to human beings ahead of profit. Maybe the parable is a special message for us Americans, for in America these days, "profitability" is the name of the game. We applaud downsizing corporations that will increase their profitability at the expense of leaving workers unemployed. What's more, we will pay their CEOs extravagantly to do the dirty work of downsizing. After all, who cares, because the market goes up. Maybe America has gone on a moral holiday all for the sake of cash down. Look, the parable steps clean past morality or profitability. Our first responsibility is not to corporate earnings but to our neighbors, neighbors whose mortal flesh is as fragile as ours, whose eyes hide deep inner agonies as do our eyes, who are ambiguous as we are. Your first responsibility is to your neighbors on the earth, not to your cash flow. And these days your neighbors on earth are hungry and hurting, frequently homeless, and, God knows—literally, God knows—they are more important than American prosperity.

Conclusion   The parable still troubles us, doesn't it? We get caught up in the parable and before you know it we're admiring a slick crook in a crooked world. Suddenly the boss praises the man and that doesn't seem right. And then we begin to see what he's done. Look at that, he's served his neighbors. Well, here we are, ambiguous people in an ambiguous world. You could change priorities, couldn't you? Neighbors. Neighbors are your number one concern.

Discussion

Prior to the sermon, verses 1–8a of the parable were read, then the three "morals" were read one at a time so the congregation could see the trouble Luke was having with the parable.

Introduction The introduction lacks visual power, though it probably worked well enough. But there are too many questions heaped up as the introduction closes. Two questions can be heard, but three in a row may merely register as rhythmic querulousness.

1 The first move is a simple system—three biblical examples and the Mark Twain reference. The allusion to President Clinton and Kenneth Starr was included because the sermon was preached the Sunday following the release of the Independent Counsel's report. I could not find the direct quote from Twain, so I described it instead.

2 The next move almost splits. In the first part of the move we chase down our own self-righteousness; in the second half I counter from a Reformed perspective. Then I add the quote from Robert Penn Warren's *All the King's Men*. I selected references to Saddam Hussein and Osama bin Laden because both were in the news during the previous week. Problem: The first two moves may sound somewhat alike.

3 In the next two moves we slide into what Bernard Brandon Scott suggested, namely, a "moral holiday." I admire the crooked manager and then excuse him on the basis of general corruption. We use dialogue to represent the manager in action. The move concludes with the Bennie Rodenbarr reference, an example of our fondness for rascals.

4 Here, I provide the congregation with exegetical background, but within a move designed to widen our moral indifference. The citation of credit card interest rates makes the indifference contemporary. Often credit cards are usurious and a sign of our cultural corruption.

5 Move five is a bit helter-skelter—I am trying to do too much in a single move. I want to show that the boss's approval shakes us up and rescues us from our "moral holiday." Then I want to work from our shock to discover in the boss's approval an image of divine mercy. The Duerrenmatt illustration may have helped. Nevertheless the move does not work very well. I should have designed two moves.

6 Here we get to the heart of the parable—not profitability but neighbor love. The reason the crook is praised is because, even though out of self-interest, he has turned to his neighbors.

Conclusion The conclusion tends to rehash the action of the sermon, which is usually a problem. Here it serves to lead us to "Neighbors are your number one concern."

Overall the sermon is a bit talky and perhaps should be more visual. The parable is difficult (as Luke also discovered), not simply because the story is somewhat scandalous, but because interpretation leads in too many directions.

RICH MAN AND LAZARUS
LUKE 16:19–31

19Now there was a certain rich man who dressed in purple and fine linen, and who partied sumptuously every day. 20And there was a certain poor man, Lazarus by name, who lay stretched at his gate covered with sores. 21He longed to be filled with the scraps that fell from the rich man's table. But only the dogs came around to lick his sores. 22It so happened that the poor man died and was carried off by angels to be at ease with Abraham.* The rich man also died and was buried. 23In Hades, suffering torments, he looked up and, in the distance, saw Father Abraham with Lazarus relaxing nearby.* 24Calling out, he said, "Father Abraham, pity me! Send Lazarus to dip the tip of his finger in water to cool my tongue, because I am suffering in this fire!" 25But Abraham said, "Child, remember, you received your good things in full during your lifetime and, likewise, Lazarus received bad things; now he is at ease and you are in pain. 26In any event, there is a great chasm between us and you, firmly fixed, so anyone wanting to cross from here to you cannot; neither can anyone cross over to us."

27He said, "Then Father, I beg you to send him to my father's house, 28for I have five brothers. He can testify to them earnestly, so that they may not come to this place of torment as well. 29Abraham answered him, "They have Moses and the prophets; let them hear them." 30But he said, "No, Father Abraham, but if someone from the dead should go to them, they will repent." 31[Abraham] said to him, "If they won't hear Moses and the prophets, they won't be persuaded, even if someone should rise from the dead."

Did Jesus tell this tall story? Most scholars say no. They suppose that Luke picked up a folktale and, because he was interested in issues of rich and poor, included the parable. Although there are scholars who suppose Jesus himself took a folktale and turned it into a parable, virtually all of them drop verses 27–31 as a later Lukan composition. The story is strange—it is set in the afterlife and features a named character, Lazarus—nevertheless, the parable is tricky and is as subtle as most Jesus material.

* Literally, "in the bosom of Abraham."

The parable looks simple enough. A rich man feeds on gourmet food every day. At the gate to his mansion lies a beggar, too weak to beg, hoping for left-over garbage from the rich man's table. Both men die and, in the afterlife, their roles reverse. Lazarus relaxes at table with Father Abraham while the rich man ends up in hot Hades.

There are subtle nuances to the story. The rich man has no name; he is merely "rich man." He dresses in purple, so he is probably either a court official or a nouveau riche social climber who aspires to royalty. He feasts elegantly not once in a while, but every day. By contrast, the poor man has a name; he is Lazarus. Ironically, his name means, "God has helped." But at the time of Christ, impoverished beggars were regarded as sinners being punished for their sins. Lazarus lies outside the wall, but near the gate to the rich man's estate. He is too weak to beg, but lies hoping for table scraps from the rich man's banquets. The only concern he receives is from wild dogs who lick his wounds, probably awaiting his death so as to eat his bones. The contrast between the rich man feasting in his house and the poor man lying outside the gate is carefully drawn.

But keep your eye on the gate.

The next section begins with a favorite Lukan phrase, "It so happened . . ." Suddenly the positions are reversed. Angels carry Lazarus to the "bosom of Abraham." The phrase suggests closeness, as well as a place beside Abraham at a banquet table. Lazarus, who hoped for scraps, now feasts in afterlife. By contrast, the rich man dies, is buried, and ends up in Hades. Once he partied every day, now he cries out for a drop of water.

Still the rich man is arrogant. He refuses to address Lazarus directly. He regards Lazarus as low-class slave labor, so he asks Abraham to order Lazarus to come and moisten his lips.

Some commentators have been distressed that rich and poor are reversed in the parable, as if riches per se were enough to condemn and poverty enough to earn merit. Certainly Luke tends in such a direction (as does the whole Bible). Recall Luke's early contrast:

> Blessed are you who are poor,
> for yours is the kingdom of God.
> Blessed are you who are hungry now,
> for you will be filled.
>
> (6:20–21a)

Luke then adds a warning to the wealthy:

> Woe to you who are rich,
> for you have received your consolation.
> Woe to you who are full now,
> for you will be hungry.
>
> (6:24–25a)

His contrast is blunt and immoderate. There do not seem to be any moral considerations. Many preachers suppose that money is somehow neutral, a medium

of exchange without moral value, saying, "It all depends on how money is used."
Luke may be wiser. There are no neutral things; money has social meaning,
whether it be power to do what we wish, or luxury to enjoy, or security.
There is always social meaning attached to things. Having money at our disposal,
however, while there are whole nations in beggar status is impossible to
condone.

Bernard Brandon Scott (1989, 159) quotes a line from Robert Frost: "Something there is that doesn't love a wall."[18] The rich man could have walked
through his gate to serve the poor man, but he did not. Even in afterlife he does
not acknowledge Lazarus directly as a fellow human being. As a result, the wall
that separated the two in life tips upside down and becomes a chasm: "There is
a great chasm between us and you, firmly fixed," says Father Abraham.

How to design a sermon? Some years ago I mapped out the following
scenario:[19]

The sermon will need an introduction that will define the parable's genre, possibly something such as the following:

> Have you ever heard a joke about the "pearly gates"? There used to be
> stories about the Irishmen, Pat and Mike, meeting Saint Peter at
> heaven's gate. Well, guess what? There were stories about heavenly
> hereafter at the time of Christ. Perhaps Jesus borrowed one of them, for
> he told a story about a rich man and a beggar meeting Abraham in the
> afterlife. Listen once again to the strange parable of Jesus.

Why would we want such an introduction? Because we must get rid of any tendency to read literal references to an afterlife in the parable. The parable proves
absolutely nothing about a hereafter; it does not document either heaven or hell.
There are Christians in every congregation eager to establish hell, particularly
for other "sinners." No, if Jesus told the story he merely was playing around with
a folktale tradition.

The first two paragraphs of your sermon will introduce the two characters
in a kind of storytelling style. A preacher need not stick to a scholarly "daily life
in Bible times" treatment of the two characters. The contrast will be more telling
if you move the figures into our contemporary world: In America today there are
more than three million homeless people. In the past two decades, the rich have
become much richer while the poor have multiplied in poverty. At the same time,
Americans are very much into conspicuous consumption; fine wines and
gourmet foods are available in most suburban malls. Description will be
easy. You may want to begin and end each of the moves with mention of the
gate—"Behind a high wall a rich man lived," "Outside the wall, down on
the ground, a beggar lay." Adjectives you apply to the fence can show up later
attached to the chasm! You don't need to labor the "message" when you can
make it happen!

There is an old Romanesque stone carving of the parable. In an upper right hand corner is the rich man in his flowing robes at table, a goblet held high in celebration. Down in a left hand corner, helplessly lying on his back, is the beggar, Lazarus. Wild dogs are lined up, waiting. The carver had read the parable well, for, diagonally, there is a wide sweep of stone like a wall dividing the two figures.

Your third move can be surprised by the reversal. Does God automatically reward the poor of the world? In capitalist countries we tend to regard poverty as the ultimate sin; to us, people on welfare are "free-loaders" at best. But Lazarus ends up feasting with Father Abraham as if he is being rewarded as a faithful Jew—which, by the way, the parable does *not* say. And the rich man, does he end up in hell simply because he is rich?

A fourth move can introduce pleading by the rich man. He appears to be down, but looking up to Lazarus. Maybe we rich nations can never understand the agony of the poor until somehow we suffer hunger and thirst. Then, suddenly, we cry out for compassion. The problem for most American Christians is that they view world poverty on the television screen; they see it from the comfort of their all-American homes. Poverty is elsewhere, Somalia or Ethiopia, but always distant. Of course, "in the distance" describes the perspective of the rich man in Hades!

Finally, we will face Abraham's terrible reply. We build fences to protect ourselves from hearing the cry of the hungry, from catching sight of desperate Lazarus-people around us. Moneyed people these days are apt to be enclaved in what realtors call "Gated Communities." But, tragically, fences can become eschatologically permanent. Most preachers seek to avoid preaching about ultimate penalties. After all, we are justified by grace and, thus, are we not assured of God's permanent affection? If we have God's permanent affection—the sunny smile on the "God Loves You" button—then the whole notion of ultimate penalty is erased forever; God accepts us as is. But we forget that though we are justified by grace we are still judged by works and, according to Matthew 25:31–46, works involve feeding our neighbors who are hungry, clothing those who are ragged, and providing space in our homes for the homeless who live hidden beyond the fences we have built. In a recent West Coast earthquake a thruway that had divided a rich from a poor neighborhood collapsed, turning into an impenetrable barrier. In the parable, what was once a wall with a gate to pass through becomes a chasm driven down unimaginable depths. Human carelessness hardens.

What can we do? The original parable ends hopelessly with a fixed chasm dividing the rich man and Lazarus. Yet, surely, the parable is told to stir concern for the poor who, whether we wish to acknowledge them or not, are our kinfolk. How would we rewrite the parable if we could? Would we not walk out of ourselves into a world where people hunger and thirst, and claim them in love as our brothers and sisters, which, of course, in God's sight they are. Only then would the walls come tumbling down.

Think of it—the gate of our indifference is a gate to and from heaven!

UNDESERVING SERVANTS

LUKE 17:7–10

7If any of you has a slave plowing or tending sheep, when the slave comes from the field, do you say, "Come and relax at table?" 8Rather won't you say, "Fix my supper, and serve me while I eat and drink. Later you can eat and drink"? 9Do you thank the slave for doing what he is supposed to be doing? 10So you, when you have done everything that's been commanded, say, "We are undeserving slaves, for we have only done what we were supposed to do."

The parable may be a little difficult to translate into our own experience. We do not have slaves—thank God. Instead we can think of a "public servant" and listen to the parable all over again:

> When the mailman delivers your mail, do you invite him in, saying, "Have a seat. Put your feet on my footstool. Let me turn on the TV for you. May I mix you up a dry martini?" No! You do not treat him specially for doing what he's supposed to do. So, when you have done all you are bound to do, say, "We are undeserving, for we have done nothing more than what we were supposed to do."

Retold, the little parable is rather amusing. But unfortunately, the parable is slight. There doesn't seem to be much to preach.

The parable is trickier than we may suppose. At the beginning Jesus has put you in the position of mastery. You are the boss, and slaves are supposed to wait on you. You do not give slaves special praise when all they are doing is what you have told them to do. Would you put them in your place at table? Would you wait on them? Not a chance! They are servants and you are the boss.

Abruptly, however, your position is switched: "So you, when you have done everything that's been commanded . . ." Now you are no longer a boss, you are merely a servant. Look at the action of the parable; it sets you up as a boss, and then without warning switches your position. You are no longer at the center of your own world; you are a slave to another. How can we design a sermon to do what the parable wants to do?

The parable speaks to us and to every human being. All two-legged human beings are "centered" selves. We think of ourselves as centered within a world so that, in consciousness, everyone else is all around us. Therefore we tend to regard others as designed to serve our needs. We forget that others are also centered in their own worlds-in-consciousness, and they regard us as adjunct to their lives.

More profoundly, because we are centered selves, we always forget that we live in relation to God, a God who is the still center around whom all things revolve: God's love is central. No wonder that the little parable has to shift our position so brutally. God, our God, has commanded our service.

The parable uses the Greek word, *doulos,* "slave." Years ago I met a man whose mother was Greek. He was one of seven children. When all the kids in the family were trying to get their mother's attention at once, she would lose her patience and shout, "You make me a *doulos!*" Do you get the picture? A *doulos* is someone who waits on you, busy catering to your every need.

The Greek also features another word, *achreios,* which can mean either "good-for-nothing" or, maybe, "miserable" (Bailey 1980, 121–24). But here "good-for-nothing" may have a different meaning, namely, serving without meriting pay, being good for no reward (i.e., "undeserving"). I have so translated the word.

Kenneth Bailey notes that the parable is related to the parable of the Returning Master in Luke 12:35–38. Here is Bailey's translation (1980, 116):

> Let your waist be girded,
>   and your lamp burning.
> And be like [those] who are waiting
>   for their master to return from the wedding,
>   so that when he comes and knocks,
> immediately they may open to him.
> Blessed are those servants
>   whom coming the master finds awake.
>   Truly I say to you, he will gird himself,
>   and have them recline at table,
> and come and serve them.

The passage in Luke 12 is a complete reversal of our little parable; the faithful servants are "blessed" and the master ends up serving them. How else can we think of God? After all, in Jesus Christ, Christians affirm a God who comes among us as a servant. Did not Jesus bend to scrub road dirt from disciples' feet? Philippians 2:5–7a, captures our convictions:

> Let the same mind be in you that was in Christ Jesus,
>   who, though he was in the form of God,
>   did not regard equality with God
>   as something to be exploited,
>   but emptied himself,
>   taking the form of a slave

As God is a servant in Christ Jesus, so we must serve one another. The motive for our obedience is neither fear nor a carping for reward, but gratitude. As God has served us, so, gratefully, we may serve God and our neighbors.

We centered selves must see that there are others, others as fragile and as demanding as we. Has God designed a world with others all around so that, transformed, we may learn to bow and serve our neighbors modestly? As Christian creatures, we live in love, peculiarly enslaved to neighbors.

In William Faulkner's astonishing work, *Requiem for a Nun,* a proud white woman learns from a black maid. The black maid, Nancy, speaks her faith: "I can get low for Jesus too. I can get low for him."[20] She believes that Christ on the cross has died for her sins and that, thankfully, she can humble herself to serve him.

There is another odd feature to the context of the parable in Luke. Following the parable is the story of the ten lepers. All ten are told to go and show themselves obediently to the priests so their cure may be certified and they may return to their communities. But one leper turns back to give thanks (*euchariston*), in effect, to worship. Thus, though the parable urges complete obedience with no rewards, the story of the lepers says that obedience is not enough—we must also give thanks to our God.[21] What is the Christian life? Nothing less than obeying God and giving God praise.

UNJUST JUDGE

LUKE 18:1–8

> [1]He told them a parable so they would pray all the time and not lose heart. [2]He said, "There was a certain judge in a certain city who neither feared God nor respected anybody. [3]And there was a widow in the same city who came to him, saying, 'Give me justice against my opponent.' [4]At first he would not, but after a while he said to himself, 'Though I don't fear God or respect anyone, [5]because this widow keeps annoying me, I will rule in her favor, lest she finally wear me down by continually bugging me.'" [6]Said the Lord, "Listen to what the crooked judge is saying! [7]Won't God decide justly for his chosen ones who cry to him day and night? Will he delay for long? [8]I tell you, God will give them justice quickly. Nevertheless, when the Son of Man comes, will he find faith on earth?"

All you have to do is to look at verses 1 and 8; they don't dovetail. In the first verse Luke tells you that the parable teaches us to pray all the time. But verse 8 asks if the Son of Man will find faith on earth when he arrives. The parable seems to split focus.

In the previous chapter there is a rather strange apocalyptic section having to do with the coming of the Son of Man (Luke 17:22–37). Luke seems to be repackaging material from Q and L. The Son of Man will come like lightning to judge the earth as "in the days of Noah" (v. 26), or "in the days of Lot" (v. 28) when God rained sudden destruction on Sodom: "I tell you on that night there will be two in one bed; one will be taken and the other left. There will be two women grinding meal together; one will be taken and the other left" (vv. 34–35). Then, according to Luke, "Jesus told them a parable. . . ." The context would appear to be the coming of the Son of Man, which, in fact, is how the parable ends. The lesson about prayer, a favorite Lukan theme, does seem to be something of an intrusion.

Here is the problem: Sermons on the second coming are not easy to preach at the indifferent cusp of the twenty-first century. The whole idea of a literal second coming strains credulity. Will Christ arrive on a fast-moving cloud to transport the elect to heavenly accommodations, while leaving unbelievers behind? For most secular souls in our era, the idea of a second coming is not doubted strenuously, it is simply regarded as too silly to waste thought over. Second-coming images seem to have lost potency rather quickly in Christian history, as attested by 2 Peter 3:3–4, penned early in the second century:

> [Y]ou must understand this, that in the last days scoffers will come, scoffing and indulging their own lusts and saying, "Where is the promise of his coming? For ever since our ancestors died, all things continue as they were from the beginning of creation!"

Luke was dealing with much the same problem; the myth of a second coming was fading fast. Thus he may have aimed the parable at prayer instead.

So what do we do with the story of a corrupt judge? Scholars have argued over the parable, particularly over verses 6–8. Are they Jesus material? Jeremias (1963, 154–56) insisted that the words were Christ's because there were Aramaisms involved, that is, phrases typical of the Aramaic that Jeremias assumed Jesus spoke. But Aramaisms indicate nothing more than that Luke's special source goes back to Palestinian soil. Eta Linnemann (1966, 187) also argues that verses 6–8 are Jesus material because, she insists, the parable must be reversed. In other words, someone, presumably Jesus, must come along and say, "Our God is not a corrupt judge." Her argument is not convincing because there are several parables that feature fairly despicable people—a ruthless boss, a king who exacts torture, a crooked manager, and so forth. Of course, according to the Jesus Seminar, none of the apocalyptic second-coming texts go back to Jesus. I concur. While we may well have a Jesus parable here, neither the second-coming sentence nor the prayer interpretation goes back to Jesus himself; both are secondary. How then do we interpret the parable?

We begin by identifying the characters as stock: a corrupt judge and a woman who at best is a determined nag. The phrase "neither feared God nor respected people" is blunt. Presumably a worthy judge would administer the law as God's law justly. But if "the fear of the Lord is the beginning of wisdom" (Ps. 111:10), the judge is rashly irreligious, for he does not fear God. What's more, he has no respect for those who appear before his court. T. W. Manson argues that the phrase "neither feared God nor respected people" means he took bribes.[22] As a circuit judge, based in the city, he would have been open to bribes from rich landowners. Though three judges were expected to rule in fiscal disputes, he is the only judge mentioned. But Israel's judicial system was in some disarray. Usually trials were held in village "gate houses." Listen to Amos on the subject of judges:

> For I know how many are your transgressions,
>   and how great are your sins —
> you who afflict the righteous, who take a bribe,
>   and push aside the needy in the gate.
>   (Amos 5:12)

Amos' words are probably a pretty good description of the corrupt judge.

The widow is also a stock figure. In a patriarchal society, widows and orphans are biblical symbols for the helpless. In first-century Palestine, the family was the source of social service. The family took care of the elderly. The family clan embraced children and children's children. But neither a widow nor an orphan has family. There were frequent court cases in which a family contested a widow's right to inheritance because, after all, she was no longer "family." Because of a widow's uncertain status, the Torah demanded special concern for her plight and special judicial sensitivity. Here is a command from Exodus 22:22–24:

> You shall not abuse any widow or orphan. If you do abuse them, when they cry out to me, I will surely heed their cry; my wrath will burn, and I will kill you with the sword, and your wives will become widows and your children orphans.

Israel must be holy as God is holy, and God cares for widows and orphans:

> The LORD your God is God of gods and Lord of lords, the great God, mighty and awesome, who is not partial and takes no bribe, who executes justice for the orphan and the widow. (Deut. 10:17–18a)

Deuteronomy describes God as a caring judge, quite the opposite of the judge in the parable. So to be holy as God is holy means a special preferential concern for the helpless widow and orphan.

The same claim is found in a famous passage from Sirach 35:14–19 where God is described as a just judge:

> Do not offer him a bribe, for he will not accept it;
>   and do not rely on a dishonest sacrifice;
>   for the Lord is the judge,
>   and with him there is no partiality.
> He will not show partiality to the poor;
>   but he will listen to the prayer of one who is wronged.
> He will not ignore the supplication of the orphan,
>   or the widow when she pours out her complaint.
> Do not the tears of the widow run down her cheek
>   as she cries out against the one who causes them to fall?

True justice, like God, will be impartial, but especially open to hearing the cries of the helpless, indeed, the complaints of widows.

In the parable, peculiarly, the widow shows up before the judge arguing her own case. Surprisingly, she has no one to represent her in court; has her husband's family turned against her? Once more we have a parable in which a woman is hero, and an assertive hero as well. She comes at the judge again and again and again, stridently demanding justice. Finally, battered and bothered, the judge grants justice, not because he cares about justice, but to get her off his back.

The parable does not have much plot. An assertive woman bugs a corrupt judge until, in spite of his lack of interest in her or her case, he gives in and grants justice. Presumably we are to reverse the judge's character. With Sirach we are to insist that our God is a God of justice, and that God wants to hear and answer our cries. Therefore we do not need to pray "all the time" because God is instantly attentive and eager for justice.

Of course, if God is loving and attentive and concerned for justice, we may want to live in constant communication with God. Obviously we don't have to nag God. Instead, we pray because God, by the Spirit, has instigated our prayers to draw us into relationship. When we pray we know God has already urged our praying. Thus we can converse with God much of the time, joining our lives to God's present and helpful grace. We need not bang incessantly on heaven's door; we can live a life of glad and grateful prayer, and do so confidently.

A corollary to the parable: We will want to be attentive to those who are oppressed. We too must be eager for justice. Thus we will be concerned for the poor who more and more may be shut out of a costly American legal system, or, if not shut out, turned into afternoon TV courtroom amusement. When justice can be bought, then the just and loving God is denied. We must be holy as God is holy; thus, both just and eager to serve the poor.

PHARISEE AND PUBLICAN
LUKE 18:9–14

9He spoke to those who were sure of their own righteousness and held everyone else in contempt, telling them this parable: 10"Two men went up to the temple to pray; one a Pharisee, the other a toll collector. 11The Pharisee stood by himself, praying, 'I thank you God that I am not like others—greedy, cheating, adulterous—in fact, like this toll collector. 12I fast twice a week, I tithe everything I earn.' 13But the toll collector, standing far off, would not even look up to heaven, but beat his chest, saying: 'God have mercy on me, a sinner.' 14Let me tell you, this one went down to his house justified, rather than the other; for those who exalt themselves shall be humbled, and those who humble themselves will be exalted."

The scene that features a Pharisee at prayer in the temple and, at a distance, a rueful toll collector is as difficult to preach as any parable. The story as it stands in Luke is simply too pat: a pompous villain, a humble antihero, and a God who seems to like breast-beating prayers. How much has Luke contributed to the story? We know that Luke has an interest in prayer. We know also that Luke has a somewhat invidious attitude toward Jewish leaders. In his eagerness to exonerate his Roman-Gentile audience, Luke is happy to condemn first-century Jewish religion. If Judaism is barren law to Luke, repentant faith in prayer is true godliness. Beneath the contrast Luke has drawn, the original parable may have hinged on v. 14: "Let me tell you, this one went down to his house justified." Why is the publican justified once he leaves the temple?

As most scholars have observed, the Pharisee's prayer is not as bad as it may sound to our more modern ears. Too many preachers have spotted recurrent "I" sentences in the prayer and, urged by neo-orthodoxy's understanding of sin as *hubris,* have labeled the prayer "self-centered" and, therefore, sinful. By contrast they remark the profound humility of the publican who acknowledges his sinfulness with a bowed head. But such sermons may not be helpful, particularly to persons who cringe within a betrammeled ego anyway. Scholars have found prayers, apparently approved in Jesus' day, that sound very much like the Pharisee's in the parable. Jeremias (1963, 142) cites a model prayer from the Talmud to be said on leaving a house of study:

> I give thanks to thee, O Lord my God, that thou hast given me my lot with those who sit in the seat of learning, and not with those who sit at the street corners [i.e., shopkeepers]; for I am early to work, and they are early to work; I am early to work on words of the Torah and they are early to work on things of no moment. I weary myself and they weary themselves, but I weary myself and profit thereby, while they weary themselves to no profit. I run and they run; I run toward the life of the Age to Come, and they run toward the pit of destruction.

Notice that the prayer also features a recurring "I." Of course, for centuries Christians have voiced similar prayers: "There but for the grace of God go I." God's amazing grace has preserved our lives from blatant criminal acts and most of us are intensely grateful. We must not read into the Pharisee's prayer our own theological judgments.

Watch out for *hubris* definitions of sin. All human beings are centered selves. In consciousness we see the world surrounding our centered awareness; we are created as centered beings. When we bump into "others" we discover that they, like us, are centered in their own "worlds." Thus, in a way, to be a centered self is to be a human being. Of course, if we fail to recognize our own broken mortality in the face of others, if instead we regard every neighbor as a threat to our freedom or a slave to our purposes, indeed as an enemy, then we are in sin. The problem with the Pharisee was not self-centeredness, but a deliberate separating of himself from his neighbor the publican.

There is some debate about the phrase I have translated as "stood off by himself praying." Does the prepositional phrase, *pros heauton,* "to himself," modify "praying" or "stood"? Greek manuscripts differ, as do interpreters (Donahue 1988, 188). Though the phrase could be translated "prayed to himself," I have followed Kenneth Bailey (1980, 145) and many others in supposing that the Pharisee "stood off by himself." His separation was not only physical distance, but a separation by self-righteous judgment.

Bailey (1980, 154–55) also speculates that the two men are standing in the temple during the afternoon sacrifice. The Pharisee gives thanks for the benefits of religion in his life. And the publican, Bailey argues, is crying out for atonement. But both are praying during temple worship.

The publican was evidently a toll collector. John Donahue has researched the role of a toll collector.[23] There were tax collectors who paid themselves by gouging their neighbors. They were small-time racketeers by our standards, not unlike those who collect "protection" money in urban areas. But there were also the toll collectors. They were doubly despised because they worked directly with and for the Romans; they were bedded down with the enemy! Not only were they gouging their own people, but they were serving the oppressors and corrupting the lesser tax collectors under their sway. Nowadays we would think of them as big-time racketeers—as "Godfather" Mafia types or worse. Would we be amiss to imagine that original listeners to the parable upon hearing the phrase, "God be merciful to me a sinner," might have burst into wry laughter? How could a just God show mercy when, obviously, the man could never make atoning restitution? He had gouged too many of too much to ever pay back his moral debts. What kind of God could whitewash such dedicated criminality? Certainly not a God of justice and truth.

How come a big-time, totally corrupt racketeer is "justified" by God? In answering the question, almost all of us clergy types go wrong. We end up saying the Pharisee is a sinner because he uses the "I" word a lot. But the publican, though a sinner, repents before God and therefore is acquitted. Although it may match Luke's understanding, such a strategy turns repentance into a "work" by which we can earn God's approval. We picture a God who does not appreciate self-centered prayer (though, inevitably, all our prayers are self-centered!) but, instead, applauds self-denigration. Advice: Repent vocally and then stand back to receive your "justification"; be saved by ruefulness! The theology is not only moralistic, but crassly unaware of complex human motivations. Yet, as long as sermons create guiltiness, we preachers can count on employment!

The parable is more sophisticated than we or Luke may imagine. Bernard Brandon Scott shrewdly notices locations in the parable (Scott 1989, 95–97). As long as the two figures are standing in the temple, and in the midst of temple theology, their moral differences can be discerned: The Pharisee is a good guy and the publican is a crook. Good guys care for their families, they are honest in their business affairs, they contribute generously to the needy and tithe to support religious institutions. On the other hand, a crook is a crook. The publican is a traitor, having sold out to the enemy; he is a corrupter, maintaining a system of exploitations, and turning every neighbor into a victim of organized greed. Within temple courts the moral "map" is unquestionably clear.

But notice that when the two men leave the temple to go home, the publican is "justified" by God. Outside religious definitions, maybe we can remember that all of us two-legged humans are beloved by God and that if we are "saved," it is by God's free grace alone. The problem with the Pharisee is that he pointed at the publican, and in his self-righteous pointing, denied their common humanity before God.

So how do we preach the parable? Shall we imagine the commander of a Nazi gas chamber chanting, "God be merciful," and with the quick, breathy prayer, winning justification? Aren't revivals wonderful! Or possibly we can picture a drug pusher in tight jeans and a torn Harley T-shirt standing on our church steps smoking a joint and saying, "I'm no damn good." Over against the young drug pusher, we may depict an active Protestant member, a church officer, who loves family and is the one to call whenever you want to get some sort of charitable program going in the parish. How will you explain to your congregation that, on leaving the church, God has justified the drug pusher?

Maybe our mistake is that we are trying to justify God's judgment by checking the character of people in the parable. Instead, perhaps, we must turn around and explore the mystery of God's "character."

Do you begin to see the only possible way to preach the passage? We are justified without qualification by the free, undeserved, gracious love of God.

End of message.

Notes

Introduction

1. Douglas R. A. Hare, *The Son of Man Tradition* (Minneapolis: Fortress Press, 1990).
2. Bernard Brandon Scott, *Hear Then the Parable: A Commentary on the Parables of Jesus* (Philadelphia: Fortress Press, 1989).
3. David Buttrick, *Homiletic: Moves and Structures* (Philadelphia: Fortress Press, 1987).
4. Funk, Robert W., Bernard Brandon Scott, and James R. Butts. *The Parables of Jesus: Red Letter Edition* (Sonoma, Calif.: Polebridge Press, 1988).
5. Robert J. Miller, ed., *The Complete Gospels: Annotated Scholars Version,* rev. and expanded ed. (Sonoma, Calif.: Polebridge Press, 1994).
6. Richmond A. Lattimore, *Four Gospels and the Revelation* (New York: Farrar, Straus, & Giroux, 1979), and, more recently, *The New Testament* (New York: North Point Press, 1996).
7. David Buttrick, *Preaching the New and the Now* (Louisville, Ky.: Westminster John Knox Press, 1998).
8. Stephen J. Patterson, *The God of Jesus: The Historical Jesus and the Search for Meaning* (Valley Forge, Pa.: Trinity Press International, 1998).

Chapter 1: The Parables of Jesus

1. Neighbors Joyce and Walter Marcotte found the quote in J. [Joseph] Bryan III, *Hodge Podge: A Commonplace Book* (New York: Ballantine Books, 1987), 20.
2. John Drury, *The Parables in the Gospels: History and Allegory* (New York: Crossroad Publishing Co., 1985), 39, 70–72, 108–10.
3. Joachim Jeremias, *The Parables of Jesus,* rev. ed. (New York: Charles Scribner's Sons, 1963), 247–48.
4. Geraint Vaughan Jones, *The Art and Truth of the Parables: A Study in Their Literary Form and Modern Interpretation* (London: SPCK, 1964), 58.
5. Clemens Thoma, "Literary and Theological Aspects of the Rabbinic Parables," in *Parable and Story in Judaism and Christianity,* ed. Clemens Thoma and Michael Wyschogrod (Mahwah, N.J.: Paulist Press, 1989), 26–41.
6. Rabbi Shimeon ben Lakish at the death of Rabbi Hiyya bar Ada. From the Palestinian Talmud, *Berakot* 5c.
7. Cited in David Stern, "Jesus' Parables from the Perspective of Rabbinic Literature: The Example of the Wicked Husbandmen," in Thoma and Wyschogrod, *Parable and Story in Judaism,* 60.
8. *Midrash Wayiqra Rabba* 13 (114b).
9. Cited in Paul Michel, "Figurative Speech: Function, Form, Exegesis—A Linguistic Approach," in Thoma and Wyschogrod, *Parable and Story in Judaism,* 142.

10. David Stern, *Parables in Midrash: Narrative and Exegesis in Rabbinic Literature* (Cambridge, Mass: Harvard University Press, 1991), 200.
11. Perhaps Matthew's community was Christian/Jewish instead; see Anthony J. Saldarini, *Matthew's Christian-Jewish Community* (Chicago: University of Chicago Press, 1994).
12. See Robert W. Funk, Bernard Brandon Scott, and James R. Butts, *The Parables of Jesus: Red Letter Edition* (Sonoma, Calif.: Polebridge Press, 1988), 19–23.
13. See, for example, *Gospel Parallels: A Synopsis of the First Three Gospels* (New York: Thomas Nelson & Sons, 1949); or, more recently, John Dominic Crossan, ed., *Sayings Parallels: A Workbook for the Jesus Tradition* (Philadelphia: Fortress Press, 1986). *Sayings Parallels* also includes other sources.
14. Several scholars have drawn up reconstructions of Q. Burton L. Mack, *The Lost Gospel: The Book of Q and Christian Origins* (San Francisco: HarperSanFrancisco, 1993), offers a lively translation. Mack's translation is based on John S. Kloppenborg, *Q Parallels: Synopsis, Critical Notes and Concordance* (Sonoma, Calif.: Polebridge Press, 1988). For discussion, see John S. Kloppenborg, ed., *The Shape of Q: Signal Essays on the Sayings Gospel* (Minneapolis: Fortress Press, 1994).
15. Jeremias, *Parables of Jesus,* chapter 2.
16. Norman Perrin, *Jesus and the Language of the Kingdom: Symbol and Metaphor in New Testament Interpretation* (Philadelphia: Fortress Press, 1976), 3.
17. John Calvin, *A Harmony of the Gospels Matthew, Mark, and Luke,* trans. A. W. Morrison (Grand Rapids: Wm. B. Eerdmans Publishing Co., 1972), 3:39.
18. R. C. Trench, *Notes on the Parables of Our Lord* (New York: Appleton, 1866).
19. Ibid, 33.
20. Adolf Jülicher, *Die Gleichnisreden Jesu,* 2 vols. (Tübingen: J. C. B. Mohr [Paul Siebeck], 1904).
21. Robert H. Stein, *An Introduction to the Parables of Jesus* (Philadelphia: Westminster Press, 1981), 56. Stein's book is useful and provides thoughtful guidance to preacher-interpreters.
22. Jülicher, *Die Gleichnisreden Jesu,* 2:511, 485, 596. Translations are from Stein, *Introduction to the Parables,* 55, 156.
23. Paul Fiebig, *Altjüdische Gleichnisse und die Gleichnisse Jesu* (Tübingen: J. C. B. Mohr, 1904).
24. C. H. Dodd, *The Parables of the Kingdom* (New York: Charles Scribner's Sons, 1961).
25. Jeremias, *Parables of Jesus.*
26. I have cited ten parables. Do all the parables have a surreal aspect—something bizarre or humorously absurd? All of the parables we will study do, except five that many scholars suspect are not original Jesus material.
27. I have argued the "surreal" in parables previously in "On Preaching a Parable: The Problem of Homiletic Method," *Reformed Liturgy and Music* 17, no. 1 (Winter 1983): 16–22; and also in *Preaching the New and the Now* (Louisville, Ky.: Westminster John Knox Press, 1998), chapter 5.
28. Paul Ricoeur, *Semeia 4: Paul Ricoeur on Biblical Hermeneutics* (Missoula, Mt.: Scholars Press, 1975), 115.
29. See, for example, the brilliant study by Robert W. Funk, "The Parable as Metaphor," in *Language, Hermeneutic, and Word of God: The Problem of*

Language in the New Testament and Contemporary Theology (New York: Harper & Row, 1966). Funk's chapter has been hugely influential. But Funk was influenced by Amos N. Wilder [see *The Language of the Gospels: Early Christian Rhetoric* (New York: Harper & Row, 1964), 80.] Wilder may have been the first to argue the metaphorical character of parables.

30. Sallie McFague TeSelle, *Speaking in Parables: A Study in Metaphor and Theology* (Philadelphia: Fortress Press, 1975), 62; see also Sallie McFague, *Metaphorical Theology: Models of God in Religious Language* (Philadelphia: Fortress Press, 1982), chapter 2.

31. John Dominic Crossan, *Raid on the Articulate: Comic Eschatology in Jesus and in Borges* (New York: Harper & Row, 1976), 63–69.

32. Bernard Brandon Scott has written a useful book that looks at teachings and parables, *Jesus, Symbol-Maker for the Kingdom* (Philadelphia: Fortress Press, 1981).

Chapter 2: The Mysterious "Kingdom of God"

1. Albert Schweitzer, *The Quest of the Historical Jesus* (New York: Macmillan Co., 1968 [1910]).
2. Dale C. Allison Jr., *The End of the Ages Has Come: An Early Interpretation of the Passion and Resurrection of Jesus* (Philadelphia: Fortress Press, 1985), 5–39.
3. C. H. Dodd, *Parables of the Kingdom,* 19.
4. Thomas Hardy, "Christmas: 1924," in *Complete Poems,* ed. James Gibson (New York: Macmillan Publishing Co., 1976), 914.
5. For a review of options, see Howard Snyder, *Models of the Kingdom* (Nashville: Abingdon Press, 1991).
6. Adolf von Harnack, *What is Christianity?* 2d ed., rev. Trans. Thomas Bailey Saunders (New York: G. P. Putnam's Sons, 1901), 60–61.
7. Alfred Loisy, *The Gospel and the Church,* trans. Christopher Home (Philadelphia: Fortress Press, 1976), 141. The volume contains a fine introduction by Bernard Brandon Scott.
8. Ibid., 166.
9. Edward Farley calls the underlying interactive human world the "interhuman." See his *Good and Evil: Interpreting a Human Condition* (Minneapolis: Fortress Press, 1990), particularly part 1.
10. Jean-Paul Sartre, *Being and Nothingness: An Essay on Phenomenological Ontology,* trans. Gazel E. Barnes (New York: Philosophical Library, 1956), 9–10. For Sartre, the nonbeing of Pierre is a presence.
11. Johannes Weiss, *Jesus' Proclamation of the Kingdom of God* (Philadelphia: Fortress Press, 1971 [1892]) and Albert Schweitzer, *The Mystery of the Kingdom of God* (New York: Schocken Books, 1914 [1901]).
12. Jack T. Sanders, *Ethics in the New Testament: Change and Development* (Philadelphia: Fortress Press, 1975), 29.
13. See, for example, "The Ethic of Jesus and the Social Problem," and "When Will Christians Stop Fooling Themselves," in *Love and Justice: Selections from the Shorter Writings of Reinhold Niebuhr,* ed. D. B. Robertson (Cleveland: World Publishing, 1967), 29–46.
14. Scott, *Hear Then the Parable,* 122.

Chapter 3: Preaching Parables

1. For example, see Harry Emerson Fosdick, "Personal Counselling and Preaching," *Pastoral Psychology* 3, no. 22 (March 1952).
2. For example, Charles L. Campbell in his *Preaching Jesus: New Directions for Homiletics in Hans Frei's Postliberal Theology* (Grand Rapids: Wm. B. Eerdmans Publishing Co., 1997). For a sharp critique of Campbell's position, see David J. Lose, "Narrative & Proclamation" (paper presented at the annual meeting of the Academy of Homiletics, Oakland, Calif., Dec. 1997), 22–45.
3. Eric Auerbach, *Mimesis: The Representation of Reality in Western Literature,* trans. Willard R. Trask (Princeton, N.J.: Princeton University Press, 1953), chapter 1.
4. Bertolt Brecht, *Parables for the Theatre: Two Plays,* rev. English versions. Trans. Eric Bently and Maja Apelman (New York: Grove Press, 1961). For a compendium of essays by Brecht on dramatic theory, see *Brecht on Theatre: The Development of an Aesthetic,* trans. John Willett (New York: Hill & Wang, 1966).
5. On assessing illustrations, see my *Homiletic: Moves and Structures* (Philadelphia: Fortress Press, 1987), chapter 9.
6. Mary Ann Tolbert, *Sowing the Gospel: Mark's World in Literary-Historical Perspective* (Minneapolis: Fortress Press, 1989).
7. The illustrations and images in the sermon are more fully explicated in my *Homiletic,* chapter 10. I analyze the images as a complete, interactive poetic system.
8. Dan Otto Via Jr., *The Parables: Their Literary and Existential Dimension* (Philadelphia: Fortress Press, 1967). In particular, see Via's chapter on "Parable and the Problems of Theological Language," 26–68.
9. The Greek *homoisos* can mean "like," or can connote "sameness." Matthew 22:34–40 is a controversy with Pharisees who are trying to trap Jesus into setting one command of God above others. Jesus answers by reciting the Shema (Deut. 6:5), but then adding Leviticus 19:18b, saying it is the same thing! Years ago David Noel Freedman insisted that Leviticus 19:18 was badly translated, "You shall love your neighbor as yourself," and that "yourself" should be "your own," meaning your own kinfolk. Obviously, 1 John 4:7–21 concurs; we cannot love God and not love neighbors.
10. Tony Kushner, *Angels in America: A Gay Fantasia on National Themes, Part Two: Perestroika* (New York: Theatre Communications Group, 1994), 158.
11. James Barr, "Biblical Scholarship and the Unity of the Church," *Nineteenth Lecture of the Robinson T. Orr Visitorship* (London, Ont.: Huron College, 1989), 14.
12. I have tried to deal with such issues twice before, in *Homiletic,* chapter 15, and in *A Captive Voice: The Liberation of Preaching* (Louisville, Ky.: Westminster John Knox Press, 1994), chapter 1.

Chapter 4: Parables in Mark

1. So argues Werner H. Kelber, *The Kingdom in Mark: A New Place and a New Time* (Philadelphia: Fortress Press, 1974), and most recent Mark scholars agree.
2. Dale C. Allison Jr., *The End of the Ages Has Come: An Early Interpretation of the Passion and Resurrection of Jesus* (Philadelphia: Fortress Press, 1985), chapters 2 and 3.

3. Norman Perrin, *A Modern Pilgrimage in New Testament Christology* (Philadelphia: Fortress Press, 1974), chapters 5 and 7.

4. Noted by Theodore J. Weeden, *Mark—Traditions in Conflict* (Philadelphia: Fortress Press, 1971), and "The Cross as Power in Weakness," in *The Passion in Mark: Studies on Mark 14—16,* ed. Werner H. Kelber (Philadelphia: Fortress Press, 1976), chapter 7.

5. John R. Donahue, S.J., "Temple, Trial, and Royal Christology (Mark 14:53–65)," in Keller, *Passion in Mark,* 61–79.

6. Mary Ann Tolbert, *Sowing the Gospel* (Minneapolis: Fortress Press, 1989), chapter 9.

7. I no longer have the playbill and am unable to document the scene.

8. Archibald M. Hunter, *The Parables Then and Now* (Philadelphia: Westminster Press, 1971), 42–43.

9. Tennessee Williams, *The Night of the Iguana* (New York: Signet, 1964), 59–60.

10. Jacob Neusner, *Mishnah: A New Translation* (New Haven, Conn.: Yale University Press, 1988), *Kil'ayim* 3:2.

11. See A. Whitman, *Christian Occasions* (Garden City, N.Y.: Doubleday & Co., 1978), 14–31.

12. *The Table Talk of Martin Luther,* ed. Thomas S. Kepler (Cleveland: World Publishing Co., 1952), 73.

13. Paul S. Minear suggests the thief image was welcomed by early Christians, because a thief can relieve us of burdensome possessions. See his *Christian Hope and the Second Coming* (Philadelphia: Westminster Press, 1957), 128–38.

Chapter 5: Parables in Matthew

1. Donahue, *Gospel in Parable,* 63.

2. Douglas R. A. Hare, *The Theme of Jewish Persecution of Christians in the Gospel According to St. Matthew* (Cambridge: Cambridge University Press, 1967).

3. Trevor Ling, *The Significance of Satan* (London: SPCK, 1961).

4. Jean-Paul Sartre, *The Devil and the Good Lord and Two Other Plays* (New York: Alfred A. Knopf, 1960), 133.

5. Alexander Miller, "The Western: A Theological Note," *The Christian Century,* 74, no. 48 (November 27, 1957): 1409–10.

6. John Milton, "Areopagitica," *The Prose Works of John Milton,* vol. 2 (London: Henry G. Bohn, n.d.), 67.

7. James Thurber, *The 13 Clocks* (New York: Simon & Schuster, 1950), 114.

8. J. A. Froude, *Short Studies on Great Subjects* (Ithaca, N.Y.: Cornell University Press, 1967), 34.

9. Henry Sloane Coffin, *God Confronts Man in History* (New York: Charles Scribner's Sons, 1947), 149.

10. *Midrash Rabbah,* trans. H. Freedman and M. Simon (London: Soncino Press, 1959).

11. The parable by Rabbi Simeon ben Shetah appears in several versions. See, for example, William B. Silverman, *Rabbinic Stories for Christian Ministers and Teachers* (Nashville: Abingdon Press, 1958), 76.

12. Otto Glombitza, "Der Perlenkaufmann," *New Testament Studies* 7 (1960–61): 153–61. Cited in Scott, *Hear Then the Parable,* 318.

13. B.E. Perry, *Babrius and Phaedrus. Newly Edited and Translated into English*, 8–11 (Cambridge: Harvard University Press, 1965). Cited in Hedrick, *Poetic Fictions*, 126, n. 41.

14. George Bernard Shaw, *Major Barbara, with an Essay as First Aid to Critics* (New York: Dodd, Mead & Co., 1907), 152.

15. The story may be legend, but has been told again and again. Denny did say something of the sort. Rejecting persons who minimize the cross, Denny remarked, "I had rather be the priest lifting up the crucifix to a dying man, and saying, "God loved like that." *The Expository Times* 60 (1949): 240.

16. From the hymn "When I Survey the Wondrous Cross" by Isaac Watts (1707).

17. W. H. Auden, "For the Time Being. A Christmas Oratorio," *The Collected Poetry of W. H. Auden* (New York: Random House, 1945), 459.

18. Walter Marshall Horton, *Our Eternal Contemporary: A Study of the Present-Day Significance of Jesus* (New York: Harper & Brothers, 1942), 83.

19. Ford said much the same thing in several different contexts. See, for example, Henry Ford, *Moving Forward* (Garden City, N.Y.: Doubleday, 1930), 280. In one speech, he insisted that the essence of the Sermon on the Mount was "just good business." See also John B. Rae, *Great Lives Observed: Henry Ford* (Englewood Cliffs, N.J.: Prentice-Hall, 1969), 61.

20. Harry K. Zeller Jr., "Why Do Good People Suffer?" *Pulpit* (June 1954): 18.

21. Maxwell Anderson, *High Tor: A Play in Three Acts* (Washington, D.C.: Anderson House, 1937), 69.

22. C. S. Lewis, *The Great Divorce* (New York: Macmillan & Co., 1946), 26–27.

23. "Beneath the Cross of Jesus" by Elizabeth Cecilia Douglas Clephane (1868).

24. Graham Greene, *A Burnt-Out Case* (New York: Viking Press, 1961), 90.

25. Rainer Maria Rilke, "Archaic Torso of Apollo," in *The Selected Poetry of Rainer Maria Rilke,* ed. and trans. Stephen Mitchell (New York: Random House, 1982), 61.

26. Samuel Beckett, *Waiting for Godot* (New York: Grove Press, 1954), 35.

27. I have been unable to locate the source of the Dorothy Day story.

Chapter 6: Parables in Thomas

1. On the *Gospel of Thomas,* see Stephen J. Patterson, *The Gospel of Thomas and Jesus* (Sonoma, Calif.: Polebridge Press, 1993); J. S. Kloppenborg, S. J. Patterson, and M. G. Steinhauser, *A Q-Thomas Reader* (Sonoma,Calif.: Polebridge Press, 1990); and Helmut Koester, *Ancient Christian Gospels: Their History and Development* (Philadelphia: Trinity Press International, 1990), 75–128.

2. On the discovery of the Nag Hammadi writings, see James M. Robinson, "Introduction," *The Nag Hammadi Library in English,* trans. James M. Robinson (San Francisco: Harper & Row, 1977), 1–25.

3. On Gnosticism, see Hans Jonas, *The Gnostic Religion: The Message of the Alien God and the Beginnings of Christianity,* 2d ed. (Boston: Beacon Press, 1963); Elaine Pagels, *The Gnostic Gospels* (New York: Random House, 1979); and Pheme Perkins, *The Gnostic Dialogue: The Early Church and the Crisis of Gnosticism* (New York: Paulist Press, 1980).

4. On parables in *Thomas,* see Ron Cameron, *Parable and Interpretation in the Gospel of Thomas* (Sonoma, Calif.: Polebridge Press, 1986).

Chapter 7: Parables from Q in Matthew and Luke

1. See Helmut Koester, *Ancient Christian Gospels, Their History and Development,* chapter 2; Burton L. Mack, *Who Wrote the New Testament? The Making of the Christian Myth* (San Francisco: HarperSanFrancisco, 1995), chapter 2; and John Dominic Crossan, *The Birth of Christianity: Discovering What Happened in the Years Immediately after the Execution of Jesus* (San Francisco: HarperSanFrancisco, 1998), chapters 14–15.
2. On Q, see John S. Kloppenborg, *The Shape of Q: Signal Essays on the Sayings Gospel* (Minneapolis: Fortress Press, 1994) as well as *Q Parallels: Synopsis, Critical Notes, and Concordance* (Sonoma, Calif.: Polebridge Press, 1988); Burton L. Mack, *The Lost Gospel: The Book of Q and Christian Origins* (San Francisco: HarperSanFrancisco, 1993); and Arland D. Jacobson, *The First Gospel: An Introduction to Q* (Sonoma, Calif.: Polebridge Press, 1992).
3. Crossan, *Birth of Christianity,* 263.
4. J. Goldin, *The Fathers according to Rabbi Nathan* (New York: Shocken Books, 1974), 103, as cited in Young, *Jesus and His Jewish Parables,* 257.
5. Douglas R. A. Hare, *Matthew* (Louisville, Ky.: John Knox Press, 1993), 123–25.
6. Christopher Isherwood, *The Berlin Stories* (New York: New Directions, 1954).
7. Epictetus, *Enchiridion* III, trans. George Long in *The Discourses of Epictetus; with the Encheridion and Fragments* (New York: United States Book Co., n.d.), 389.
8. Marc Connelly, *The Green Pastures* (New York: Farrar & Rinehart, [© 1929]), act 2, scene 8.
9. Albert Schweitzer, *Memoirs of Childhood and Youth,* trans. C. T. Campion (New York: Macmillan Co., 1949), 71.
10. Ivan Turgenev, *Poems in Prose in Russian and English,* ed. André Mazon, trans. Constance Garnett and Roger Rees (Oxford: Basil Blackwell, 1951), 35–37.
11. Paul V. Carroll, *Shadow and Substance: A Play in Four Acts* (New York: Random House, 1937), act 3, scene 1.
12. T. S. Eliot, "The Hollow Men," in *Collected Poems 1909–1935* (New York: Harcourt, Brace & Co., 1936), 101.
13. In January 1964, Columbia Records issued a Bob Dylan album titled "The Times They Are a-Changin'."
14. I remembered the quote from a secondary source, but after consulting Islamic scholars who agree the citation is surely Ghazzali, I (and they) have been unable to locate the original source.
15. B. Shabbat 153a. As quoted in B. H. Young, *Jesus and His Jewish Parables,* 103.
16. The twelfth-century hymn, "Jerusalem the Golden" by Bernard of Cluny, as translated by the Reverend John M. Neale in 1851.
17. Ignazio Silone, *Bread and Wine,* trans. Gwenda David and Eric Mosbacher (New York: Signet, 1937), 226–27.
18. Edith Lovejoy Pierce, "Main Street U.S.A.," in *Wind Has No Home* (Evanston, Ill.: E. L. Pierce, 1950).

Chapter 8: Parables in Luke

1. John A. Darr, *On Character Building: The Reader and the Rhetoric of Characterization in Luke-Acts* (Louisville, Ky.: Westminster/John Knox Press, 1992).

2. Mary Ann Beavis, "Expecting Nothing in Return: Luke's Picture of the Marginalized," *Interpretation* 48, no. 4 (October 1994): 357–68. See also David L. Mealand, *Poverty and Expectation in the Gospels* (London: SPCK, 1980), chapters 3–4.
3. Samuel Beckett, *Waiting for Godot* (New York: Grove Press, 1954), 51.
4. Jacob Neusner, *Mishnah: A New Translation* (New Haven, Conn.: Yale University Press, 1988), *Horayat* 3:8.
5. Plutarch, "On the Fortune of Alexander," *Plutarch's Moralia,* Loeb Classical Library (Cambridge: Harvard University Press), 336. Cited in Scott, *Hear Then the Parable,* 136.
6. *Institutes* 4.16.
7. Neusner, *Mishnah, Shebit* 1:8
8. David Daube, "Inheritance in Two Lukan Pericopes," *Zeitschrift der Savigny-Stiftung für Rechtsgeschichte, Romantistische Abteilung* 72 (1955): 326–34. Cited by Bailey, *Poet & Peasant,* 169.
9. *The Confessions of Saint Augustine,* trans. Rex Warner (New York: Mentor-Omega Books, 1963), 52.
10. The novel was in my parents' library, which was given away twenty years ago. I have been unable to recall title or author.
11. Frederick Buechner, *Love Feast* (New York: Atheneum, 1974), 60–64.
12. For a review of different positions, see Joseph A. Fitzmyer, S.J., *The Gospel According to St. Luke X—XXIV* (Garden City, N.Y.: Doubleday & Co., 1985), 1096–97.
13. Ibid., 1097–99
14. Robert Penn Warren, *All the King's Men* (New York: Bantam Books, 1959), 257.
15. The blurb from the *San Francisco Examiner* appears on the back cover of Lawrence Block, *The Burglar Who Studied Spinoza* (New York: Signet, 1998).
16. The refrain runs through Kurt Vonnegut Jr., *Slaughterhouse-Five or The Children's Crusade* (New York: Delta Books, 1969).
17. Friedrich Duerrenmatt, *Traps* (New York: Alfred A. Knopf, 1960), 94–98.
18. "Mending Wall," in *Complete Poems of Robert Frost* (New York: Henry Holt & Co., 1959), 47–48.
19. Much of the material on the Rich Man and Lazarus is drawn from my earlier book, *A Captive Voice: The Liberation of Preaching* (Louisville, Ky.: Westminster John Knox Press, 1994), 91–99.
20. William Faulkner, *Sanctuary* and *Requiem for a Nun* (New York: Signet, 1961), 329.
21. See my *Homiletic: Moves and Structures* (Philadelphia: Fortress Press, 1987), 333–47.
22. T. W. Manson, *The Sayings of Jesus* (London: SCM Press, 1957), 305.
23. John R. Donahue, "Tax Collectors and Sinners: An Attempt at Identification," *Catholic Biblical Quarterly* 33 (1971): 39–61.

Bibliography
Books on the Parables of Jesus

Bailey, Kenneth E. *Poet & Peasant and Through Peasant Eyes: A Literary-Cultural Approach to the Parables in Luke*. Combined ed. Grand Rapids: Wm. B. Eerdmans Publishing Co., 1983.

_____. *Poet & Peasant*. Grand Rapids: Wm. B. Eerdmans Publishing Co., 1976.

_____. *Through Peasant Eyes*. Grand Rapids: Wm. B. Eerdmans Publishing Co., 1980.

Boucher, Madeleine. *The Mysterious Parable: A Literary Study*. Washington, D.C.: Catholic Biblical Association of America, 1977.

Breech, James. *Jesus and Postmodernism*. Minneapolis: Fortress Press, 1989.

_____. *The Silence of Jesus: The Authentic Voice of the Historical Man*. Philadelphia: Fortress Press, 1983.

Bultmann, Rudolf. *The History of the Synoptic Tradition*. 2d ed. Trans. John Marsh. New York: Harper & Row, 1968.

Crossan, John Dominic. *Cliffs of Fall: Paradox and Polyvalance in the Parables of Jesus*. New York: Seabury Press, 1980.

_____. *Finding Is the First Act: Trove Folktales and Jesus' Treasure Parable*. Philadelphia: Fortress Press, 1979.

_____. *Semeia 9: Polyvalent Narration*. Missoula, Mont.: Scholars Press, 1977.

_____. *Raid on the Articulate: Comic Eschatology in Jesus and Borges*. New York: Harper & Row, 1976.

_____. *The Dark Interval: Toward a Theology of Story*. Niles, Ill.: Argus Communications, 1975.

_____. *In Parables: The Challenge of the Historical Jesus*. New York: Harper & Row, 1973.

Derrett, J. Duncan M. *Law in the New Testament*. London: Darton, Longman & Todd, 1970.

Dodd, C. H. *The Parables of the Kingdom*. New York: Charles Scribner's Sons, 1961.

Donahue, John R., S.J. *The Gospel in Parable: Metaphor, Narrative, and Theology in the Synoptic Gospels*. Philadelphia: Fortress Press, 1988.

Drury, John. *The Parables in the Gospels: History and Allegory*. New York: Crossroad, 1985.

Findlay, J. Alexander. *Jesus and His Parables*. London: Epworth Press, 1950.

Fisher, Neal. F. *The Parables of Jesus: Glimpses of the New Age*. New York: Women's Division, Board of Global Ministries, The United Methodist Church, 1979.

Ford, Richard Q. *The Parables of Jesus: Recovering the Art of Listening*. Minneapolis: Fortress Press, 1997.

Funk, Robert W. *Parables and Presence: Forms of the New Testament Tradition*. Philadelphia: Fortress Press, 1982.

_____. *Jesus as Precursor*. Philadelphia: Fortress Press, 1975.

_____. *Language, Hermeneutic, and Word of God*. New York: Harper & Row, 1966.

Funk, Robert W., Bernard Brandon Scott, and James R. Butts. *The Parables of Jesus: Red Letter Edition.* Sonoma, Calif.: Polebridge Press, 1988.

Hedrick, Charles. *Parables as Poetic Fictions: The Creative Voice of Jesus.* Peabody, Mass.: Hendrickson, 1994.

Herzog, William R. II. *Parables as Subversive Speech: Jesus as Pedagogue of the Oppressed.* Louisville, Ky.: Westminster John Knox Press, 1994.

Hunter, Archibald M. *The Parables Then and Now.* Philadelphia: Westminster Press, 1971.

_____. *Interpreting the Parables.* Philadelphia: Westminster Press, 1960.

Jeremias, Joachim. *The Parables of Jesus.* Rev. ed. New York: Charles Scribner's Sons, 1963.

Jones, Geraint Vaughan. *The Art and Truth of the Parables: A Study in Their Literary Form and Modern Interpretation.* London: SPCK, 1964.

Kingsbury, Jack Dean. *The Parables of Jesus in Matthew 13: A Study in Redaction Criticism.* Richmond: John Knox Press, 1969.

Lambrecht, Jan, S.J. *Out of the Treasure: The Parables in the Gospel of Matthew.* Grand Rapids: Wm. B. Eerdmans Publishing Co., 1991.

_____. *Parables of Jesus: Insight and Challenge.* Bangalore: Theological Publications in India, 1976.

Linnemann, Eta. *Jesus of the Parables: Introduction and Exposition.* New York: Harper & Row, 1966.

Patterson, Stephen J. *The God of Jesus: The Historical Jesus and the Search for Meaning.* Harrisburg, Pa.: Trinity Press International, 1998.

Perrin, Norman. *Jesus and the Language of the Kingdom: Symbol and Metaphor in New Testament Interpretation.* Philadelphia: Fortress Press, 1976.

_____. *Rediscovering the Teaching of Jesus.* New York: Harper & Row, 1967.

_____. *The Kingdom of God in the Teaching of Jesus.* Philadelphia: Westminster Press, 1963.

Scott, Bernard Brandon. *Hollywood Dreams and Biblical Stories.* Minneapolis: Fortress Press, 1994.

_____. *Hear Then the Parable: A Commentary on the Parables of Jesus.* Minneapolis: Fortress Press, 1989.

_____. *Jesus, Symbol-Maker for the Kingdom.* Philadelphia: Fortress Press, 1981.

Shillington, V. George, ed. *Jesus and His Parables: Interpreting the Parables of Jesus Today.* Edinburgh: T. & T. Clark, 1997.

Stein, Robert H. *An Introduction to the Parables of Jesus.* Philadelphia: Westminster Press, 1981.

TeSelle, Sallie McFague. *Speaking in Parables: A Study in Metaphor and Theology.* Philadelphia: Fortress Press, 1975.

Tolbert, Mary Ann. *Perspectives on the Parables: An Approach to Multiple Interpretations.* Philadelphia: Fortress Press, 1979.

Via, Dan Otto, Jr. *The Parables: Their Literary and Existential Dimension.* Philadelphia: Fortress Press, 1967.

Wilder, Amos N. *Jesus' Parables and the War of Myths: Essays on Imagination in the Scriptures.* Edited by James Breech. Philadelphia: Fortress Press, 1982.

Books on Jewish Meshalim

Culbertson, Philip L. *Word Fitly Spoken: Context, Transmission, and Adoption of the Parables of Jesus.* Albany, N.Y.: State University of New York Press, 1995.

Feldman, Asher. *The Parables and the Similes of the Rabbis: Agricultural and Pastoral.* London: Cambridge University Press, 1924.

Osterley, William Oscar Emil. *The Gospel Parables in the Light of Their Jewish Background.* London: SPCK, 1936.

Stern, David. *Parables in Midrash: Narrative and Exegesis in Rabbinic Literature.* Cambridge, Mass.: Harvard University Press, 1991.

Thoma, Clemens and Michael Wyschogrod, eds. *Parable and Story in Judaism and Christianity.* New York: Paulist Press, 1989.

Westermann, Claus. *The Parables of Jesus in the Light of the Old Testament.* Minneapolis: Fortress Press, 1990.

Young, Brad H. *Jesus and His Jewish Parables: Rediscovering the Roots of Jesus' Teaching.* New York: Paulist Press, 1989.

On Preaching Parables

Allen, Ronald J. "Shaping Sermons by the Language of the Text" In *Preaching Biblically: Creating Sermons in the Shape of Scripture,* edited by Don M. Wardlaw, 29–59. Philadelphia: Westminster Press, 1983.

Buttrick, George Arthur. *The Parables of Jesus.* Garden City, N.Y.: Doubleday, Doran & Co., 1928.

Capon, Robert Farrar. *The Parables of Judgment.* Grand Rapids: Wm. B. Eerdmans Publishing Co., 1989.

_____. *The Parables of Grace.* Grand Rapids: Wm. B. Eerdmans Publishing Co., 1988.

_____. *The Parables of the Kingdom.* Grand Rapids: Zondervan Publishing House, 1985.

Carroll, John T. and James R. Carroll. *Preaching the Hard Sayings of Jesus.* Peabody, Mass.: Hendrickson, 1996.

Graskow, David M. *Preaching on the Parables.* Philadelphia: Fortress Press, 1972.

Graves, Mike. *The Sermon as Symphony: Preaching the Literary Forms of the New Testament.* Valley Forge, Pa.: Judson Press, 1997. (Chapter 4)

Long, Thomas G. *Preaching and the Literary Forms of the Bible.* Philadelphia: Fortress Press, 1989. (Chapter 6)

Lowry, Eugene L. *How to Preach a Parable: Designs for Narrative Sermons.* Nashville: Abingdon Press, 1989.

Schweizer, Eduard. "Preaching on the Parables." In *Biblical Preaching: An Expositor's Treasury,* edited by James W. Cox. Philadelphia: Westminster Press, 1983.

Sermons on the Parables

Bosley, Harold. *He Spoke to Them in Parables.* New York: Harper & Row, 1963.

Brunner, Emil. *Sowing and Reaping: The Parables of Jesus.* Trans. Thomas Wieser. Richmond: John Knox Press, 1964.

Chappell, Clovis Gillham. *Sermons from the Parables.* Nashville: Cokesbury Press, 1933.

Crowe, Charles M. S*ermons on the Parables of Jesus.* Nashville: Abingdon-Cokesbury, 1953.

Keating, Thomas. *The Kingdom of God is Like—*. New York: Crossroad, 1993.
Thielicke, Helmut. *The Waiting Father: Sermons on the Parables of Jesus*. Trans. John W. Doberstein. New York: Harper & Brothers, 1959.
Trotter, Mark. *What Are You Waiting For? Sermons on the Parables of Jesus*. Nashville: Abingdon Press, 1993.
Van Wyk, William Peter. *My Sermon Notes on Parables and Metaphors*. Grand Rapids: Baker Book House, 1947.

Parable Bibliographies

Crossan, John Dominic. "A Basic Bibliography for Parables Research." *Semeia 1*. Missoula, Mont.: Scholars Press, 1974.
Kissinger, Warren S. *The Parables of Jesus: A History of Interpretation and Bibliography*. Metuchen, N.J.: American Theological Library Association, 1979.

Acknowledgments

These pages constitute a continuation of the copyright page. Grateful acknowledgment is made to the following for permission to quote from copyrighted material:

Anderson House. Excerpt from Maxwell Anderson, *High Tor: A Play in Three Acts* (Washington, D.C.: Anderson House, 1937), 69. Used by permission.

Augsburg Fortress. Reprinted from *Homiletic: Moves and Structures* by David Buttrick, copyright © 1987 Fortress Press. Used by permission of Augsburg Fortress.

Christian Century Foundation. Excerpt from David Buttrick, "The Children at Play," *Pulpit* (July 1958): 9-10. Copyright 1958 Christian Century Foundation. Reprinted by permission from the July, 1958, issue of *The Christian Pulpit*.

Wm. B. Eerdmans Publishing Co. Excerpt from John Calvin, *A Harmony of the Gospels Matthew, Mark, and Luke,* translated by A. W. Morrison (Grand Rapids: Wm. B. Eerdmans Publishing Co., 1972), 3:39.

The estate of Edith Lovejoy Pierce. Excerpt from Edith Lovejoy Pierce, "Main Street U.S.A.," *Wind Has No Home* (Evanston, Ill.: E. L. Pierce, 1950). Used by permission.

Grove Press. Excerpt from Samuel Beckett, *Waiting for Godot* (New York: Grove Press, 1954), 35. Used by permission.

Harcourt, Inc. and Faber & Faber Ltd. Excerpt from "The Hollow Men" in *Collected Poems 1909–1962* by T. S. Eliot, copyright 1936 by Harcourt, Inc., copyright ©1964, 1963 by T. S. Eliot, reprinted by permission of the publishers.

Harcourt, Inc. Excerpt from Robert Penn Warren, *All the King's Men* (New York: Bantam Books, 1959), 257. Excerpt from *All the King's Men*, copyright 1946 and renewed 1974 by Robert Penn Warren, reprinted by permission of Harcourt, Inc.

HarperCollins Publishers, Inc. and Brill Academic Publishers. Selected parables from the *Gospel of Thomas* from The Nag Hammadi Library in English, 3rd, completely revised ed. by James M. Robinson, general editor. Copyright © 1978, 1988 by E. J. Brill, Leiden, The Netherlands. Reprinted by permission of HarperCollins Publishers, Inc. and Brill Academic Publishers.

Harvard University Press. Excerpt from B. E. Perry, *Babrius and Phaedrus.* Reprinted by permission of the publishers and the Loeb Classical Library from *Babrius and Phaedrus,* translated by Ben E. Perry, Cambridge, Mass.: Harvard University Press, 1965.

Henry Holt and Company. Excerpt from "Mending Wall" from *The Poetry of Robert Frost*, edited by Edward Connery Lathem, Copyright © 1958 by Robert Frost. Copyright 1930, 1939, © 1969 by Henry Holt and Company, LLC. Reprinted by permission of Henry Holt & Co., LLC.

Alfred A. Knopf. Excerpt from Jean-Paul Sartre, *The Devil and the Good Lord and Two Other Plays* (New York: Alfred A. Knopf, 1960), 133. Used by permission.

Lectionary Homiletics, for sermon preached by David Buttrick at "A Festival of Homiletics," Williamsburg, Va., May 4, 1993. Used by permission.

C. S. Lewis Co. Ltd. Excerpt from *The Great Divorce* by C. S. Lewis, copyright © C. S. Lewis Pte. Ltd. 1945. Extracts reprinted by permission.

Logos Productions, Inc. Excerpt of edited text of David Buttrick, "A Fool Farmer and the Grace of God," *Pulpit Digest* (November/ December 1983): 57-60. Used by permission.

Logos Productions, Inc. Excerpt of edited text of David Buttrick, "A God Who Is Mercy," *Pulpit Digest* (March/April 1990): 56-59. Used by permission.

New Directions Publishing Corp., and Casarotto Ramsay & Associates Ltd. Excerpt by Tennessee Williams, from *The Night of the Iguana*. Copyright © 1961 by Two Rivers Enterprises, Inc. Published and reprinted by permission of New Directions Publishing Corp. Also reprinted by permission of The University of the South, Sewanee, Tennessee. All rights whatsoever in this play are strictly reserved and application for performance, etc., must be made before rehearsal to Casarotto Ramsay & Associates Ltd., National House, 60–66 Wardour Street, London W1V 4ND. No performance may be given unless a license has been obtained.

New Directions Publishing Corp. and Curtis Brown, Ltd. Excerpt by Christopher Isherwood, from *Berlin Stories*. Copyright © 1935 by Christopher Isherwood. Reprinted by permission of New Directions Publishing Corp. Copyright © 1954 by Christopher Isherwood. Reprinted by permission of Curtis Brown, Ltd.

Penguin Putnam Inc. Excerpt from Ignazio Silone, *Bread and Wine*, trans. Gwenda David and Eric Mosbacher (New York: Signet Book, 1937), 226-27.

Random House, Inc., Curtis Brown Group Ltd., and Chatto & Windus. Excerpt from William Faulkner, *Sanctuary* and *Requiem for a Nun* (New York: Signet, 1961), 329. Used by permission. William Faulkner, *Requiem for a Nun*, published by Chatto & Windus, and William Faulkner, *Sanctuary*, published by Curtis Brown Group Ltd.

Random House, Inc. Excerpt from Paul V. Carroll, *Shadow and Substance: A Play in Four Acts* (New York: Random House, 1957), act 3, scene 1.

Random House, Inc. and Faber and Faber. Excerpt from "For the Time Being: A Christmas Oratorio," *The Collected Poetry of W. H. Auden* (New York: Random House; London: Faber and Faber, 1945, 1994). Used by permission.

Simon & Schuster, Inc. Excerpt from C. H. Dodd, *The Parables of the Kingdom*. Reprinted with the permission of Scribner, a Division of Simon & Schuster, from *The Parables of the Kingdom* by C. H. Dodd. Copyright ©1961 by C. H. Dodd.

Simon & Schuster, Inc. Excerpt from James Gibson, editor, *The Complete Poems of Thomas Hardy*. Reprinted with the permission of Simon & Schuster, Inc. from *The Complete Poems of Thomas Hardy* edited by James Gibson. Copyright © 1978 by Macmillan London Ltd.

National Cathedral (Washington, D.C.). Excerpt of edited text of David Buttrick, "God's Word," *College of Preachers* [Newsletter] 37, no. 1 (Fall 1996): 6-7. Used by permission.

Westminster John Knox Press. Excerpt of edited text of David Buttrick, *The Captive Voice: The Liberation of Preaching* (Louisville, Ky.: Westminster John Knox Press, 1994), 91-99. Used by permission.

Westminster Press and SCM Press. Excerpt from Archibald M. Hunter, *The Parables Then and Now* (Philadelphia: Westminster Press; London: SCM Press, 1971), 42-43.

Index of Subjects

243

Index of Scriptural References

Index of Modern Authors

251

The Sermons

1958   Children in the Marketplace: Preached at the First Presbyterian Church of Fredonia, New York, on January 26, 1958. Subsequently published as "The Children at Play," *The Pulpit* (July 1958): 9–10.

1960   Planted Weeds: Preached at the First Presbyterian Church of Fredonia, New York, on February 21, 1960.

1965   Two Children: Preached at the Fourth Presbyterian Church, Chicago, Illinois, (Pastor: The Reverend Elam Davis) on April 11, 1965. Subsequently published as "I Will and I Won't" in *Presbyterian Life* (September 1, 1965): 2.

1965   Tenants: Preached at Fourth Presbyterian Church, Chicago, Illinois, on April 12, 1965. Rewritten for Muhlenberg College Chapel on March 31, 1974.

1965   Feast: Preached at Fourth Presbyterian Church, Chicago, Illinois, on April 13, 1965. Rewritten to be preached at Beechwood Baptist Church in Louisville, Kentucky (Pastor: The Reverend Howard Hovde) on April 10, 1974.

1965   Closed Door: Preached at Fourth Presbyterian Church, Chicago, Illinois, on April 14, 1965. Subsequently published as "Be Prepared," *Presbyterian Life* (February 1, 1967): 6.

1965   Last Judgment: Preached at Fourth Presbyterian Church, Chicago, Ilinois, on April 15, 1965. Subsequently published as "Last Judgment," *Presbyterian Life* (September 15, 1965): 2.

1974   Vineyard Laborers: I do not know where the sermon was first preached—probably somewhere in the Pittsburgh area—but it was revised and then preached at Beechwood Baptist Church in Louisville, Kentucky, on April 7, 1974.

1980   Sower: The sermon was preached on September 16, 1980, at the ordination of the Reverend Joan M. Marshall at Westminster Presbyterian Church in Washington, Indiana. Subsequently it was published as "The Seed Parable," in *Kairos* [Saint Meinrad School of Theology] 2, nos. 1–2 (March 1982), and also as "A Fool Farmer and the Grace of God," *Pulpit Digest* (November/ December 1983): 57–60. In another version, the sermon is discussed in my book, *Homiletic: Moves and Structures* (Philadelphia: Fortress Press, 1987), 158–60.

1982   Entrusted Money: Prepared for a brief chapel service at Louisville Presbyterian Seminary, Louisville, Kentucky, on November 8, 1982, then revised for the installation of the Reverend William L. Steele as Minister of the Reformed Church of Bronxville, New York, on November 8, 1998.

1989   Prodigal Son: Preached for a workshop under the direction of Dr. Robert Giuliano at Huron School of Theology in London, Ontario, on March 7, 1989. It was subsequently published as "A God Who Is Mercy," *Pulpit Digest* (March/ April 1990): 56–59.

1993   Unmerciful Servant: Preached at "A Festival of Homiletics," sponsored by *Lectionary Homiletics* (Editor: The Reverend David B. Howell) in Williamsburg, Virginia, on May 4, 1993.

1996   Rich Farmer: Preached at the National Cathedral in Washington, D.C., on May 15, 1996, for the College of Preachers. It was subsequently published as "God's Word," *College of Preachers* [Newsletter] 37, no. 1 (Fall 1996): 6–7. Editor: The Reverend Canon Erica B. Wood.

1998   Dishonest Steward: Preached at the First Presbyterian Church in Buffalo, New York, on September 20, 1998. Interim Pastor: The Reverend Angus M. Watkins. Subsequently published in *Pulpit Digest* (January–March 2000).

Index of the Parables